BEYOND THE NOTES
Journeys with Chamber Music

Susan Tomes

Photo: Julia Hedgecoe

BEYOND THE NOTES

Journeys with Chamber Music

Susan Tomes

THE BOYDELL PRESS

First published 2004
The Boydell Press, Woodbridge
Reprinted in hardback 2004
Reprinted in paperback 2005

ISBN 1 84383 045 0 hardback
ISBN 1 84383 160 0 paperback

The Boydell Press is an imprint of Boydell & Brewer Ltd
PO Box 9, Woodbridge, Suffolk IP12 3DF, UK
and of Boydell & Brewer Inc.
668 Mt Hope Avenue, Rochester, NY 14620, USA
website: www.boydellandbrewer.com

A catalogue record for this book is available
from the British Library

Library of Congress Cataloging-in-Publication Data
Tomes, Susan.
  Beyond the notes : journeys with chamber music / Susan Tomes.
    p. cm.
Includes index.
  ISBN 1–84383–045–0 (alk. paper)
1. Ensemble playing.   I. Title.
MT728.T65 2004
785.04'3 – dc22   2003017410

This publication is printed on acid-free paper

Printed in Great Britain by
Athenaeum Press Ltd, Gateshead, Tyne & Wear

Contents

PART TWO
Preparing and Performing

List of Illustrations

Frontispiece: Susan Tomes

Foreword

There was a time in my life when I toyed with the idea of becoming a professional musician. Admittedly, I was simultaneously toying with the idea of opening the batting for England. There was no great likelihood of either fantasy ever coming true. To be more precise, there was never the faintest possibility that I would ever have made it into even the seventh eleven of the most struggling minor county as a cricketer, whereas my daydreams of earning a living by playing the clarinet did somehow persist until my mid to late teens.

It was not to be. My lack of talent was ultimately matched by my lack of application and I drifted into editing the school magazine while my friend Alastair was practising his tonguing, scales and arpeggios three or more hours a day. He went on to be a much-in-demand professional bassoonist. I went on to become a little-in-demand amateur clarinettist and a never-in-demand amateur pianist.

In common with, I suspect, most amateur musicians there have been times in my life when I've wondered what I missed out on. The satisfaction of having a perfect technique – of being able to dash off pages of Beethoven or Schubert without blinking – is, to most of us, only just imaginable. But then so are the endless days, weeks and years of meticulous rehearsal; of perpetually aching wrists and shoulders; of struggling with out of tune pianos; of living in cheerless hotel rooms; of fighting against constant jet lag; and of playing in half-empty halls to moderately-interested audiences for inadequate reward.

I wonder no more. This book by Susan Tomes describes the life of the dedicated professional musician more vividly and honestly than any other work I've read. What she has to say is both depressing and profoundly inspiring. Depressing because the daily sacrifices, minor humiliations and sheer grind involved in making music to an extraordinarily high standard are unflinchingly laid bare in these pages. There is no better account I know of which captures the insecurity – technical, emotional, financial, physical – of the chosen path. And inspiring because of the way in which a more important message shines through: the way in which great music can provoke and nourish such passion and dedication in those who truly respond to it.

Susan not only responds to it, but captures it in endlessly clear, fluent and perceptive writing. This is not good for the morale of those of us who ended up earning a living from writing rather than music.

The veteran former editor of the Daily Telegraph, William Deedes, once identified an annual syndrome known to all amateur golfers as post-Open depression – the feeling of utter inadequacy in your own game as you watch the Woods, the Garcias and the Parneviks gracefully glide around a championship courses with such dismissive ease.

After the American golfer, Tom Lehman, won the 1996 Open, Deedes described his technique for coping with this sense of despondency. It went as as follows: 'Close your eyes, clear the mind and try to imagine Lehman taking over your job. Then think what sort of a fist he would make of it. For myself, I try to imagine Tom Lehman on his first day in our leader-writing circle and asking him to do 450 words during the next hour or so on whether or not we should join a single European currency. In my optimistic moods, I see my golf as relatively better than the leader he would turn out.'

I've tried this technique on Susan Tomes, and it has, if anything, the reverse effect. Not only is she a brilliant pianist, but she could walk into a writing job on most national papers (though possibly not writing about the single European currency). She seems to derive the same sort of pleasure and pride in her 'hobby' of writing as most amateur musicians gain from our hobby of playing chamber music. But, whereas we would be mortified to allow anyone, let alone Susan, hear our playing, she has the confidence – the sheer effrontery – to publish this endlessly absorbing book of writing on music.

I think I speak for us all when I ask: is this fair?

Alan Rusbridger

Acknowledgements

In writing about chamber music it helps to have interesting colleagues. I am indebted to the members of Domus and to my present colleagues in the Florestan Trio, with whom I have been fortunate to enjoy years of stimulating and satisfying collaboration. Their idealism and commitment have provided much of the material for description and discussion in this book. They have been unforgettable companions on our journeys with chamber music.

My hundreds of pages of notes would never have been shaped into a book without the wise counsel of my partner Robert Philip, not only a brilliant writer himself but a wonderful touchstone and editor too. Somehow he found time to help me find a path through the accumulated material while writing a book of his own. I am, as always, so grateful for his wholehearted and unwavering support.

I am also aware that the book might never have been published without the support and encouragement of Bruce Phillips, Laurence Dreyfus and Cyril Ehrlich, and of Alan Rusbridger, Annalena McAfee and Charlotte Higgins at *The Guardian*. Caroline Palmer at Boydell & Brewer has been an exemplary editor.

One person has lived with the gradual assembling of this book during her whole life. Special thanks are due to my daughter Maya, whose precious companionship and lively mind have sustained me throughout.

Several of the essays in Part Two have been previously published, sometimes in shorter form. Here they appear in expanded form, and I have also taken the opportunity to correct any errors I noticed later.

Making music in a big kiln, Looking Involved, Recording Schubert's E flat Trio, and *Practice makes Imperfect* all appeared in *The Guardian*.

Rehearsing Beethoven's opus 1 appeared in *BBC Music Magazine*.

The recording process from the performer's point of view was a talk given at a conference on recording held at the Jerusalem Music Centre, Jerusalem, in 1998, and translated into Hebrew for publication in Israel.

A puzzling Schubert Quintet was incorporated into an interval talk given for BBC Radio 3.

Am I too soft? appeared in shorter form in the *Financial Times*.

Introduction

This book began years ago as a diary that I kept about our chamber music group Domus and its travels with its own portable concert hall, a white geodesic dome. At the beginning I thought I might try to be a kind of official scribe for the group, keeping a record of our adventures so that we would all remember how they unfolded. However, in practice I found it impossible not to add my own comments and reflections. I soon realised, and so did everyone else, that the diary was going to be my personal account of our project.

The bulk of the Domus diary was written on an old manual typewriter that I dragged about from concert to concert, often typing late at night as a way of letting off steam. I stopped writing it at a time when our future with the dome seemed to hang in the balance. The diary remained on a shelf in my bedroom until 1995, when the group disbanded. At that point, feeling nostalgic, I took it down and read it through after a gap of many years. As I did so, I realised that the project had really been very interesting, and that a record of it deserved to be kept and even publicised. I took advice on whether it would make a book, but was told that all kinds of supplements would need to be written.

There was no more to write, as Domus had come to an end, and so the diary went back onto the shelf. In the same year I became the pianist of the Florestan Trio. Gradually I started keeping diaries of the Florestan's tours; partly this was to keep a sense of focus and balance during our times away from home. I also wrote about our experiences of rehearsing and recording.

Much more recently I had the good fortune to be invited to write occasional wide-ranging pieces for *The Guardian*. Gradually I realised that with the Domus diary, my writing about the Florestan Trio, and my newspaper articles, I had amassed enough for a book of collected essays covering twenty years of performing life. By this time, also, such writing had become more welcome. Universities increasingly value 'primary material', or evidence from the performers themselves, which allows them to study music performance from the inside.

Although there are lots of autobiographies by musicians, there aren't many books written by performing musicians about the inner dynamics of a musical life. Interestingly, most such books have been written by pianists. I've often wondered why this is. Pianists do tend to be a distinct species within the world of musicians – a fact often remarked on by other players, though not always with approval. Traditions of professional life force many pianists to be loners, and the very self-sufficiency of the piano imposes its own isolation. Because the piano can play both melody and harmony at the same time, piano pieces are complete in themselves, whereas single-line instruments generally require partners (usually pianists) to supply the harmonies.

Since the piano is not an orchestral instrument, most pianists have little opportunity to socialise with other musicians. They're completely cut off from the social life that thrives within all orchestras. Many pianists don't belong to a chamber group, and even if they do, its members are probably the only other musicians they see regularly. Pianists don't have the opportunity, as my string-playing colleagues do, of reviving freelance links with orchestras if they need to make some money when solo or chamber concerts are scarce. They spend a great deal more time alone than do players of other instruments. This can make them slightly loony, or it can make them reflective, or both.

In my experience, pianists tend to read and study more than many other players. 'Bloody intellectuals', as a colleague once grumbled. It's true that their relative isolation within the world of musicians gives them plenty of time to think. I've also sometimes wondered if the fact that pianists don't have to hold or lift their instrument gives them a different sort of relationship to the process of performing. Of course, there are plenty of pianists who seem physically obsessed with the piano, but I can also think of many who benefit from being able to look and listen more than other players can. In a purely physical sense, pianists have a wide range of freedoms because the piano sits there without help.

Pianists have also been very much influenced by the publisher's habit of printing the full score – i.e. everyone's parts – in the piano part only (other instrumentalists play from parts containing only their own notes). This has inculcated in pianists the feeling of having a fuller and deeper knowledge of what's going on than other musicians do. A pianist colleague of mine once memorably likened it to being linked to a satellite Global Positioning System while everyone else is trying to figure out where they are just from what they see around them. There's also the fact that pianists play a different set of notes with each hand, which I'm sure must heighten their sense of perspective, perhaps even influence the way their brain works. Because they always play harmony as well as melody, pianists have to think vertically and horizontally at the same time, and I have no doubt that this expands their mental view. Pianists are always aware not only of their own part, but of what everyone else plays as well, because they can see it at a glance. Certainly they see the *whole picture* earlier than others do. In my experience pianists are usually the only ones who know all about the music before rehearsals begin. Indeed, they have known for months, because it takes that long to learn a difficult piano part properly. Not for pianists the insouciant habit of sight-reading at the first rehearsal!

After rehearsals begin, the process of learning the piece is one that involves all the players, leading eventually to a 'shared knowledge' that belongs to them all. However, I would contend that even after that process has occurred, pianists often continue to feel that they are in possession of *more information*. In my case this led to a certain feeling of pressure to shake off that extra information by writing it down.

I've noticed that fellow musicians feel quite superstitious about putting into words things about music that they feel are better unsaid. To some extent I share those feelings, which is why I've omitted from the diaries a certain layer of personal comment and insights. Many performers dig deep into themselves to fulfil their wish to communicate with listeners; as a colleague one often sees the raw side of others, which on the whole I have not included in my descriptions except insofar as it was an ingredient of our rehearsals and concerts. Yet without discussing colleagues' private lives (that would make a very different book) there is an enormous amount to say about everyone's way of preparing, rehearsing and performing. A player's *musical* personality is a slightly separate thing from their social personality, and it's largely the musical personality that the audience perceives, thus making it the proper subject of description here.

I mentioned earlier that when I was first keeping a diary for and about Domus, my colleagues were curious about it only now and then. Music is an evanescent art, and one of the most precious things about musical performance is that each one is different, unique, the result of all its ingredients whether fleeting, lucky, haphazard, or consciously chosen. When an audience is added, it multiplies the random ingredients, which can blend into a memorable whole. It's exactly this serendipitous quality of performance that many musicians like about their profession.

So am I not like them? Well, yes and no. I love the 'unique moment' of performance, but I also regret the traceless passing of all the effort that goes into it. I'm only 'a creature of the moment' when actually playing a concert. Otherwise, I like to remember and analyse, especially recalling the things people say. Words have always been tremendously important to me, and though I acknowledge completely that music doesn't have exact parallels in words, I seem to feel an occasional but recurring and even imperative need to try to describe some of our musical experiences. To that extent I'm not a typical musician. All the reports are filtered through my consciousness, of course, which means that my colleagues might not have described things in the same way, or might not have described them at all.

Sometimes friends have asked why I can't just let my concerts and recordings represent me. The answer seems to change as time goes on. When I was younger I did think that one's playing should explain everything, *pars pro toto*. As the years went by, and I realised how fragile aural memories are, I felt a need to supplement them by writing down something about what went on. This is partly because I've always loved writing and would have written in any case, whether about music or something else. But my writing self is only an aspect of my artistic self, and I would not like it if all the evidence of my playing were erased from the world and only my writing remained. This book is supposed to work in tandem with my life as a player; I don't like the idea of someone who's never heard me play trying to sum me up just by reading the book. Yet for my own emotional reasons I do feel glad – even relieved – that I have tried to capture some of our experiences in writing.

Underpinning all our different performances is the continuous effort that musicians make to learn, to understand, to discuss and experiment. They work on their instruments, on the pieces they play, and on themselves too. In the lives of all serious musicians there's a continuum of enquiry and discovery, which the audience rarely has a chance to see. I have quite a few colleagues who actually prefer the rehearsal process to the performance, because it's then that they can interact with the work in various ways and explore how best to bring it to life. To some extent they also bring themselves to life through such work. This, too, is never witnessed by the audience.

When I started writing on the subject, many people told me that they had always wondered what goes on in private practice and rehearsal. Some people, indeed, were not even aware that rehearsal goes on in any serious way. Even now I'm sometimes asked questions that reveal startling depths of ignorance, even among concert-goers.

I was once asked after a concert in New Zealand, 'And is this all you do – or do you also work?' Recently someone asked my trio, 'Do you ever get together on days when you don't have a concert?' Sometimes people seem to think that 'being musical' is a natural gift that doesn't need working on; we can just do it, so all we need to do is to turn up at the concert hall and play what we see in front of us on the music stand. When we tell people that our rehearsal days are often like theirs, working office hours, they are astounded. And then they begin to wonder what on earth we talk about. This book gives an idea of what two particular chamber groups talked about, and how they gathered up all the elements of their performances.

When we started the Domus project, we wanted to bring music we loved to new listeners. I started writing the diary in 1981. Re-reading it twenty years later, I am repeatedly struck by the extent to which the problems of music-making and concert-giving that I described then are still present in my mind. In one sense this is depressing: the problems we tried to tackle with our portable concert hall have not been solved. In particular, we find as time goes by that the better-known we become, the less contact we have with our listeners. People now assume that we wish to be left alone, or are too grand to talk to. They're also handicapped by a fear of saying the wrong thing if they find their way backstage. Curiously, when I am in an audience I find myself similarly tongue-tied!

I still look forward to finding out what the listeners thought about our concerts, but these days I rarely do. This is partly because of the layout of traditional concert halls, where the players depart from the stage to backstage rooms and separate exits difficult for the audience to find, even if they are brave enough to try. There have been many concerts in recent years where we had no contact with listeners at all. Often this doesn't bother my colleagues – if they are happy with their performance they don't need extra reassurance – but it bothers me. Often our only substantial feedback after a concert comes days later in the form of a newspaper review. As all concert-goers will know, reviews often bear only a tangential relationship to how the concert was experienced by most of the people there, so they are not a guide to how members of the audience felt.

At the moment, attempts to bring classical music to 'the people' tend to take the form of commercial trivialisation, with massively overpaid celebrities, usually opera stars, belting out the most popular tunes into microphones, in arenas and parks that hold an audience of thousands. These raise, in grotesquely exaggerated form, the misgivings we had about trying to make great music 'fun'. Such events are like rock concerts, and bear no resemblance to what we were trying to do. They pretend that classical music is 'easy listening' – inflating the easiest bits of it into something that it is not, so that the mass audience will accept it. Our aim was to enable audiences to experience classical music as we, the musicians, experience it: as a vital, intimate part of our lives, something to share on a human scale. The difference between these two 'popularising' enterprises is like the difference between setting up a hamburger chain, and inviting people into your home for lunch.

There are other themes that run through the diary, and these are constant in the lives of chamber musicians, because they are at the heart of what we do and why we are musicians. They are to do with what the music is, how to make sense of it, to 'interpret' it, how to convey its meaning to one another and to an audience, how to balance technical problem-solving with the exploration of the spiritual dimensions of music. Though these are a constant source of debate among musicians, verbally and non-verbally, the ways in which we try to tackle them are rarely described in print. It's very important to some that their experience of music is non-verbal. Perhaps, also, even those who are good at talking about these matters fear that they might be revealing 'trade secrets' if they broadcast them to the wider world. I feel, however, that the more people learn about what we do, the better, and that the deeper the audience's understanding of what we do, the deeper their understanding of the music will be. Moreover, the deeper the audience's understanding, the more we understand why we spend so much time preparing the performance.

This book divides into two parts; firstly, the Domus diary and a collection of diaries about touring with the Florestan Trio. As the Domus and Florestan episodes were separated by some years, readers will notice a change of emphasis between one and the other, reflecting everyone's changing lifestyle and priorities in the intervening years. Secondly, there is a collection of essays musing on teachers and on performance topics such as rehearsing, practice and recording. The whole book is about the questions which have preoccupied me for twenty years: how to make sense of music and of a life in music. These questions continue to hold my attention.

PART ONE

Journeys with Chamber Music: Touring with Domus and Florestan

A Portable Concert Hall: the Domus Diary

My Domus diary was written twenty years ago and has not been revised (except for abridging it) for publication. Its way of expressing things, typical of me then, is not quite typical of me now. And of course the same applies to everyone whose opinions and behaviour are described in the diary. However, I have kept the original wording because it conveys a sense of the involvement and commitment we all felt at the time.

The diary entries were often written moments after the incidents described. We were all in the thick of things, and probably lacked objectivity – indeed, if we'd possessed objectivity we wouldn't have been there in the first place. So I hope they will be read as despatches from the musical front, written in the midst of a huge endeavour when none of us had much experience of our profession, and giving a flavour of time and place that was precious to all involved. Indeed, the time we spent with Domus was important in many different ways, and had a lasting influence on us all.

This is the story of the first years of Domus, a group that later travelled the world as a piano quartet, and won numerous record awards. Its original members are now spread out internationally, and follow distinguished musical careers as soloists, conductors, chamber musicians and members of symphony orchestras.

Domus was formed in 1979 by a group of young professional musicians who had met up at the International Musicians' Seminar, founded by the Hungarian violinist Sandor Végh, at Prussia Cove in Cornwall, England. Its founder members were Felix Wurman (cello), Robin Ireland (viola), Krysia Osostowicz (violin), Richard Lester (cello) and me, Susan Tomes (piano). We were then at the beginning of our professional careers, and were already slightly dismayed at the lack of contact we had with our audiences. We had all been educated to believe that music was a potent form of communication, and we expected to be closely in touch with our listeners – just as one is when learning and practising music in the home – but it was not so in the concert hall.

We were united by the feeling that formal concerts often inhibited both players and listeners, and also by the feeling that concert-giving should not be so entirely dislocated from the rest of the day's activities. Admittedly, many performers find the Otherness of concerts both necessary and compelling because it gives the sense of a special occasion, and draws the best out of them. But this Otherness has a life of its own, independent of the performers; it doesn't always amount to the feeling of a special occasion, but sometimes just feels stiff, and makes people feel they are not free to behave normally. We felt this very much when we experienced the formal atmosphere of many long-established concert series. Much as we longed to be invited to play in them, we also regretted the air of constraint that seemed to descend on the audience.

The idea of building our own portable concert hall emerged from a series of conversations during the seminars at Prussia Cove. These courses take place twice a year in an incomparably beautiful setting by the sea, and attract student and professional musicians from around the world. As the constant theme of the classes was 'communication' – with the music, with one another, with audiences – it was natural that we all discussed how what we were learning could be incorporated into our budding professional lives. Gradually we all confessed we were worried that professional musical life was less 'communicative' in several senses than we had hoped it would be, and were concerned how little contact there was with listeners. During mealtime and late-night conversations we came up, almost jokingly, with the idea that we should get together and build our own concert venue, where we could do things as we liked. 'We've got to build a portable concert hall!' was the merry refrain.

Our idea was to put up our portable hall in places where there were no concert halls, and to give informal concerts of chamber music. We wanted to cut through the stiffness of the atmosphere that sometimes prevails in traditional concert buildings. We also thought that if nobody was obliged to behave like this or that, we could share our love of chamber music at close quarters with many new kinds of listeners who would grow to love it as we did.

When I look back on it, I see that we were brought together not so much by musical compatibility as by idealism and shared ideas. Curiously, these don't always go together. People can go well together musically without going well together socially, and vice versa. In our case, we were a peculiar mixture of practical, spiritual and intellectual qualities, though the shared wish to live a different kind of musical life brought us close together, close enough to become very good chamber music partners in due course. In the beginning, however, it was a philosophy that bound us together.

The idea of building a portable concert hall might never have become a reality without the inspirational adventurousness of our American cellist Felix Wurman. Felix had always had an extraordinary gift for starting exciting new projects and motivating people to become involved with them. When the idea of the portable concert hall came up, he immediately thought of the geodesic dome structure, which he had studied at school and had always wanted to build in earnest. It was Felix who translated our ideas into reality by going off and working out how to gather the materials for a prototype dome. The rest of us might eventually have figured out how to get our hands on some kind of large tent, but I don't think we would ever have hit on the idea of a geodesic dome – the lovely shape that became synonymous with the project, and inspired the group's name, Domus. The name carried a double significance: it was partly a reference to the dome itself, and partly to the Latin word for 'home', showing how we felt about the dome.

'It couldn't be just any old kind of tent,' said Felix, who built the first dome in the cellar of his cello teacher's house in Germany in 1980. 'It just had to be a dome.' The first dome was made of plastic tubes, a rudimentary connecting system for them, and a cover made from a pink silk parachute kindly donated by the RAF. Once we had seen that a geodesic dome was entrancingly beautiful, but also could easily blow over the edge of a cliff, as it once nearly did in Cornwall, we set about reproducing it in sturdier materials. Our dome seated 200 people, and obviously it had to be safe.

Having swapped plastic for aluminium tubes and the parachute for a PVC cover, Felix found us a Bedford van in which to transport it. Eventually we also acquired a specially made trailer, the size of a horse-box, in which to carry a piano. At first we had an upright, but later we graduated to a grand piano – mad as that seems. The trailer had an ingenious, if cumbersome design, which allowed its sides to be unfolded, and had uprights that dropped down to become legs, thus forming a concert platform. The piano remained on the trailer throughout, either lying on its side for transport purposes, or turned onto its legs when the trailer became a stage.

Domus had to learn the hard way that a breathtakingly simple shape is not breathtakingly simple to build. We did everything ourselves – partly on principle, and partly because our budget never allowed us to employ any outside help. We put up and took down the dome, did all the technical maintenance, did the driving, all the administration, all the concert organisation, and all the publicity, such as it was – as well as all the playing. Thus we were all thrown in at the deep end of professional life, for which our training as performing musicians had scarcely prepared us.

When I look back on this, I realise how bizarre it was that someone like me – bored by nuts and bolts both actual and metaphorical – should have become involved with a project that was so demanding on the practical front. Though I loved the sight of the dome when it was up, I was never gripped by the technical side of it, and indeed resented the vast amount of time that had to be spent on it. My non-musical skills were on the planning and administrative side, and these became essential as Domus tried to get itself known. Luckily, several of our original members turned out to be gifted and enthusiastic dome-builders. Without the practical skills, adventurousness and technical know-how of Felix, Robin Ireland and Richard (then known as 'Dickie') Lester, *Domus* would never have become a reality.

The final form of the dome, with which we began touring in 1980, took half a day to put up, often starting more or less at dawn. Aluminium tubes were locked together at various points by a specially designed 'hub system' to form the geodesic skeleton, and the fireproof PVC cover was hung inside the dome from ropes tethering the cover to the hubs overhead. We also installed, with some difficulty, a platform, which hung from the roof of the dome and was strong enough to support a person's weight. This was useful partly because it provided access to the 'roof', for installing electric cables and so on; it also provided a platform from which an enterprising person with a portable instrument could, and did, deliver an unusual serenade from on high. From the platform hung an electric fan, which could be turned on when the atmosphere became stuffy.

During the rest of the day, we installed electric cable, lights and sometimes microphones, brought in chairs (often making arrangements to borrow them from a local school) or cushions for the audience, and converted the trailer into a stage for the grand piano, which travelled inside the trailer from place to place, and had to be turned on its side for purposes of transport. This physical work was relished by some, tolerated by others, for although we were proud of the fact that we put up our own concert hall, it could and sometimes did strain our hands.

'Oh no – it must never not be *fun!*' Felix once said in an anguished tone in reply to someone who complained that everything had become too difficult. This reply became a catchphrase of ours, and was used for years afterwards whenever anyone said that things were hard. 'It must never not be fun!' seemed to sum up the spirit of the early days of Domus.

We used the dome firstly as a summer project, taking it to Italy and erecting it on a hillside outside Assisi. All we knew at this stage was that music should be fun, and our experimental concerts stumbled on a formula that guided us over several years of touring. We greeted the audience, introduced each piece to them, and invited them to stay for a drink with us after the concert. In these pleasant exchanges we discovered the perfect antidote to post-concert blues, as well as a good many home truths about classical music and what people think about it. The audience, mostly of villagers and holiday-makers, were not constrained by their surroundings to be stiff or shy, and they were delighted with the dome.

Because assembling and dismantling the dome took so much time and energy, we tried to stay in each venue for at least five days. This arrangement, imposed for practical reasons, turned out to be humanly rewarding. Instead of being condemned to one-night stands, with cities dimly perceived through the fatigue of travel, we could get to know and be known by every local audience, many of whom made an effort to come to every concert once they knew us. Concerts became the natural culmination of days spent rehearsing, eating and sleeping in the dome, and listeners often said how much easier it was for them to relax in a space so obviously enjoyed, and 'inhabited' in the real sense of the word, by its guardians.

'You're doing well with your portable concert hall,' a listener told us in Hamburg on our second tour. 'If this goes on, will you be able to graduate to real concert halls soon?' 'It's the other way round,' we explained for the umpteenth time. 'We moved *out* of real concert halls into the dome because we prefer playing here.' This clearly confirmed the listener's notion of English eccentricity; he went off bemused by the thought that a 'real' concert hall was less attractive than a tent visited by all kinds of weather.

When you have your own concert hall, the possibilities seem endless. In addition to regular concerts, we began improvising, doing theatre exercises, and playing primitive jazz with metal boxes as drums and aluminium tubes as Alpenhorns. We then wondered whether we could include such improvisations in our concerts. Could we expect people to pay to hear us uprooting ourselves in public, or should we confine ourselves to playing what we play well? At this point we came across John Heilpern's book, *Conference of the Birds*,[1] describing Peter Brook's journey across Africa with a group of actors dedicated to finding out whether theatre was a universal language. Not only their ideals, but their problems were uncannily like ours. They, however, had Peter Brook to resolve their arguments, whereas ours were often circular. We formed a plan to go to Paris and discuss our ideas with Peter Brook, and eventually we did so.

By this time we had more or less decided to become a compendium of entertain-

---

1   *Conference of the Birds, The Story of Peter Brook in Africa*, by John Heilpern, Penguin Books, 1979.

ments, supplementing our musical skills with jazz, improvisation, comedy, film, juggling and culinary display (I am not making this up). Brook, however, thought we were on a dangerous track. He advised us to remember our real field of contribution. Private rehearsals could be as multi-disciplinary as we liked, but we should remember that in each concert we were responsible for two hours of the audience's lives, and should not assume that theatrical experiment that gratified us would gratify them. He thought there was a danger of the dome being more noteworthy than the concert in it, and advised us to make sure that the playing was as potent as the environment. This advice was undoubtedly among the best we ever received. We came back from Paris purged of the lust for variety, and decided instead to make sure that, purely as musicians, we deserved the attention we were beginning to get.

The next season, in Germany in 1982, bore the fruit of this decision. We seemed to get the balance right; audiences commented on the music first and the dome afterwards. Musically we felt much greater self-respect, and in the Sternschanzenpark in Hamburg we gave a week of concerts, which generated a wonderful concentration among players and listeners alike.

Then, on the way to the Bonn Festival, our van was involved in a serious motorway accident when a forty-ton truck hit it from behind. Three players were injured; two cellos and our piano were destroyed. The trailer and its contents – the tubes that formed the dome, the lights and our tools – were strewn over the motorway. The remaining players, travelling in another van, were plunged into a nightmare series of visits to police, lawyers and hospitals – all without advice or expertise, and all in a foreign language.

Eventually we hired a removal van and drove the debris (including my mangled typewriter) back to England, where we set about salvaging the remainder of the concert season. Somehow, by hiring, repairing and borrowing the equipment lost in the crash, we managed to play at the Cheltenham Festival and in Battersea Park. Felix, convalescing with both legs in plaster, played his cello in a wheelchair. David Lockington, our guest cellist, was still recovering in hospital with back injuries and severe burns.

People often asked us where we found the energy to survive such a setback. In fact, a less serious setback might have finished the group. As it was, the magnitude of this one simply activated our collective will to survive. We never received a penny of compensation for all that we lost. The lorry driver claimed in court that our van was showing no lights, and without an effective lawyer – and indeed without the money to go to Germany to represent ourselves in court – we were unable to prove the contrary.

This dramatic end to the season destroyed our good resolutions about putting music first. Luckily we soon had the chance to do so. We had all won scholarships to the Banff Centre for the Arts in Canada, where we spent the first three months of 1983. Amid the peaceful Rockies, and away from the practical responsibilities of the dome, we concentrated on our playing. It was our first opportunity in several years to be single-minded. We explored new rehearsal techniques, learned new works, and in a leisurely way confronted personal problems that usually had to be squeezed into the five minutes between tidying the last row of chairs, and changing (usually in the back of a car) for the concert. Banff was ideal for us; the authorities let us set our own pace, and we cherished the chance to 'confine ourselves finer' than we normally are. We were not, however, introverted. We pioneered a series of inter-arts seminars, gave performances of new works, played at exhibition openings, in the bar, at poetry readings, in masterclasses and in the art gallery. All this (and going for walks to the top of snowy mountains) gave us back our appetite for the future.

In 1983, the last year of the diary, Domus had its longest-ever concert season in the dome, pushing back the weather frontiers at both ends of the summer. We started at the Bath Festival, appeared at the Bracknell Festival and visited Germany and Italy. Our programmes mixed light and serious classical music, usually with a first half composed of short pieces linked by theme or narrative, and a big chamber work after the interval. Thus new audiences were not asked immediately to develop a big concentration span, and the players had the chance to play solos and duos as well as piano trios and quartets.

We didn't see ourselves as missionaries for classical music. Rather we felt that we were conducting a permanent cheerful enquiry into the meaning of the music we play. Having tackled widely different audiences in all sorts of settings from urban to idyllic, we discovered that we couldn't predict the ones who would really appreciate live chamber music. This was the most exciting aspect of our work. A new audience meets the music with few of the trappings of the 'real' concert hall, and their fresh response to the music refreshes it for the players, who then see it not through a glass, darkly, but face to face.

The 'dome' project came to an end in 1985 because the magnitude of the technical task we had set ourselves outweighed our practical skills and energies. We were essentially idealists grappling with the hard realities of geodesic frame construction, repairs and maintenance, trailer building, piano moving, electricity connection, seat hire, civic park regulations, lighting, and the unkindness of the English weather – to say nothing of the work involved in developing our own playing and preparing many different programmes for each venue. The group was still a highly-motivated unit, but we felt the time had come to leave the dome behind and concentrate on music.

There was another reason that the dome part of the project came to an end, and that was the gradually growing sense that the music we played was maybe not best served by a fun atmosphere and a lighthearted presentation. All our favourite pieces of chamber music had in fact taken days, weeks, months of preparation, private practice and serious rehearsal. Many of us measured our lives with those pieces as milestones and used them as lodestones for our emotional lives. We came to feel that presenting them with nonchalant informality was betraying their real importance, and possibly even making it harder for the audience to sense their true dimensions. This has remained a thorny issue even years after the events. We realised all along that this music could touch people's lives, and by taking away the 'scary' and alienating aspects of formal concerts, we sought to remove the obstacles to the audience's bonding with the music. In other words, we wanted people to get close to the music we loved, and we tried to make that easy for them.

In the years that followed, however, we very often noticed that great music needs and gets serious attention and absorption from players and audience alike. Everyone needs to acknowledge that profound immersion is the most rewarding way to perform and to listen. In order for this to happen, one needs distractions to be kept to a minimum. This was always going to be an uphill struggle in a portable concert hall, which was basically an outdoor setting, and whose practical demands were not only distracting, but often overwhelming for the young musicians in charge of it. The nature of these demands is clearly shown by the sudden ending of the diary at a difficult time in Germany.

After this diary ceases, the group felt that the phase of its life dominated by the dome had come to a natural end, and began to seek opportunities in the 'ordinary' concert hall. We did in fact continue using the dome in the summer season, and even took it to Australia after Domus had reduced to four people and become a piano quartet.

We later found that the project with the dome had in fact come to mean a lot to many people in different parts of the world, and even twenty years later people often speak to us about it with fond nostalgia. Other musicians, who basically agreed with us about the misguided 'elitist' image of chamber music, had derived great vicarious satisfaction from our struggles to change its image. Many of our audiences declared that their experience of concerts in the dome was the most meaningful they had ever had. They continued to follow our career as a piano quartet, but said they missed the atmosphere of the dome. Ironically, of course, had we felt supported like this during the lifetime of the project, we might have felt strong enough to continue and develop it. It should be remembered that we dreamed up this 'outreach' work at a time when such 'customer-oriented' projects were extremely rare, so in a sense we were ahead of our time in Britain and suffered accordingly.

Had the project ever attracted sponsorship, or made enough money to pay people to help us with the practical side of things, the concerts in the dome would no doubt have continued for much longer. As it was, we didn't even make enough money to support ourselves. The lack of sponsorship was an aspect of basing the project in Britain that was often bitterly commented on by Felix, our American founder. He always maintained that we would have had a lot more support of every kind in the USA, not to mention more suitable weather.

But in ideal circumstances, perhaps our concerts would not have had the same flavour of reckless dedication, achievement against the odds and commitment that people seemed to value so greatly and to remember long afterwards. This, at least, is how a British artist reconciles herself to her fate.

Principal players mentioned in the diary

Felix Wurman	cello
Krysia Osostowicz	violin
Robin Ireland	viola
Richard (then 'Dickie') Lester	cello
Michael Faust	flute
David Lockington	cello
Susan Tomes	piano

Guest players

Steven Isserlis	cello
Roger Dean	jazz piano
Ruth Ehrlich	violin
Richard Ireland	violin
Leo Phillips	violin
Gabi Lester	violin
Eva Tomasi	violin
Janet Hilton	clarinet
Ashley Brown	drums
Maggie Nichols	singer
Chi Chi Nwanoku	double bass

DOMUS DIARY

Preparing for the Cheltenham Festival, 1981

Being invited to be a 'fringe event' in the Cheltenham Festival was rather a coup for Domus at the beginning of its career. The Cheltenham Festival is one of Britain's most prestigious international classical music festivals, taking place each July. The festival authorities, aware of us as individual musicians and prepared to give our project a try, had invited us to put up the dome on the extensive gardens in front of the Cheltenham Town Hall, and to give two weeks of informal concerts there. Our programmes were much like those of the Official Festival, but ours was a 'fringe' event in the sense that it was not funded by the festival. We had a spectacular, very central site surrounded by elegant Georgian buildings, but it was up to us to organise, publicise and sell tickets for our own concerts.

This was our first major appearance, though we had been preparing intensively for more than a year, giving open rehearsals and informal concerts both in the dome and in house concerts, and refining aspects of dome-building. We were desperate to meet our public properly. Being invited to Cheltenham didn't represent progress on every front, though, since the concert fees were only what we could take in ticket money at the door of our dome, and we had to pay for our meals and accommodation out of that. Because we didn't want anyone to feel excluded from the concerts, we set ticket prices very low. Money was always incredibly scarce in Domus, and as we had to economise on accommodation, we were always living in crowded conditions when on tour.

The thought of having the paying public inside our dome, and of having visits from some of the internationally respected musicians who appear at the festival, concentrated our mind on the technical safety of the dome. Everything had to stay up, be reliable, be waterproof, and not fall on people's heads. We should have spent most of our time on rehearsal and private practice, but as Cheltenham drew nearer, we seemed to be spending all our time on designing and making things for the dome.

We had also experimented with a new way of connecting the aluminium tubes that formed the skeleton of the dome. This produced unforeseen problems – the new 'hub system' being too flexible to hold the tubes in precise alignment – and shortly before the festival we concluded that we would have to go back to the clumsier but more predictable old hub system. There was so much to think about, with music and rehearsal often being pushed into last place in the day, while at the same time we were miserably aware that they should have been first. We had been really looking forward to our first official festival, but by the time it opened, we were already in what was to become a character-istic state of fatigue, wondering how on earth we were going to manage a fortnight in the public gaze. At the last minute, several concerned friends offered to come down and help with tasks such as making posters, preparing food to sell to the audience, and so on. The opening pages of my account show clearly the sense we all had of having bitten off more than we could chew – something that characterised most of our adventures.

Nuts and bolts, July 1981

In the week or two before going to Cheltenham the group has never been so brittle. Even though the chance of performing is getting nearer, we have never been so overwhelmed by the fatigue of administrative and practical duties, and it's very bad luck that so many things have had to be done at the last moment. The specially made cover for the dome has only just been collected; the trailer is being made this week by a group of inspired amateurs, the cushions are being designed and made, and everyone is depressed by the failure of the new hub system and the need to return to the clumsy old one, which takes twice as long to assemble. It still takes us most of a day to put up the dome and to arrange the stage, piano, seating and lighting.

If only I could work out the dynamics which make the air clear and make the air heavy with antagonism in the group. I hesitate to believe in a group dynamic which is other than – I mean not simply more than – the sum of its parts. When I'm aware of what each individual person feels, and yet the whole group suddenly moves according to an impetus which is greater than, or different from, what I assume the sum of our feelings is.

After our long and agitated discussions about the tension in the group, rather intensified by the arrival of Richard Ireland fresh from the Royal Northern College of Music, and telling us how disheartening it was for him to find us in this state, it was most odd to find ourselves serenely tackling a Shostakovich rehearsal this morning and everyone beaming with enjoyment of small details during the morning. And yet not one of us, on our own, felt at all sanguine about even seeing each other today. I suppose it's just as well that incalculable influences work upon us when we're together. Just as well, anyway, when they're beneficial influences. It can be equally disarming, of course, when things go sour for no discernible reason.

I often feel that I could draw a kind of graph of the dynamics of a group during rehearsal. It's fascinating that people whom I feel socially close to and at ease with are sometimes quite remote from me, or I from them, while playing. And conversely: people with whom I feel quite awkward in conversation can feel like extensions of my own thinking during a piece of music. How can it be that one feels a musical rapport with someone to whom one has little to say? Or how can it be that I feel musically distant from someone with whom I've just shared an intimate exchange of confidences about our private lives? There must be something about one's musical being which is *not paralleled* by one's social being. What forces guide one's musical personality? Is the musical self actually drawn from ingredients which have no other outlet? Or does it mirror one's private feelings about the world rather than one's social experience?

Sometimes I feel that when we start playing, people draw boundaries around themselves which seem to correspond to some peculiar idea of dignified platform behaviour. I often feel that this is not even their own idea, but has been unthinkingly imbibed somewhere along the route from teachers, parents and other authorities. In concert it can be quite hard to make contact with certain people, other than a kind of 'pantomime contact' which is almost done as though projecting what they imagine the audience wants to see. Actually I hate it when I glance across the platform and see someone give me an 'emotional look' of the kind that I never see on their face in ordinary life. Other people seem more buried in their music, cooler in their smiles and leanings, and for someone like me who feels at their most alert and relaxed during a performance, it makes me feel sort of lonely on the stage. I wonder how the others would describe their sensations?

In this week before the real start of the Domus season, several of us are wondering privately if the group momentum has run its course, and if we will even survive a fortnight in Cheltenham, feeling so inflammable as we all do. We are definitely trying to be all things to all people – responsible for not only the music but the huge spectrum of practical tasks as well. Everyone sees the problem, but no-one knows how to resolve it, and perhaps no-one feels that they have the authority to do so.

Saturday 4 July

Everyone in the group is struck by how different in size the Dome looks according to its context. Here, in the Imperial Gardens in Cheltenham, looking (as Dickie observed) rather erotic against a backdrop of white Georgian houses and highly trained lawns, the Dome seems friendly, small, and all of us want to protect it.

This was our easiest Dome assembly yet, we all agree. No unforeseen flaws in the procedure, no running around to drill different holes and unbolt tubes wrongly bolted together; instead, we have constant breaks for sitting on the lawn and everyone feels how pleasant it is not to be working against the clock as we usually are.

Felix manages to strike up a friendship with three local lads who are hanging around watching us, and not sure whether to be mocking or not. Within five minutes he has them carrying huge numbers of chairs from the Town Hall, helping to tighten nuts around the bottom layer of the Dome, and trying to reach high enough to pull down the other end of a rope he has pulled too far over its pulley under the roof of the Dome. They try very hard to form a kind of human pyramid in an effort to reach the knotted end, but overbalance at the last minute and, grabbing at the long end to save themselves, send the knotted end flying to the roof, where we shall never reach it. We realise the disadvantages of a project unencumbered by ladders, scaffolding and other tools of the normal Dome-builder.

The white cover, only a fortnight old, looks dirty already. We have a temporary groundsheet which is also made of a certain plastic, and we are astonished (and dismayed) by its echo properties when combined with the PVC cover. Michael laughs experimentally inside the dome while we are all outside it, and it sounds like those recordings of the song of the hump-backed whale, penetrating through miles of water.

The upright piano is lodged inside its horsebox of a trailer, and while the others are doing manly things with spanners, I play the piano inside the trailer. The trailer encloses me from everything happening around me, and it's a most peculiar sensation to finish a piece and hear voices floating over the trailer walls in response. A number of tourists climb up and photograph me giving this impromptu concert, like a Jack playing at the bottom of his box.

We then move the trailer (only just small enough to pass through the door) into the Dome, and put it in place at the far end, where the sides of the trailer are to be dropped down and the ingenious legs dropped into position, converting the trailer into an instant stage already equipped with piano. We pause for a brief argument about the best place within the Dome for eliminating the echo, about which I am much the most sensitive because it seems to affect the sound of the piano more than any of the other instruments. The echo, we find, is now stronger than before, presumably because of the short grass. The general opinion is that it makes little difference where the stage goes, and we also find a disorienting extra echo at the very centre of the Dome, standing under the clear plastic canopy over the rosette. This feels like speaking into a microphone, and we wonder if this exciting effect is audible only to the person perpetrating it, or if it could be used to good effect in, for example, a piece specially composed for Dome acoustics.

Felix's American friend Mary Ann makes a poster to hang outside the Dome, advertising our next programme. We realise how little publicity we have done, and start to devise various strategies such as playing serenades in the beer tent, busking on the Promenade, walking around with a handbell, and the like. There is a debate about locking the piano, whose lock was mysteriously broken while the dome was up in the Purcell School, perhaps by people curious to see inside. Felix and Richard offer to sleep in the Dome to act as security guards, but their resolve is shaken in the evening when we find the Dome being used as a sanctuary for various local thugs and their tape-players, and even we, feeling so protective about our things, are quite nervous when we go inside and find strangers installed and looking malevolently at us. This is the day after the 'skinhead' riots in Southall, and we suddenly feel superconscious of the threat to the Dome. The dome is not insured, because our funds wouldn't stretch to paying the premium, especially for public liability. So everything depends on luck being on our side. Eventually it's decided that Felix will put his van as near as possible to the Dome and sleep in that, as we all feel that sleeping on an unguarded stage would make him just too vulnerable. Robin also phones the local police to ask them to keep a special eye on the Dome, and they say they will.

It's interesting to sit outside the Dome and watch people strolling up to it, reading the notice, peering inside, and commenting to each other. Most seem baffled or bored by the notice of our programme, and we realise that it's not enough just to advertise in the usual way. There's also quite a lot of comment about the £1 entrance fee, which we decided was the lowest possible realistic fee. People seem to think it's a lot, but of course the people who would think otherwise are probably not hanging around the gardens at 9.30 on a Saturday night. We feel that we shall learn a lot about projecting an image.

Sunday 5 July

The day dawns dull and windy for our first Cheltenham concert, and over breakfast at our digs we all wonder why on earth we chose white as the colour of our concert dress when we must have the highest dirt risks of any group in classical music. Keeping clean in the Dome is certainly a problem, exacerbated by the lack of nearby running water and, for those with cold hands, the lack of hot water. Not everyone feels happy in the white costume; Michael parades self-consciously around in one of the white shirts with the Elizabethan sleeves and eventually declares that, as he has a bad cold, it would be unwise for him to appear in an open-air concert so scantily clad. Actually, if we had known the weather forecast for this dreadful summer, we would have been wiser to choose white Aran sweaters and seven-league boots as our uniform.

As 2 p.m. approaches – the time of our opening concert – we can't help noticing that the Imperial Gardens are more or less deserted, and some spirited busking in the beer tent by Felix and Michael fails to arouse great local interest. By the starting time, some twenty people are sitting in the Dome, and we are all a bit disconcerted by the smallness of the audience. No-one quite wants to begin, all believing that at any minute the entire Berlin Symphony Orchestra will issue from their rehearsal in the Town Hall and decide to spend their lunch hour in the Dome concert, but three passing members of same are accosted in German by Michael, and decline the invitation with no attempt to disguise their distaste. So we begin; Felix makes a nice speech to the audience, who all smile back encouragingly, and try to look as though they were each occupying several seats. But the opening piece, Mozart's *Kleine Nachtmusik*, feels a little flat, and we can all sense it. Then Michael explains to the audience the history of the next piece, Debussy's *Syrinx* for solo flute, and how he sometimes played it from the platform suspended from the roof of the dome, as a kind of signature-tune. This clearly engages the audience's attention, and Michael's lovely performance follows. Then I decide to introduce the players to the audience, and find myself rambling on about what it's like to be a performer as opposed to being an audience, and how easy it is to proceed through the whole concert without meeting any of the listeners, and how nice it would be if they would not vanish at the end, but would stay behind and eat cakes with us and chat about the concert.

I explain about the Kawai upright piano, and about how its reflective front surface allows me to survey the expressions on the audience's faces while playing. All this suddenly lightens the atmosphere in the room, and when we get on stage to tune up for the Shostakovich, everyone is noticeably more relaxed. Once again I conclude that one can really take nothing for granted in the audience; one assumes that the audience sees through the mask of dignity which we wear on the platform to the loveable souls underneath, but in most cases this is simply not possible for them to do, given so little evidence.

The performance of the Shostakovich feels much more like what we have been aiming at; it's lively, intense and the chamber music spirit suddenly begins to stir amongst the group. At the end the audience, as requested, sits tight in its seats and the players immediately start to mingle. Mary Ann brings out her tins of delicious fruit and nut cakes, and gallons of apple juice, and these are acquired by audience and players on a fairly random basis in which some are given away and some are paid for, as is also the case with the Domus badges and the brochures.

The first people I pick on to chat to say just the right things; they heard the Shostakovich the previous year in the Pittville Pump Room and found it terribly solemn and alienating, but this afternoon they found it full of life and humour. One person, quoting from Felix's speech about how we 'love chamber music but don't like what is commonly known as the chamber music experience' (by which he meant solemn platform behaviour and over-respectful audiences) said that as far as he was concerned, the 'chamber music experience' was far more authentic in our concert than it usually is in traditional concerts. Nobody mentions the Mozart, but everyone is kind about Debussy and Shostakovich, which I think is simply a measure of how much they felt taken into the confidence of the players, and I'm sure that, had the order of the programme been different and the Mozart following instead of preceding our friendly speeches, the response to the Mozart would have been warm too. It's very interesting; the quality of the playing seems to be registered on one level, but the quality of the contact is what people long for, and once that has been established, it seems to open whole new channels of possibility for the quality of the playing as well.

Derek Ashley, a writer and teacher who's an old friend of Robin's family, said later that he had been feeling more and more convinced that the influence of The Establishment has taken a stranglehold on people's lives, and that the only thing worth striving for artistically is the re-establishment of human contact on a small scale. He said that he felt terribly pleased to be there when he felt what we were trying to do; it matched what he was feeling in general, and he was sure that the small size of the project was conducive to the kind of individual contact we wanted to make. So we end the first concert with a feeling of relief outweighing our disappointment at the smallness of the first audience.

The interior of the Dome is converted into a croquet course, and two teams of players and remaining audience are formed. While this croquet game is in progress, it gets round to tea-time and dozens of people, suddenly materialising in the Gardens for their afternoon stroll, pop into the Dome and ask for leaflets and details of the programmes. Lots of them express surprise that our concert was at such a funny time, and when we think of it, we feel that we should have foreseen the Sunday lunch habits of Cheltenham people. Many more people come into the Dome and express interest in the whole project than were present at the concert, but it gives us hope for next week.

Monday 6 July

No concert in the Dome today; everyone does private practice. Everyone else practises in the house where we are staying, but as there is no piano, I have to practise in the Dome, and I discover all sorts of occupational hazards of being a member of Domus. The Dome is playing host to various local youths apparently dealing in illegal substances, which activity they think is unobserved, but is easy for me to see in the aforementioned shiny black frontage of the Kawai piano as I play. They heckle me a bit, shouting at me to play various pop songs, and generally sniggering at my efforts to practise phrasing. I feel rather helpless and realise the naiveté of our wish to make everybody like chamber music.

A high wind is blowing, and it really feels as though the Dome will take off. Felix and Dickie staked it down yesterday, but one can still see the rim of the Dome trying to rise from the ground, and several of the nodes of the cover have pulled loose from the hubs, indicating that the knot we used was the wrong one. There also seems to be undue strain on the doorway, where we left out the crossbar, and Dickie realises that this is because we took out the crossbar at one of the only places where there is a straight line from the roof of the Dome to the ground, thus destroying the strong vaulting. We put the crossbar back in – a feat of some ingenuity considering how much tension the other bars are supporting – and move the doorway round to the left.

Later we get a thousand Domus leaflets printed on pink paper, in memory of the pink parachute which was the dome's first cover (not that anyone will know this), and distribute them to nearby bars and hotels, where they excite not a huge amount of attention.

Tuesday 7 July

In the morning Robin and I find that the Dome has been used as a hostelry during the night. Beer has been poured on the tarpaulin covering the piano and on the stage; the cushions have been made into beds for couples, and half of our piano blanket has been torn off and removed. It's astonishing how quickly we have all come to feel protective about our Dome: Ruth and Dickie appear during our rehearsal and rush around sweeping up, cleaning the table, collecting fragments of rubbish in paper bags, perhaps more diligently than they do in their own houses. Dickie has an excellent idea about the large poster-board we need: he saws a triangular piece of red wood which can be hung inside one of the triangles of the lowest layer of the dome, and to this board we pin notices of our concerts.

Our second concert, consisting of three *Miniatures* by Frank Bridge, a Honneger flute piece, the Rachmaninov *Vocalise* and the Bach B minor Flute Suite, is far easier than the first. This is partly because there are a lot of children, and Felix evidently feels more comfortable in introducing the concert to them; I'm delighted because the Allegri Quartet manages to get over to the Dome after their concert in the Pittville Pump Room, and seeing Bruno [Schrecker, the quartet's cellist] makes me want him to be impressed with everything. The Bridge *Miniatures*, rescued from obscurity by Felix who played them in the hotel lobby in Chicago, score quite a success with the audience, and it's obvious that we need more such light-hearted pieces to set the tone of some of the concerts.

Michael charmingly introduces his Honneger piece: 'This is called *Danse de la Chèvre*, which means . . . what does it mean, Sue?' which he then plays with his usual absorption, and Robin plays his Rachmaninov *Vocalise* on the viola, which causes several people in the audience to decide to learn it, as they afterwards reveal. But Robin is unhappy with his performance; it's a long time since he did any solo playing in concerts, and he says he felt the bell-jar descending, cutting him off in a private anguish which runs counter to all that he wants to feel in a Dome concert. This feeling, which he explains later, leads to an interesting discussion about musical concentration, a topic near to Dickie's heart at the moment as he explores various ways of creating it in his practising.

The Bach Flute Suite, which gave so much trouble in rehearsal and seemed to elude firm decisions about its direction and mood, is very warmly received by the audience, who, having been entertained for half an hour, are willing to concentrate on a more serious piece at the end of the programme. After this, most of the audience stays behind, and in the course of chatting to some of them, it becomes more and more clear that this part of the concert – the mutual feedback – is going to be one of the most rewarding parts of the project, and even addictive.

It's noticeable that people do not try to say the silly, nervous things they sometimes say in the Green Rooms of big concert halls; if they do stay behind, they say fresh and honest things, and it's such a relief to see one's efforts measured against people's response. Several people who were at the first concert came to the second;

several say that they will come every day, and one delightful lady takes a pile of our pink leaflets and goes off to distribute them to the newspapers, shops, and her hairdresser, from whose emporium she returns later with a gleaming new hairstyle to report on her progress with publicity. A couple of people ask about booking the group; one man asks if he can book us simply as a group of players without the Dome. This time there is much less interest in the Dome itself than there is in the players, which redresses an imbalance we were worried about.

In the afternoon we have a Mozart rehearsal, which is attended by a large crowd of sunbathers and strollers, and outside the Dome there are concentric rings of people happy to read their books or play with their children in the vicinity of nice music. David Roth stays for the rehearsal and makes many useful comments about the string playing, including analyses of how it sounds from the back of the Dome, which we rarely have a chance to know about. It's strange to be playing a Mozart concerto on an upright Japanese piano; I can't seem to find the right angle for the piano so that the audience can see me, but I can also see my colleagues.

In the evening we decide to have a walk in the Cotswolds, which are miraculously nearby, and depart in two cars for Sudeley Castle, once the home of Katherine Parr, last wife of Henry VIII. It's actually the first summer evening, or the first sunny evening since May, and it feels marvellous to be doing something so relaxing together. We always comment on the need to build in a relaxing part of each day that we have to spend as a group, but rarely get round to organising it, as there are always so many unfinished tasks.

But this evening it seems so easy to shed the concerns of the town as we meander in a huge circle around the castle and its fields, and finally end up at The Old Corner Cupboard Inn in Winchcombe. Robin, crowned with a daisy chain, immediately succumbs to Flower's Original Bitter, much to his brother's amusement. There is a magical moment when a huge hot air balloon sails silently into the lilac evening sky above the village, and we all watch quietly as it passes overhead, the sound of its gas jet travelling through the air some seconds after we see it, like a lion roaring on the next planet.

Wednesday 8 July

The Dome's most undisturbed night yet. I wonder if there is any site in any other town that would be so free from vandalism. Certainly we could not leave the Dome unattended in any comparable site in London. There is a growing confidence amongst the group now that we begin to sense the function that we play in this Festival, and see it reflected in the support of a few loyal members of the audience. The comment most often made to us is that we 'show up the official Festival', that the atmosphere in Domus concerts is 'far more memorable' than in the big Festival concerts, and this is exactly the condition to which we have been aspiring.

I personally feel that the kind of concert we are now evolving is much closer to my ideal kind of performing situation; I feel none of the alienation which usually descends on me as I traipse up and down the aisle of big concert halls, and none of the anti-climax which usually hits immediately the concert is over. Something about Domus has evidently caught the imagination of some of the audience; people have been really kind in taking it upon themselves to publicise us, and today a member of the audience dropped in to say that he had been over to the local radio station to suggest that they recorded one of our concerts. Another lady said that she would go home and telephone her friends about us. An elderly couple took a pile of leaflets and brochures to give to their friends. This sort of thing does not happen after traditional concerts, or not, at least, to groups that I have been involved in. It's tremendous to see people who have been at all three of our concerts here, and it keeps us on our toes, preventing us from saying the same things at each event.

Felix's introductory speech gains more panache at each repetition, though he still forgets half of what he means to say, and has to be shouted at by the rest of us. Ideally I would like everyone to take it in turns to introduce the concert, or the players, or the pieces, but as it works out, the bulk of the announcing is done by Felix, Robin and me, and the others repeatedly decline to join us. It's very nice being able simply to speak at a normal level and be heard by everyone in the hall, which takes away a lot of the anxiety I usually experience when I have to announce things.

Today's concert is the Claude Bolling Suite for flute and piano, and the Fauré Piano Quartet. The Fauré has mysteriously erased several of its problems since we last played it, and seems to have partaken of that odd process whereby unconscious work is done on it in the intervals between rehearsing it, in this case an interval of two weeks. Certain of its tempi, previously a subject of dispute, have settled down, and the directions of many of the phrases, which remained obscure to us because of the peculiarly French hingeing, have clarified. It was thus a pleasant experience to perform it, though afterwards several people said that the piano had been too loud, which is the opposite of what the audience said when we performed the same piece at Harrow. It seems to be generally the case that people sitting on the right side of the dome (with the back of the piano facing them) find it too loud, whereas people sitting on the left complain that they hear too much of the strings. This problem is probably more extreme in the dome than in a normal hall.

The Bolling is a great success, with people clapping between the movements. We decide that we should put at least one 'up-tempo' piece in every programme, and everyone notices that if the audience has been entertained or seduced by something cheerful, they are more willing to make the effort of listening to something serious at the end.

We have a visit from a group of wind-playing colleagues who are performing in the official festival, and it's odd to exchange ideas and impressions with a group of our own age who have chosen to go for the glossy side of the profession, in contrast to us who are trying to go for more and more informality. They ask all the questions appropriate to such a group: how much do we make out of it, how high-powered is our publicity; they warn us of the dangers of presenting too friendly an image, because it detracts from the convincing image of the players, and they feel in general that we should present ourselves as a group of international quality which has chosen, rather than been forced, to take their music to unusual venues in an unusual setting.

It's nice to see them, but just listening to the conversation I become aware of how greatly our ideas and wishes for our careers have changed in the process of getting Domus together, and even in the last week as we've seen the relief of the new audiences at our new approach. I wonder how many people in the group, if offered a magic series of high-powered concerts and a glamorous career at this moment by a fairy godmother, would abandon Domus in favour of that? I think we might be split half and half on that decision, and I could guess exactly who would choose what. I wonder if this balance will change in the course of the summer.

Wednesday evening is the most amicable we have had in Cheltenham, due largely to the fact that people have spent the afternoon either alone or with one other person. Felix has been with his Mum; Robin has been practising and writing to a friend; Dickie and Mary Ann, having accomplished various things to do with posters, are in The Cotswold pub, and Ruth and Michael have gone for a drive to the country. An ingenious vegetable dinner is prepared, and Felix unveils his latest idea, for a tour of the National Parks in America. His mother aids and abets this plan, saying that she will help him to raise money for what he describes as a Big Yellow Bus, fitted out for sleeping and cooking.

An energetic discussion about the merits of different countries ensues. In today's *Guardian* there are about five different articles on the aftermath of the Toxteth Riots, and having read them, several of us are gripped by a desire to emigrate. We make a pretend plan to tour the national parks of the USA next summer, and to plan a Domus tour of Africa for the winter of 1982. Everyone enters into the playful and optimistic spirit of this discussion, and I can't help noticing how changed the atmosphere is from last week, or indeed any of the preceding several weeks, when such suggestions would have been greeted by groans and vows of solitary meditation.

Thursday 9 July

The weather has suffered a relapse, and introducing the lunchtime concert I announce that we are thinking of renaming the concert series 'Recitals in the Rain', 'Classics under Canvas', 'Mozart in the Monsoon', or 'Dvorak in the Downpour'. Robin afterwards claims that no-one could hear a word I was saying because of the noise of the rain on the PVC dome cover.

Actually the rain, pattering gently on the skin of the dome, provides rather a hypnotic accompaniment to today's music, which is a Bach Cello Suite and the Mozart Piano Concerto K.414, in the version for piano and string quartet. Although there is rain, it's still quite warm, and I see people looking contented and drowsy as they watch rain falling on the canopy and listen to the playing. The audience, or those members who are at all the concerts, are becoming quite confident in their pronouncements, as we encourage them to be. Several people later say that although the Bach was beautifully played by Dickie, it was too long for the sort of new audiences we're trying to win over, and others are quite critical of the acoustics, at least from certain parts of the dome where, for example, the piano overwhelms the strings, or where the bass is lost. Actually today is the first time that we have felt really happy with the balance between piano and strings, as the balance required by a piano concerto naturally favours the soloist. This is my first experience of playing a Mozart concerto with four instead of thirty players, and it's so much more enjoyable to be able to offset one delicate texture with another, instead of pushing against the inertia of whole string sections, and so on.

One lady from the audience offers us the use of her washing-machine to clean our white concert clothes, and this confirms my suspicion that a certain section of the audience is attracted to us because they want to mother us. I see some of them looking at us with kindly concern as though they would like to be able to dress us in clothes which actually fit, and to give Robin a hearty meal, and to dust our piano. Even Felix's Mum, who arrived from the States yesterday, would not let him play in that night's concert until he had had a shave.

Felix's sister Nina and her boyfriend, Thomas Goritzki, arrive just before the lunchtime concert begins, and after the concert Felix and Thomas get right down to the serious business of juggling routines, which they practise in a corner of the dome. We've often talked about interspersing music with juggling or other tricks – as indeed was sometimes done in Beethoven's time – but it's very difficult to strike the right balance between giving the audience the impression that we're serious musicians, and giving them the feeling that we're lovable amateurs who dabble in various entertaining things, one of them being music. Derek and Joan Ashley, who come to the lunchtime concert, not having been since last Sunday, say that we have now struck the right balance. Derek says that on Sunday he felt that there was a danger of presenting the concert in such an informal and relaxed way that the audience would be unprepared for the intensity of the playing, and that there was too great a contrast between the amiable way we described our project, and the seriousness of the playing which followed. This is more or less what the visiting wind players were saying yesterday, though in their case it was simply projection, as they hadn't heard us introducing the concert or playing in it. There clearly is a right tone to strike, and we probably need to try even harder – I notice that the audience likes to have real information to digest, and that any amount of facts about the dome, the cover, the piano, the composers of the works, the players, and so on, does not make them restless.

I have recently been interested in jazz, and have invited a few jazz-playing friends to come and join me in the dome for an experimental jazz concert, to give some variety to our week's programming. So in the evening, the Dome is transformed by microphones, wine bottles, and a red standard lamp on the stage. Maggie Nichols, Roger Dean and Ashley Brown arrive from London and we decide on a blend of straight and free jazz, which suits me very well, though I feel that the others would be happier doing free jazz all evening. But the blend is evidently the right thing for the Cheltenham Audience, and there are one of two juxtapositions – such as the opening one between Rogers and Hart's 'I Could Write a Book' and the free improvising which follows it, and the one between a frenetic improvisation and Maggie's slow ballad 'Touching Faces' – which quite absorb the audience. It's always the juxtaposition between the known and the unknown which sets people thinking, and if it's skilfully done, as Maggie does it this evening, the listeners can really be wooed into attentiveness to something they wouldn't normally consider listening to.

One of the highlights of this evening is Felix's juggling debut in public. We only have this idea at the interval, and Felix is immediately seized by panic, but we make the juggling improvisation the first number in the second half, so that he has no opportunity to run away. Maggie improvises some words, and I try to follow the rhythm of the juggling balls on electric piano. This is a big hit with the audience, who immediately enter into the spirit of the thing and applaud enthusiastically every time Felix manages a long 'break'. It's so successful, in fact, that it's a difficult act to follow, and we could certainly incorporate such a number in a later concert, perhaps in Piccadilly.

This is in fact the first time I have played in the Dome with non-Domus members, and that sensation is most odd. I try to impress on them how wonderful our Dome is, but I can see that they are all preoccupied with other things, and regard it as no more interesting to play in than one of the marquees at Bracknell, for example. Their only comments about the Dome itself refer to the difficult acoustics, and I realise how defensive we all are about our project. I want it to be as impressive on the strength of one visit as it becomes when you have the chance of living with it. I can't bear it that other musicians should think of it as just a tent!

I am really looking forward to having a talk with Roger Dean, but at the end of the evening I'm so exhausted by the day – rehearsing and playing a concerto at lunchtime, and rehearsing and playing jazz in the evening – that I can hardly speak by the time we get to the Indian restaurant. Ashley's head is practically resting on the table cloth, but Roger seems as lively as ever, bursting with ideas, and stays until after midnight before setting off on the two-hour drive to London. I wish I had his magic metabolism.

Friday 10 July

At 5 p.m. there is a rehearsal of the Bach Flute Suite in the Dome, and immediately the music resumes its ambiguous quality, which had seemed to disappear in the last concert. The group is divided into two parts, one of which wants the music to be more flowing and more directional in its phrasing, while the other wants poise, the slow swing of the musical pendulum. The acoustical problems of the last performance are greatly relieved by the addition of Nina Wurman on double bass, and listening from outside the Dome I'm aware of what, for the first time, seems the correct balance between treble and bass instruments. I get chatting to the Head of the BBC Transcription Service, who compliments the group on its playing and compares it very favourably to the Baroque playing of a well-known group appearing in the Official Festival.

Saturday 11 July

The janitor of the Town Hall reveals to us that a group of skinheads were caught climbing on the frame of the Dome last night and were warned off by police. Various chairs have been tipped off the stage, but inside everything seems to be more or less undisturbed.

Even after one day's rest, I find it quite hard to get into the swing of the lunchtime concert, which may be partly because Ruth and Robin do the introduction (extremely well) and I'm not buzzing with adrenalin when the time comes to play. Dickie opens the concert with two light pieces – one by Glazunov, and one Fauré – which set the tone beautifully. Then we play the Fauré Piano Quartet, introduced by Robin, who has clearly derived some benefit from his day in the cathedral, and sounds very relaxed. Sir Lennox Berkeley and his wife are at the concert, and Robin notes with trepidation that they are sitting in just the worst place, acoustically – on the extreme right of the audience, where the volume of the piano is too great. Nevertheless Sir Lennox generously says afterwards that he didn't mind the over-balancing, as he liked the piano part so much. Everyone else says that the acoustic was perfect, now that we have faced the piano more away from the audience.

The Fauré has changed subtly since our last performance. I felt that none of us was nearly so alert as we were the other day, but I also felt a new spaciousness in the music, and felt that I had time to bring out some of the passing detail in a new way. Felix says that we all made stupid mistakes and played lots of wrong notes, but everyone who heard both performances said very positively that today's was much better, and I'm baffled by the gap between the performers' impression of how the piece is going, and the audience's response to it. Richard Ireland, who complained that all the detail was glossed over in the first performance, was much happier with today's and said that it felt really settled and grandiose where it needed to be.

A discussion on acoustics follows the concert. Sir Lennox, the Head of the BBC Transcription Service, and one or two interested members of the audience debate various solutions such as a sounding-board behind the piano, an absorbent disc hung from the roof, a cloth hung behind the stage to muffle some of the reflective surfaces, and so on. We decide to try the sounding-board, since we have one in the form of the front wall of the trailer, now lying unused under the stage.

The Saturday evening concert unfortunately attracts only a small audience, probably because of the cold and rain. Nobody feels like changing into our flimsy white concert clothes. We begin with two movements from the Bolling Suite, which suddenly seem more tedious than they did in the last performance. Then the Bach Flute Suite is introduced by Robin in a 10-minute speech laden with deprecatory remarks. 'We've had a huge amount of trouble rehearsing this . . . with our different backgrounds we all have different ideas on authentic Bach playing . . . in this movement we can never agree whether to use this bow stroke, or this one . . . the overture isn't really meant to be listened to . . .' and the like. The players are all consumed with amusement, but I wonder how wise it is to reveal to the audience the dissent amongst the players. It seems significant that, having alerted the audience to the number of compromises that had to be made, the performance sounds a bit like that. Nevertheless it's delightful to see the two Ireland faces (two brothers) and the two Wurman faces (brother and sister) next to each other on the platform, each with their characteristic family facial expressions as they play.

Robin and I begin the second half with the Rachmaninov *Vocalise* arranged for viola and piano. I insist on introducing it, so that he doesn't have a chance to say that we found it difficult, and the performance is far more relaxed than it was the other day. Then comes the Shostakovich piano quintet, which is also much quirkier and more spacious than before. I have a curious synaesthetic sensation while playing it that each phrase is like a trench that one can walk along, scattering things or picking them out of the earth.

After the concert a van-load of people departs for the Cotswold Beer Festival in the Tithe Barn at Postlip. This festival is one of the most extraordinary sights I've ever seen, located in a mediaeval tithe barn of beautiful Cotswold stone, with Real Ale stalls packed around the perimeter. Outside, where sausages are being cooked over an open fire, there are groups of people singing, dancing, lying in heaps in the grass, serenading the moon, accosting strangers, competing with one another to sing rude canons, and so on, while inside the barn there is a folk band which is being good-naturedly heckled and booed by an appreciative audience. We immediately start saying how wonderful the Dome would look here, but also realise that even these good-humoured beer drinkers probably wouldn't want to hear the sort of music we would be playing if we were playing here.

Sunday 12 July

The lunchtime concert today – Beethoven Serenade and Mozart K.414 – attracts one of our fullest audiences yet, and the playing is given extra impetus by the presence of the Irelands, and in particular by Patrick (Robin's Dad), who sits very centrally on a cushion and looks unusually attentive. Michael later says that he did several things in the Beethoven only because of Patrick, and playing the Mozart concerto, I keep seeing Patrick's smile of comprehension reflected in the front of the piano, which inspires me to do various new things with phrasing and dynamics in an attempt to keep that smile sustained.

After this concert the Irelands all comment on the startling improvement in presentation since our opening concert in Harrow, and Peggy says that we have now got it 'exactly right'. I'm pleased to have gained confidence in speaking to the audience, which I want to do because I think it's important, but which makes my heart beat so violently that I can't control my hands when I sit down to play afterwards. It's funny that playing the piano to an audience doesn't make me shake, but speaking to them does.

We are all rather irritated by a Festival visitor who seems to have adopted us, or to have cast himself in the role of Stage Manager, which he claims is his profession. He hangs around us at all possible times, sitting in the dome during all rehearsals, during private practice, when we're relaxing, and now has taken it upon himself to sleep in the dome at nights, though God knows why, to protect it. He's a man in his fifties who seems knowledgeable about the arts, but it's unnerving to see the confidence with which he attaches himself to us, in the belief that we shall welcome his help and advice on everything from the hanging of mobiles to the introduction of pieces. I tried to make it clear to him this morning that his sleeping in the dome was an unnecessary piece of self-sacrifice, but he simply said that he was happy to help, and that he would be installed in there at night until the end of the week. I don't understand what he gets out of it.

We all depart after the concert for a walk in the Forest of Dean, and on the way back we discuss the events of the past week and try to assess how everything is going.

Basically everyone feels that it has been a very good week, the only disappointment being that the audiences have numbered on average 50, instead of 150. But Richard Ireland feels that the atmosphere at Dome concerts, while friendly and conducive to a general sense of well-being in the music, is not quite right for subtle playing. I try to ask what exactly it is that he feels militates against subtle playing, as so many things seem to be in its favour: the intimacy, the support of the audience, the acoustical enhancing of detail – and he agrees, saying that he can't quite put a finger on what it is. But after some discussion with Dickie, they both agree that not enough thought is given to the homogeneity of playing styles within the group. Not all of us play well with each other, and yet the group is divided up more or less randomly, or at any rate democratically, for each large piece of chamber music. They both feel that the subtlety will never rise above a certain level if the group contains so many diverse musical styles and performing personalities.

I mention this to Michael and Ruth, both of whom disagree. They both feel that the most important element to share in a group like Domus is the sense of ideals about performing. We all came together because we wanted a certain atmosphere and a certain contact with our listeners, and they feel that this is a far better basis for developing a homogeneous group sound than to start with similar musical styles and disregard the diverse aspirations and motives of the players. Both of them feel that Richard Ireland, for example, does not appreciate Domus because he does not have the years of experience of deadening orchestral playing, or ad hoc chamber music, or of playing in ensembles where the players get away from each other as quickly as possible when the rehearsal ends, and are indifferent to each other's lifestyles. Both feel that for Richard, playing in Domus may not be so different from playing in college to an audience of friendly colleagues, and that we, having encountered the problematic freelance scene in London, are in a better position to appreciate the qualities of Domus concerts. My own position is pretty near this, though I do agree with Richard and Dickie that not enough thought is given to exactly who plays with whom in the various pieces. It's very nice to feel that everyone's playing can be trusted enough that names can be drawn almost out of a hat for whatever piece needs to be cast, but I often feel uncomfortable with a particular player in a particular piece, and know very well that someone else in the group would have done better. We have so far been remarkably free of discrimination, and have favoured no single player at the expense of another, or made it clear that we value one person's playing more than another's – so it seems a pity to begin a policy of scrutiny, of considering the wisdom of certain people's participation in certain pieces. But I see the shadow of such a policy looming up.

Monday 13 July

Unwisely, we have agreed to lend the Dome to a visiting fringe group from Manchester, but wish we hadn't, as it feels such an intrusion. Wishing to rehearse ourselves, we are forced to find somewhere else because our own venue isn't available, and then get in a very bad mood because poor communication and organisation among us lead to a whole series of delays, sadly rather typical of us these days. Leisure time is badly needed, yet we seem to squander every chance we have of obtaining it, as though we are addicted to being 'on duty'.

In the evening several members of the group go to hear the first half of the Philharmonia concert, and Felix and I have a drink in the Gardens while waiting for them to emerge at the interval. Felix has begun to think about next year, and is concerned about the possibility that members of Domus may be seduced away from the project by financially more secure employment. Felix wants to know if I might also come to this sort of decision, and I tell him that I can't imagine a group with which I would feel it more worthwhile to play. In fact, as a pianist, there is much less chance that I will be offered this kind of job anyway, as pianists are not needed in orchestras.

Felix feels, quite rightly, that people's commitment to Domus would be much less fragile if we were able to offer more money. If, for example, we were backed by a big firm (which Felix thinks is much more likely to happen in America) or if we had a large bursary from the Arts Council or similar, we would not be in the position of having to ask people to make actual sacrifices to be in the group. Everyone is happy to give up a part of the summer for no remuneration, and even to pay their expenses themselves, but clearly this attitude could not hold fast over the rest of the year. It seems appalling that a project so optimistic should be put in jeopardy because it can't attract any funding. Felix wonders whether, if we found a substantial sum in sponsorship, Domus members would stick with the group for a greater part of the year, and we conclude that the answer would be about half and half.

Again, this is all bound up with money. Part of the strain of being 'on tour' with Domus is the multiple occupation of small flats, the three people sharing rooms, the feeling of encroaching on other people's hospitality, the constant worrying about spending fairly large amounts of money on things like petrol, food and drink when we never know if we shall be able to claim any of it back from the Domus account. But if we were more secure financially, we could buy ourselves more space and more varied food, and would not always be working through sacks of brown rice, and confronting our slender budget.

We realise now that we should have arranged Cheltenham on the same basis as we've arranged Piccadilly – being paid a pre-arranged sum, and leaving the gate money to the Festival. Here in Cheltenham we can have made no more than £50 per concert in total, and usually quite a lot less, which is a much worse outcome than we anticipated. We have not tried to divide it up yet, but it's clear that if we stick to our original scheme of paying back people's expenses before dividing up the remainder equally amongst the players, the whole amount of our takings could disappear in the expenses.

When I contemplate going back to the traditional concert format after a glimpse of how different everything could be, I really feel a sense of waste that Domus should pack up after only a month, and have to start building momentum again in a year's time. Despite our failure to make a profit, it has felt artistically so worthwhile.

Tuesday 14 July

In the morning a rather tense rehearsal of the Dvořák Quintet for Strings is interrupted by the arrival of hordes of tiny children under the impression that there is a children's theatre show in the Dome – a mistake, not of our making, in the Fringe brochure. Half the group wants to improvise a little concert for them, and the other half feels that it's not our responsibility to compensate for the mistake of the administrators, and wants to abandon the tinies to their disappointment. In the end Robin plays his *Vocalise* and Michael plays *Danse de la Chèvre*, both of which hold the tinies' attention for about one minute. Then Felix's Mum offers to do some group play-exercises with them, and teaches them all how to get up on the stage and bow, and how to recognise the difference between A and E on the violin, as demonstrated by Ruth. The tinies are a bit bewildered by this mixture of being entertained and then entertaining the audience, but some of them have a fine time.

In the evening we all go to Stratford, where we manage to get tickets for the new production of *Midsummer Night's Dream*. It's slightly disappointing to find such a gimmicky and commercial production; the mostly American audience responds noisily to the slapstick and to the innuendo, and fidgets during the serious bits. As Ruth says, it's a production geared very much to the tourist trade in Stratford. It strikes a peculiarly sour note to see excellent actors in such a commercial produc-tion, and we feel it's a lesson in the dangers of orienting things too much towards what you imagine the audience wants of you. People do to a large extent accept the image you choose to present of yourself, and we've already found that presenting our concerts too informally dissipates people's concentration on the music, while presenting them with a proper sense of self-respect induces that same respect in the listeners.

We're incredulous to hear that the local newspaper, which has been constantly badgered by both Fringe and Festival organisers to review one of our concerts, has announced its intention to come to the Dome to photograph a local theatre group inside it, and to write about them, but not to mention us. We contemplate refusing them entry, but eventually decide simply not to abet them in any way. Later we realise that they won't even have noticed this subtle reproach.

Wednesday 15 July

Some of us go to the morning concert given by the Orlando Quartet in the Pump Room. It's most odd, at first, to be at such a formal concert attended by the usual Official Festival audience, and to see the players so serious and silent on the stage. But it's true that in such an atmosphere it's easy to concentrate, if you want to concentrate, and this is perhaps what Richard Ireland wants in his concert performing. I think all of us are struck by several things in the concert, enviable and unenviable. It's obvious, for one thing, that the players are completely free to think about the music, having emerged from their cosy hotel rooms to play to their guar-anteed audience of highly cultured people. It's also obvious that the unifying factor in the quartet is the sound, which is astonishingly unanimous. Of course one can't tell, not hearing them speak or being allowed any glimpse of their personalities, whether they are also unified in social respects, but from what little I know about them I guess that this is perhaps not so important to them as it is to us.

I'm also struck by the fact that they don't do anything to draw attention to them-selves in their playing - only to things in the music. This is very different from our concerts, in which people frequently try to draw attention to themselves, or at any rate to demonstrate visually to the audience their delight in the ingredients of chamber music playing. None of the Orlando Quartet smiled once during the performance, whereas we smile all the time, and it's one of the things that listeners most often comment about. Yet we, I suppose, are at least as much interested in the effect that we, specifically *we*, have on the interpretation, and want to alert the audi-ence to our personal qualities and the diversity of endearing things which define the group's image. If the Orlando Quartet's bodies had disappeared, and music issued magically from the instruments alone, I don't think it would have made any differ-ence to the way I heard them, or to my admiration of their musicianship. But if the members of Domus became invisible, I should think about thirty per cent of the attractive features of our playing would be lost. Is this good or bad?

I'm not sure which is a better approach to *performing*, quite apart from which is better in the abstract, but I feel rather glad that we reach the audience on more levels than simply instrumental. Of course, with a structure like the Dome, there is the danger that the visual appeal will relieve the players of the need to concentrate all their appeal in the sound, but I think we're all conscious of this. Nina remarked the other day that she was surprised to find that just the atmosphere of the Dome alone wasn't enough to create a special atmosphere in the concerts, but the rest of us realised it last year, and perhaps most forcibly in Harrow, where we suddenly didn't know what to do once the audience had got over its surprise and delight at the Dome itself.

Johannes Goritzki [Felix's cello teacher in Germany] in fact may have been the first person to realise the danger of relaxing in the shadow of the Dome, and it may have been two years ago that he tried to impress on Felix that having a novel shell for concerts would never be enough to keep the players satisfied and keep the concerts interesting. He said that our sense of worth had to come from our playing, not just from having had a novel and enterprising idea, and how true that has turned out to be, now that we've solved most of the technical problems of the Dome.

Robin and I have a typical afternoon on the phone, trying to fix up, confirm, and arrange things for the Piccadilly Festival. While waiting for Robin to book piano movers, I have an idea about a new kind of Open Rehearsal in which the players would actively solicit the audience's participation in making an interpretation. We could each support a different approach to the piece, and would try out all the possibilities, encouraging the audience to say which they liked, and to comment on individual players. We'd try to show how an interpretation is arrived at, because I'm sure that inexperienced listeners often get the impression that it's simply a question of learning the notes and playing together, and have no idea of how many alternatives are proposed in the course of rehearsing. We'd try to show how, once you've made certain decisions about beginning a piece, you have to follow them with certain others, and so on. Robin says you'd need a pretty sophisticated audience, but perhaps it could be done more simply – with instant composition workshops, for example? We decide that improvising should be the next priority for Domus, to loosen us all up.

Listening to the Dvořák Quintet in today's lunchtime concert, I'm aware of various things which could be worked upon in the group's approach. One is conscious of the players trying to match each other point by point along the phrases, at every place they know they have a chord together, at every point where they know that their part combines significantly with other parts. Thus the momentum of the performance is no more than the sum of five players trying to co-ordinate their phrases with one another, and the élan is a kind of orchestral élan, with no individual player taking the responsibility for the direction of the music.

I remember David Waterman [the cellist of the Endellion Quartet] saying, apropos of Endellion rehearsals, that one could only progress so far by trying to subordinate one's own part to the existence of others. He said that it was easier for a quartet if the leader simply played with the confidence of his own momentum, and that it was surprisingly easy to follow someone who took charge of a phrase, or section, without constant reference to the other parts. After he said this I tried it out myself in the next available rehearsal, and found that it really worked, so I still try to do it, and know that when other people do it, it is indeed easy to follow.

At an advanced level, as with the Orlando Quartet, they clearly knew the piece so well that they all agreed on its momentum and played practically without reference to each other, the charge being distributed evenly amongst the four players, as far as I could see. They did not make a point of matching each other at large and small milestones in the music, as we do, and the result was a kind of seamless phrasing which erased all traces of rehearsal procedure. This is probably largely a question of knowing the music, and each other's playing very, very well, which we have hardly had a chance to do.

But when I think about the Dvořák Quintet I see that the group's approach is too confined to small units of time and of music. And that everyone tries democratically to be aware of everyone else, almost to the extent of giving the impression that they don't trust the others to know where they are in the music and trying therefore to make everything clear. I wonder how it would work to rehearse things with a different player each time being the 'leader', playing at his or her own momentum and forcing the others to play *with*, not simply at the same time as them.

Thursday 16 July

On the way to a morning concert, a discussion about the wisdom of participating in an established festival as part of its 'fringe'. Several members of the group have come to dislike the comparisons constantly being made between the atmosphere of Official concerts and the atmosphere of ours, even when the comparison is in our favour. Every time we go to an Official Concert, we notice the effortlessly large audience they attract, almost regardless of the quality of the players, and we resent the fact that we have to struggle so hard to publicise ourselves. We wonder whether, if we came back here, we would be able to come back as part of the Official Festival, simply to guarantee ourselves some automatic attention.

We feel that in Cheltenham the authorities have encouraged our presence here simply to display their liberal attitude, but aren't prepared to help us in concrete ways. The organiser of the Festival has not even been to one of our concerts, and yet declares himself happy with the alternative image we've brought to the hitherto rather formal Festival. We don't want to be set up as the 'token black' in a famous festival, and would rather be the only event in the place we were playing, so that people have to judge us simply according to whether they like our playing or not. Here, we feel that people either say, 'They're part of the Fringe, but they're jolly good', or the converse, 'They're all highly trained classical players, but they're jolly informal', neither of which strikes quite the right note.

Michael continues his discourse on the problems of eating well while on tour. He claims that he now feels as though he hasn't eaten a proper meal for five days, and that he notices the detrimental effect on his energy supply. We all more or less concur in this, and as Ruth says, it's a pity that our restricted budget forces us to buy the sort of things which take ages to cook, like the beans/lentils/rice and vegetables which we ate at Finemere during the rehearsal week. Michael declares that when we next go on Domus tour, we have to take along a cook. I must say it's a great relief when, in between the afternoon rehearsal and evening concert, Felix's mother arrives with trays of salad and boxes of quiche, and we are spared another meal of pasties and sandwiches from the tea-tent.

Felix and Dickie open the concert with seven Bartók Duos which go down very well, and are very entertaining to watch, with Dickie's face expressing all the grand and serious emotions, and Felix's all the mischievous and extrovert. Then Ruth, Michael and Robin play the Beethoven Serenade, this time standing up to play it. They play it very well, but the piece is about double the length it needs to be, and after the fourth movement, even the other players begin to fidget. Felix and I agree that it's not a good idea to play music which has a built-in fidget ingredient to an audience which is not sure if it can sit through a classical concert or not.

Unfortunately this is one of our smallest audiences yet, and is relieved only by the presence of some unexpected people, including the composer Robin Holloway. We're glad that we changed the programme from the Dvořák Quintet (insufficiently rehearsed) to the Fauré piano quartet, now that he is in the audience and expresses excitement about hearing it. This inspires me with a wish to demonstrate to him how well we understand the music, and it turns out to be our most spontaneous performance of the three, and to please him a lot. In the middle of the last movement Michael (who is listening) says that he has a sudden realisation of how important it is for him to be in Domus.

On the way home we try to work out the finances of these two weeks. It's clear that, if we allow £20 petrol expenses for each of five cars, and Ruth's train fare, it will leave us with about £100 in the bank, out of which have to be paid seven players, and the bills for various things like spanners, gloves, communal food and drink. Thus each player will earn less than ten pounds for two weeks of very hard work. This is a harsh and unjust ending to the fortnight.

Friday 17 July

In the morning we are dismayed by the appearance of the dome after the onslaught of the theatre group, who have arranged all the chairs in straight rows as they would in a rectangular theatre, and have cluttered up our stage with screens, electrical equipment, band instruments, dressing-room accessories and the like. We are sad that they are insensitive to the shape of the dome, and we're also surprised how little it takes to obscure that shape. We rearrange as many as we can of the chairs in our old arcs, with cushions at the front.

At lunchtime we're coming out of the shed after having changed, and are amazed to see a queue of people waiting outside the dome for more seats to be added, those inside being already full. At a quick glance there must be more than a hundred people, and we wonder why, on this particular day, Domus has suddenly leapt into the consciousness of the festival public. I ask the audience what inspired them to come to this particular programme, and the consensus is that word of mouth has delivered great opinions of us – though too late, of course. Various people describe how their neighbours at concerts in the official festival recommended us, and others were phoned by their friends. Everyone seems to think that if we stayed for another week, our concerts would certainly be full, but Thomas says that, from his experience in theatre work, there's no rhyme or reason for the behaviour of audiences during a 'run' of concerts, and that the audience's prediction may not be true.

At any rate the Dome is packed for the first time in England, and this makes Thomas decide that today is the day to improvise his mime about the relationship of a non-musician to musical instruments, in which (he reveals later) the cello becomes a buxom wench, the double bass an interfering mother, the viola a cute toddler, the violin a passive baby between a bored couple, and the piano a car. He decides to insert the mime between the Bach solo flute Partita and Schubert's Trout Quintet, but it quickly becomes evident that this is the wrong programme for it, partly because of the length of the programme in relation to people's lunch hours, and partly because of the personality of this audience.

After Michael has given a splendid performance of the Bach, Thomas goes and sits cross-legged on the stage with a book, and gradually the audience realises that they are meant to be looking at him. But he misjudges the length of his preamble, which consists of picking his nose with various implements ranging from violin bows to shoulder pads, and with Robin's yellow duster. He then makes three bows into a 'Venetian blind', held by three members of the front row, and pretends to go to sleep behind them. Then he breaks into speech and tries to explain to the audience the fact that he doesn't speak English, and at this point the audience starts getting restless. One man shouts from the back, 'Get on with the music!' and a bit later, 'We've come to hear a concert', which brings murmurs of agreement from a section of the audience. Thomas falters, decides to give up, and ends with a little apology for his experiment, which is applauded by another section of the audience.

It's a pity that this improvised section of the concert doesn't work, and we wish it had been inserted into a more suitable programme, and into one where time is less important. The Trout is about 40 minutes long, and it really is the Trout that people have come to hear, as is clear from their blissful faces during the performance. Towards the end there is a sudden rainstorm which sounds quite deafening on the cover, and it almost obscures the forte passages on the last page. People comment afterwards on how nice it was to listen to music in the rain, and in particular a sort of watery piece like the Trout. The applause is fairly deafening too, but I'm surprised to find that in many ways I prefer our smaller audiences, the quality of whose attention seems finer, at least judging from the sort of things they say afterwards.

We all go for supper to Michael Hunt's house, where formation juggling practice takes place, people pass around e.e.cummings and read things aloud, the merits of opera are hotly debated, and conscientious members of the group go off to hear the Northern Sinfonia concert and return some time later to find the rest of us considerably the worse for several more bottles of wine. When I drive Patrick back to the dome to guard it, I decide that the time has come to have a serious word with our self-appointed guardian who continues to sleep there despite our own watchman being there too. But both Patrick and Robin are worried about my tackling him so late at night. In fact Robin is so agitated about my plan that he refuses even to witness the possibility, and jumps out of the car and runs off into the darkness. I agree to pick a less vulnerable time for this confrontation.

Saturday 18 July

We have our first Money Meeting, at which we abandon all previous policies of dividing the money in various subtle ways (such as paying people's rent) and opt simply for refunding Felix money he has spent on various technical things, repaying petrol expenses and dividing the remainder in seven. This leaves us with about £17 each for two weeks of work. It is shocking, and rouses us angrily to denounce the festival authorities who claim that we enhanced the festival, but did so little to help us in concrete ways.

As always, on a day when we don't have a concert, I feel quite disorientated by the lack of focus in the day, and I do notice that, over the fortnight, I've been able both to charge up my usual state of being and to feel more relaxed in performance. What I usually dislike about being a performing artist is the lack of integration between the performance days and the other days in one's life. Life is either super-charged or under-charged, and trying to leap from one state into the other is quite a strain. Here, because the performances have been so frequent, one simply can't treat them as events to build towards, and one can sustain a pleasantly high level of concentration around a performance which makes the concert less isolated from the other events of the day. I don't feel that concert-giving becomes ordinary, but rather that everything becomes more alive because of the ongoing Adrenalin Factor. But when I mention this to Richard Ireland he disagrees, saying that he would prefer there to be fewer concerts, more rehearsal, and more sense of occasion.

We have a session with the actor David Gann to work out some poetry for him to read in tomorrow's final concert. The programme opens with Bartók Duos, and David experiments with various kinds of accompanying poem, from Eliot's *Quartets*: 'Words move. Music moves only in time' etc. to poems by Gerard Manley Hopkins, but in the end we decide that these are too complex and serious for Bartok, and for a Sunday lunchtime audience, and try instead some poems on the opposite side of the emotional scale, such as Roger McGough's poem about making love on the bus, and Herrick's poems about his mistress's anatomy. Eventually we decide on the McGough, an e.e. cummings poem about a car and an exciting journey in it, and some pastoral Hopkins to precede the Trout.

David, who has heard us debating our various tours and the community arts side of our project, mentions that we may be wrong to think primarily of playing chamber music to people who aren't used to it and don't go to concerts. He thinks that, even if we succeeded in intriguing people or alerting them to something new, their response nevertheless would not be satisfying enough to the players to justify weeks of intensive rehearsal, and that we need, in some measure, the sort of informed response one gets from listeners who really know what they're listening to, and know the significance of our approach. He said it would be at least as valuable to come to established festivals like this one to demonstrate to jaded audiences that chamber music can be fresh, friendly and still of a high standard. That our role may be as least as much to re-orient stale ears which have been attending concerts for years and are thoroughly versed in the formal traditions of them. This seems a good idea: a blend of taking new music to the inexperienced listener, and taking enthusiastic, idealistic performances to a jaded festival audience.

Cheltenham was not our only festival that summer, but I have described it in detail as representative of our first public season. Later in the summer we took the Dome – again with a very poor financial outcome – to the Piccadilly Festival in London, where the nearby street was dreadfully noisy, and the weather very unkind to us. Because we had nowhere else to put them, we hung our concert clothes from the frame of the Dome, and they were damp when we came to put them on! The keys of the piano were actually wet when we opened the lid in the morning, and during concerts, the wind blew the music off our stands. These were hardly conditions in which musicians could flourish.

It was during this period that I started to feel really oppressed by all the administration I was doing for the group. There was so much to do that music was often the last thing on my mind, and playing the piano was often postponed until the late evening, when I had hardly the energy to practice. Nobody had ever officially asked me to take charge of the administration, but as often happens with these things, I ended up doing it because I could see what needed to be done. Obviously my talents didn't lie in the practical dome-building activities, so it seemed natural that I should do some office work – though of course after the dome-building problems were largely solved, the administration just grew and grew until it became more than a full-time job. I began to feel that I couldn't keep up the standard of my piano playing if I was spending twelve-hour days on office work. I began to flag the idea that we should try to raise some money to pay a part-time administrator.

Talks with Russell Hoban, February–March 1982

Krysia and I have been reading Russell Hoban's new book, *Riddley Walker*. We have both been fans of his work for a while, since reading *Turtle Diary*, a good example of his whimsical, humorous yet spiritual approach. We get the idea of writing to Russell Hoban to ask if he would be at all interested in writing us a kind of music-theatre piece, or something for us to speak and improvise music to. For Krysia and me, the idea of writing to him is as magnetic as the idea of mystical union with a sort of Doppelgänger. After much procrastination from both of us, it's me who writes the letter. I tell him about the number of times that Krysia and I egged one another on to phone him from call boxes in mainline stations at midnight, on our way home from concerts, to tell him how much we liked his books (fortunately he was never in).

A few days later, as I have exhausted all the avenues down which I have been trying telepathically to witness his reaction, he telephones. He says he *is* interested in writing something for musicians, and would like to come to tea. After this I am in a state of pleasurable anticipation which I express by making a notice that says 'Russell Hoban is coming to tea' with silver stars around it and green hearts like turtle hearts. I pin it on the kitchen board, and it's still there when he comes to tea ten days later, much to my embarrassment.

To our amazement Russell Hoban views my letter, and our appearance in his creative life generally, as 'a propitious thing'. He has been writing a new book, *Pilgermann*, and thinking about popular music; he says he's become more and more aware that his next project would involve music in some way, and our letter seemed to be the confirmation. The whole of his conversation is permeated with his belief more than belief, his *knowing* – that nothing is random, that you have to listen intelligently to the interference in your ordered life and in your plans and allow apparently chance elements to guide you into new areas.

He describes how he works in a room with two short-wave radios and a tape

player, and says that he listens constantly to stations like All-India Radio and
Chinese Radio while he writes, deliberately disengaging part of his mind from the
writing process so that space is left for new ingredients supplied by things that
happen on the radio, or on the tapes. He says that the popular conception of 'concentration' is a hoax. Shutting out everything but your own thoughts is no way to
play intelligently in the universe. This approach is, of course, one that deeply
touches me because I've always felt exactly the same; if stuck in the groove of my
own thinking, I simply go round in circles unless I deliberately take myself somewhere where someone or something else can articulate a new thought that I can use
as a door.

Russell Hoban thinks that popular music is maybe the best; the most profound
because it reaches such large numbers of people, and is about things that matter to
them. For a while I'm afraid that I'm not going to like him if he can't see that great
classical music is also about things that matter to people, but after half an hour of
mild misunderstanding we agree that it's not enough simply to be about things that
matter, but to say them in a way that people understand. With classical music you
have to make quite an effort to understand, even when you are an initiate; thus
popular music does have what Russell Hoban calls 'cheap profundity', meaning
available profundity.

Krysia and I play him some Szymanowski, and a whole Mozart sonata, K.376.
He makes a couple of notes in his notebook; says he hasn't sat so close to musicians
for years and years, recalls how he once set up an easel in the middle of a string
quartet to sketch them, and how the thought came to him that the music was insep-
arable from the effort of making it. This leads us to talking about how important the
live element is; he thinks that even a record of so 'physical' a player as Casals is a
mere simulacrum, but Krysia disagrees, saying that even though it's a record you still
have a powerful sense of Casals sitting there breathing and wheezing over the cello
clamped between his knees. It may not be a problem for writers; there isn't 'live'
writing and mummified writing in the same way.

One interesting thing is that he can't quite understand, or pretends not to understand, why we want to be known by our audiences as *people* as well as musicians.
Isn't our musical personality enough? Do we feel that we would somehow make
ourselves viable as human beings by speaking to the audience? Do we feel more
completely represented by our speaking than by our playing? I ask him if he doesn't
feel a discrepancy between his literary persona and his social one, and he says no.
This is obviously completely true; everything he says is like the voice in his books –
self-contained, reserved, direct, mysteriously whimsical.

We try to explain the qualities which seem to be available to us in music-making,
but not available in our social selves. He says it doesn't mean that the qualities are
magically bestowed upon us by a higher authority when we abandon ourselves to
music; just that music calls for those qualities, whereas our lives probably don't, 'or
haven't done so yet', he says prophetically. He asks us to play him something, and
seeing that we're still a bit nervous, he asks us not to try to be efficient in giving
account of ourselves. Everything will turn out to be significant, he feels sure, so we
should just say whatever comes into our heads and not filter out things which seem
to be unworthy, because even chance elements may give him the clue to a connection. He's like the connection man in *Riddley Walker*, and watching him out of the

corner of my eye while I'm playing, his face dryly alert like an intelligent frog's, I have the strongest feeling that he is not well represented by his physical self, that he doesn't *really* look as he appears to look. My instinct is that he 'really' looks like a Paul Klee drawing, but of course a drawing is just an image too, not the way a real person could look.

Just before his visit the *I Ching* predicts the importance of 'yellow lines on a black background', which I take to be a reference to Russell Hoban's letter to me: black ink on yellow paper.

February 1982

Russell Hoban says he can't understand why people succumb to the pressure to specialise – or can't see why versatile people can't step aside from the hypocrisy of the pressure – and so I think that perhaps it *is* time to become active on lots of musical fronts, and to be part of the process of change back to a kind of Renaissance versatility. We've all always said how much we envy the Renaissance its values, and now perhaps it's time for us to play a significant role in the transition to a better sense of values in the twentieth century.

Writing this I'm reminded of yesterday, when Russell Hoban asked what it was that identified a composer as himself when you hear his music. I replied that very often it's the manner of transition that identifies the composer. Not even one idea, or another, but the way of arriving at an idea, or leaving one. Transitions have always fascinated me and I believe they fascinate all of us in Domus. Certainly we find ourselves discussing them in rehearsal a great deal.

As I sat down to write this I had forgotten the preceding couple of pages in which I described Russell Hoban's first visit, and when I read them over just now I realised what a wealth of telling detail would have been left out of my account composed a month after the event; I therefore decided to write down all that has happened since, on the grounds that all of it will, as Russell would assure us, turn out to be significant.

After his first visit I got on the phone to the Greater London Arts Association and asked them if they would consider funding a commissioned work from Russell Hoban. The Literature Dept said that no-one had ever asked such a question before, and it took them a week or so to formulate a reply, which was basically Yes. I wrote to Russell to tell him this, and had back a prompt letter which made me feel rather as if I had been too forward with a new boyfriend, projecting our relationship into a future which he did not wish to share. He said that he didn't want a commission fee because he didn't want to have to promise to write us anything, didn't want to have a deadline or feel the pressure of expectation. The letter, however, changed tone with relieving speed, and he went on to say that he'd been thinking of Mozart in connection with two watercolours of tracks across a heath, towards an unseen sea; he connected this to the idea of geography in music, saying that there are places in music like there are places in everything. I replied to this, telling him of my old fantasy of the places in music where I felt that, if only I could slow down my perception of time enough, I could 'part' the musical fabric and rush through between two chords to a safe place where I would be invisible. *In* the music, as though it were a knoll in a forest, as though it had the sort of depth one could dig one's fingers into, instead of merely the metaphorical 'depth' we refer to in analysing harmony or texture.

He replied, continuing the thought and saying that we put notes together like we put words together, as a map of places to go, or as a map of a way to go. Reading this I remembered the curious sensation I once had during an Italian church concert in which Végh played the Bach D minor partita. It was partly an illusion caused by his 'speaking' tone on the violin, and partly it was the very real contours of his sound, like contours on a map, but I felt that instead of listening to music I was listening to *information*, and that I could not afford to miss a single link in the sense of it. I had no urge to drift in and out of the music as I so often do. It was like being lost in a maze and hearing someone explain, just once, the way out of it. Lots of good performers give me the sensation of knowing how to get lost *in* the music, but not many make me feel certain they can find their way out.

Our fragile relationship with Russell took a turn for the worse when we told him about some of our other projects and plans. Unfortunately some of them involved people and notions that he disliked. He felt that if we liked them, we couldn't like him, or at any rate we couldn't be in sympathy with both at the same time. We had to try hard to persuade him that we were not merely grabbing at every idea that came our way, and that we had a wide range of reference points amongst the group. To our great relief, Russell accepted this and agreed to write to us again with more of his views on the creative process.

In the next letter he talked about duplicates. Records, photographs, cassettes, and Borges's idea of a map of the town as big as the town it's a map of. Although Russell is an equipment freak, or so he says, he's thinking more and more of the evils of recording. One of his essays jokes about a super-sophisticated recording machine that will extend rearward in time to replace the sound it was designed to record. He wants a world that will not pass away, in other words. Through the bitter tone of the joking one senses the same emotion that visiting India aroused in me, and curiously enough it is Indian music via All-India Radio that aroused it in him, too. We envied deeply the music that does not depend on memory, that doesn't ask to be remembered. 'It gives us a place to be,' Russell says later. *A place to be* is, perhaps, different from a place to think.

Although it sounds wonderful, this music which doesn't ask to be remembered, there are good and bad examples. Lots of trivial music isn't meant to last. Some music doesn't seek to last because it perfectly expresses our sense of 'now'. Classical music seems to fall into another category, asking to be remembered, and even seeking to replace 'now' with its own sense of time and place.

Russell elaborates his feelings about music in a paragraph that makes us realise sadly that perhaps he is moving away from us. 'What's happened is that I've come to a time where I don't want much emotion in my music; I don't require either to be uplifted or downput by it. . . . I don't want much emotion; I want the dance in the stone. That's how I think of it; the dance in the stone, not the foam for ever fading in the wake of our forward motion. As I write this I'm listening to Haydn opus 54 no. 2 in C; it is lean, muscular, brilliantly brooding; the adagio always breaks my heart. But I find that breaking the heart with music isn't the thrill it once was. What I'm after more and more is on the other side of heartbreak; it's in the stone of things, with bare, spare music that not only doesn't ask to be remembered, it doesn't ask for anything at all, makes no attempt to hold on to the hearer or to anything else.'

A few days later he comes to tea again. This time only I am at home, and we have a very good talk for four hours; my favourite kind of conversation, in which things remind us of other things, and everything seems to be connected, with each topic bringing up a whole network of possible tangents between which I can hardly choose, and stammer as I try to grasp them all. We talk about why Domus needs to speak to its audiences; the first question he asked us, and one which still puzzles him. I explain to him that I'd love to be able to read out his 'cruising' pages to our audiences, but feel that it would be wrong or hypocritical to pretend to do so casually; I want to set it up properly, so that everyone will prepare themselves for the words in the same way that they would prepare for the music. In silence, and with respect.

He agrees, but keeps saying that our own reflections on music and why we play it will be far more interesting than his. Of course this is possible in theory, and it's odd how panicky I feel at the notion that he might pull out of the project, leaving us to dredge our own imaginations for all that we do and say in the dome, instead of allying our imaginations to his, which is so powerful a register. (I almost said 'recording ear', but that, of course, is what he doesn't want to be. I think that I may just have understood his reluctance to commit words about music to paper.)

I feel like one feels when a good teacher gently tries to ease one out of his orbit, to fend for oneself; I know it must be right, in the long run, only that we haven't had a long run on a secure base from which to jump into the unknown of our own resources. We agree that Domus will try to put together a programme in which we really talk about the music, our feelings about it, what it's like to play, etc., and that he will come and listen to this programme and we'll go from there. Not simply talking like programme-notes talk or like a radio announcer talks, but really putting together our knowledge and vulnerability and our wish to make contact with the listener, if we really have one,

Meanwhile Krysia has written to Russell about triangles, and he likes her ideas, replying that he imagines the triangles of the dome outlined in neon, and various configurations of triangles, three players, and the like inside. He says we couldn't do better than put together our musical, alchemical and structural triangles; he's been studying an old alchemical symbol composed of triangles and called the 'Hidden Lion', perhaps like the one in his book *The Lion of Boaz-Jachin and Jachin-Boaz*. Then he warns us that he's going to dive back into his current novel, *Pilgermann*, and that we won't hear from him for a while. But we are heartened; the tone of his letter is once again warm and energetic. Not that one should read this as any more permanent than 'the foam fading in the wake of forward motion'.

Alas, Russell did dive back thoroughly into his novel-writing, and to our great regret, nothing came of the project for him to write us a music theatre piece.

Our visit to Peter Brook in Paris, March 1982

After reading about Peter Brook's theatre experiments, we have long wanted to consult him about Domus. We try to make arrangements to meet him in Paris where he lives, but this turns out to be enormously complicated. After almost a year of negotiation and delay, our visit is finally arranged with the help of a small Arts Council travel grant, but at a time when only Krysia and I are free. But we are so glad to have the chance of talking to him that we we submit to his proposal of an hour's interview, this having been whittled down from a period of several weeks in Paris as observers of his rehearsals, to a day spent with him, and latterly to fractions of a day. On the day before our meeting, his secretary says that he is only free during his lunch-hour, which feels so humiliating that we almost abstain from going. But we go, and I fortify myself mentally for the split-second timing that 1 will need to get from the airport at 11.30 to the Café Le Bastille at 12.30. Of course it goes wrong; the plane is more than half an hour delayed and I miss half of the famous lunch-hour. Luckily Krysia is there for the whole period and in any case Brook says, when our time is up, that we obviously can't stop talking at such an interesting juncture, so we agree to go back after the performance of *Carmen* that evening (which he is directing) and talk to him again.

Brook's flat is in the Escalier Avril in the Passage du Cheval Blanc next to Lucien Gau's lamp shop. An old printing studio has been beautifully renovated and furnished in the Japanese style with all the furniture more or less at floor level. Brook sits on the edge of a floor mattress in Buddha position and listens with the bodily attentiveness he later describes having witnessed in the bazaars of India and Afghanistan. His solid sensual face is enlivened by pale blue eyes unflinching in gaze. When one speaks to him he listens without moving, as a Buddha statue would listen to a supplicant; at pauses he shifts slightly without moving his blue gaze. The tables are piled with books about the Mahabharata, elementary Sanskrit grammars, books on mysticism, records of Indian music.

Brook does not speak much unless asked the right question, and then he replies in a measured flow of perfectly controlled and intricate ideas which roll from level to level, now enigmatic, now practical. He doesn't spare us the full strength of his insight into the arts, and I'm grateful to him for that; nor does he spare us the long egg-shaped silences of consideration before he replies. But these long pauses don't utterly convince me; I almost feel they're inserted like deliberate flaws, to avoid infuriating the gods with too perfect an articulacy. He speaks like an upper-class Englishman and in such a civilised way that one is lulled into listening casually; suddenly one realises with a shock that what he is saying is as strong as pure alcohol.

Brook speaks of the need for gurus; at a certain stage of preparation, he says, no matter how zealous one is in searching out the right path for oneself, one needs the intervention of a guru to raise the search onto the next level. The way he says this, with an enviable lack of self-deprecation, makes me wonder if he sees himself as fulfilling the guru role for us. And in the bright white light of his kitchen, facing him across a table and watching his calm head measured against a great white expense of bright wall, he seems so still and sure that he is indeed magnetic. I wonder how he feels about the people who regard him as a guru; if he feels no pawing of alarm. You can endow something with power by venerating it. Even if someone is venerated against their will, perhaps a power *is* called into being. It certainly feels like it during our talk.

First we speak about the stages of development of a performance. Brook constantly uses the analogy of cooking, and says that so many performances are arrested at the stage of preparation, 'the chopping of the food'. Even if they pass from preparation to development, very few people know how to get the impetus which turns development into fruition. He talks about how this is done in his own company: how the three casts worked for 12 hours every day for 3 months on *Carmen*, for example. Brook says that he has always envied music its attitude to each performance as a fresh and unique event, and says that actors could learn from that. But he thinks that musicians could learn from the momentum that develops in a performance given many times, as happens in the theatre.

In his experience, he said, when a show goes into performance it has a natural curve; it improves for a while and then starts to go stale. But the improvement part of the curve is much longer than one would imagine; in the case of *Carmen* each cast has done the show 50 times, making 150 performances, and he says that each cast is still improving and consolidating. We are envious; we describe how we never get the chance to perform anything more than a couple of times. Last summer, we recall, we felt quite daring when we repeated a work several times in the course of the summer.

Brook thinks this is a terrible waste of the energy put into a rehearsal, and says that from the point of view of performance the work can only ever stay at the 'preparation' stage; that it's a pity to deny the work the chance of gathering its own speed and finding its own proportions in a long 'run' of performances. He says that he has never heard a classical concert which struck him as having made its peace with its potential, as he says his *Carmen* casts have done after three months of intensive rehearsal and three months of performance.

He goes on to speak about classical concerts in general. He never goes to them any more because he can't bear the atmosphere. People arrive to listen, people arrive to play, and somehow both parties seem to think that their dual presence constitutes an agreement as to why they're all there, as if the concert process had been agreed upon. But it hasn't; Brook says he feels as if he's at a cinema which consistently starts its films in the middle, so that no matter how often you go you'll never quite grasp the mise-en-scène. An important chunk has been left out, and and though performer and audience are there, there is no *meeting*. Platform manner in concerts is so rigid and uninformative, and one has no sense of the individuals on the stage, only their *personalities* (a word he uses scornfully).

We speak of how to open the music up for an audience. Brook describes a schools performance of Chekhov's *The Cherry Orchard* which began with one of the actors talking about the play for twenty minutes. This went down very well with the children but, he said, it wouldn't have been possible in a big theatre where that sort of technique would look like 'slumming'. We describe our own difficulties with talking to the audience. Pretending that the music is 'easy' is the wrong approach, because it usually isn't, and so they feel misled; pretending that it's difficult is wrong too. Brook says that there *is* a way of starting a performance from cold, which has the same effect as a twenty-minute speech initiating the audience into one's confidence, and he goes on to speak of how his own company tries to create this supra-normal atmosphere before the show begins.

This gives us lots of ideas. He describes how the company has a ritual of meeting a quarter of an hour before the show and just sitting quietly like they would in a Quaker meeting, making the occasional comment if it's relevant to what they're about to do. Then as soon as the show finishes, they meet again to have a quick but intense post-mortem, usually on the subject of why that night's show was different to the last night's, what was different and who initiated it, and so on. Krysia and I say that we'd be frightened of such a post-mortem. But Brook says that it's one of the parts of the whole process which his actors most look forward to.

We go on to speak about attitudes to performance, and I describe the curious conclusion we came to at the end of last summer, when it seemed that the most successful performers were the ones who knew how to preserve a stillness between themselves and the music, not the ones who tried to feel as the music feels, changing as the music changes. Brook says that there are various fallacies connected with performing attitudes. Several attitudes traditionally held to be good he thinks are really unproductive; for example the player who regards himself merely as a channel for Mozart, or whoever, to live again. Brook says we shouldn't forget that Mozart is dead, and his music is not rampaging around the universe seeking a medium for its earthly existence. The music only lives if we give it life, and the kind of life we give it is crucially dependent on our individual resources. He has an analogy for how music works on different people; it's like dropping red dye on different materials. When you drop red dye onto a ball of wool, the wool retains its woolness, but when you drop some onto cotton, the cotton seems radically changed.

He describes also the fallacy of 'thinking yourself into the role'. Once a theatre group visiting Zagreb began to work on a production of *Hamlet*, and as an initial exercise the director told each actor to take a few lines of his or her role and walk around Zagreb that evening saying the lines over and over again until it felt as though 'they' were saying the lines, not as though they were saying lines by Shakespeare. Of course the surreal effect of this can be imagined.

By contrast he describes how his company rehearsed for '*The Ik*', which was about starving tribes in Africa. At the beginning of rehearsals a healthy American girl in the company suggested that they ought all to go into the country for four days and starve so that they would have first-hand experience of what it's like to starve. Brook thought this was laughable, and went to describe what they actually did. They studied the outward manifestations of hunger, with the aid of medical reports, diagrams, movement experts and so on. They learned how a starving man walks, sits, moves to conserve energy. With a clinical detachment they learned how to ape the outward signs of hunger, and having, done so, he said, they actually felt an inward correspondence. Working *from the outside in*, he said, they managed to simulate a powerful sense of hunger which convinced the audiences that they all knew just what it was like. He describes also an exercise they did with a speech by Aeschylus in the original Greek. No-one knew what the words meant, but simply working from the sound alone they built up an intricate improvisation which, according to Brook who knew what the speech was about, would have convinced the most learned expert that all the actors could speak Ancient Greek. It's as if the *meaning were enshrined in the sound* of the words as well as in their significance.

Then he describes how the three casts of *Carmen* (a total of eighteen people) worked on the details on their interpretation. I asked him whether all three versions were different, and he replies that in external details they are exactly the same. All the actors were present at all the rehearsals, and all exponents of a particular role contributed to the making of it – suggesting moves, vetoing moves, criticising and inventing until the best suggestion was mutually agreed upon – so that the final version was the same in all three versions. But the effect of each one is different because of the vocal timbre, the physical presence and so on of the participants. Listening to him saying this it seems like a mere academic distinction, but when we go to a concert in which all three Carmens are singing, it is easy to see what he means. The actual effect of each is so profoundly different that at once we start to think how it would be to rehearse a string quartet with eight people present at all rehearsals, agreeing on details of phrasing and tone which seemed identical but which were given quite different ambiences by the physical demeanours of the individual players.

Brook speaks of the stillness which every performer needs, and says that there are two 'bad' ways conventionally accepted. In one, the performer 'squashes' the dimensions of the role into the confined space of his personality which, anyway, is a cliché; in another, the 'classical' approach is adopted to distance the performer artificially from his role, and this results in a process of which the best result can only be intelligent sophistication. There *is* one good way, Brook thought (and this is where I despair of being able to represent him faithfully): somehow to allow the role to impregnate one, and thereafter to give it back to the listener. He tried to make clear this distinction between 'being' the role; keeping deliberately distant from the role, and this third way of taking on willingly the lineaments of the role without surrendering the lineaments of the psyche. He repeated that there is a difference between personality and individuality; the latter being many-layered, the deeps mysterious because they are not of our devising.

Then he talks about how they paced the 12-hour rehearsals which preceded *Carmen*. He says the important element was a leader (namely him) who acted like an expedition leader, mindful of how far they had to get by the end of the day, but alert also to the need to relax, have fun, etc. He said that all groups need this kind of leader; left to their own devices the actors couldn't get nearly so far as they do with him. He gave analogies for the leadership process, how the wheel-spokes radiate from a hub; how the branches radiate from the stem. He recommends us to adopt the leader principle as well. We try to describe the mixture of dominant personalities within the group, and our reluctance to let any one of them dominate artificially; but he says we could try rotating leaders, or electing leaders. With his own company he said that the more they worked with him, the more they could work on their own, but, he said, 'of course it's childish to think one can be both necessary and unnecessary at the same time. I *am* necessary to them at the moment.'

Much of what he says arises from the idea of 'right timing'; both in the sense of the right time to do things, and the right length of time for a movement or action. He describes how impressed he was in the East, when he saw how differently people moved and used their bodies. In India he felt that people were in tune with a fundamental pattern; like a tide welling up in their collective unconscious. These bazaar people, though physically 'slow', were quick with the rhythms and sound which were right for that time, and they were completely involved in their actions.

Coming back to England, Brook went to visit Harrod's and saw that, although everyone was physically 'quick', bustling and jerky, their actual movement was slow and they had no sense of the time factor for each movement and went on doing it for too long, or not long enough.

One has to find the right length of time for a movement. (Writing this I remember Sandor Végh's comment, at the Prussia Cove seminars, that he likes the English term 'movement' rather than the German *Satz* because the English implies *movement*.) Everything has its right length; what we usually experience is softer and flabbier than the firm proportions of the fundamental patterns which flow under everything. This reminds me, too, of Russell Hoban's latest novel *Pilgermann* in which, as he described it to me, the two principal characters conduct an enquiry into the point where stillness becomes motion and vice versa, with special reference to a mosaic floor. The builder of the mosaic floor tells them that it's very dangerous to use a floor for other than floor purposes, and he's probably right.

We try to talk about our plans to do mime, street theatre, poetry, juggling, cake making, jazz and other tangential things. Brook reminds us, in perhaps the most important part of the meeting, of our 'real field of contribution'. He says that we must always remember that our most valuable time is the time of performance, not the time of self-indulgent rehearsal, or the experiments with things we are not really conversant with. Though one feels obliged to be a right-thinking citizen, conscious of community needs and willing to tackle a hundred unconventional areas, none-theless we must not forget that our claim on the attention of 200 people is our expertise in the field of classical music, and it is there that we can make our real impact. Not in rehearsal, not in private practice, but *in performance*, when we are totally responsible for two hours of the audience's life. He points out that we want to be properly responsible, securely responsible; not to run the risk of frittering away the audience's time with amateurish display. He says we must remember that in sitting alone in private practice, or even in experimental rehearsal, with juggling, mime and personal invective, we are not contributing; that part is only preparation, like the chopping up of vegetables before cooking. All our efforts should be based on the question: Why make music at all? What is the sense of it? One has to assume (he said) that all traditions are wrong, all existing answers inadequate. If one has a sense of something deeply lacking in professional musical life, as we do, one must cling to that sense as the driving force and not be tempted to seek immediate reassurance. One is swimming against the waterfall with a group like Domus which has to exist in contradiction to so many things currently valued and rewarded; one has to have the fuel of searching.

I try to describe how impressed I was, some years ago when I visited India, with the notion of different kinds of music being appropriate to different times of day, and how I'd like to try out something like that in Domus. Brook tells us to be careful of working purely on the level of ideas. Our lives are not regulated as Indian lives are, and we don't live according to the time of sunrise and the sunset. Therefore to pretend to regulate our lives with Haydn, Brahms and Ravel would be a purely intel-lectual exercise, and he cautions us against it, saying that we should become conscious of the dynamics of our own lives and not adopt other people's, simply for the sake of an artistic translation of them.

At the end of the talk he tells us about a visit to Buenos Aires, where he met an experimental theatre group composed of people who worked in ordinary jobs during the day and met each night to work on improvisation. The pressures of making a living and of sacrificing all their spare time to a theatre group which seemed to be making no headway with reputation was getting them all down, and they felt that if the difficulties continued at the same intensity, the group would break up. They asked Brook to give them some exercises which would infuse new life into their rehearsals. He did, but it didn't seem to cheer them up.

Then he had an inspired idea: he told them that their 'exercise' was to undertake every rehearsal with the specific aim of ensuring the survival of the group. Whatever they discussed, whatever they tried out, was to be done with that survival in mind. A year later one of the Argentinian actors visited Paris and he told Brook that this 'exercise' had made all the difference. Instead of watching themselves gloomily for signs of dissolution and decay, they had been vigilant with a view to prolonging the life of the group, and it had been prolonged. After we leave Brook's studio at 2 a.m. I realise why he told us this story, and it was of course because our description of the difficulties within Domus had reminded him of the group in Buenos Aires. His idea of the 'exercise' of Thinking Survival does indeed seem inspired, and we feel we could adopt it as a motto for this summer.

Seedorf, Schleswig-Holstein, Germany, June 1982

Our German flute player, Michael Faust, had been working very hard to create a small tour of Germany for us. Our first stop was at the Schleswig-Holstein festival, one of Germany's prestigious classical music festivals, where we were again a sort of 'fringe event'. The elegant audience there was unprepared for the rigours of going to a virtually outdoor classical concert in a dome.

Our first site in Germany is a beautiful old 'Hof' or courtyard with mansion house, tower house and a courtyard of farm buildings in the midst of which we set our dome, angering the aged ladies whose washing-line poles we remove from the lawn in question. The lake and forest behind the house are like Sibelius, and we find a crouching-place in between the reeds in a certain spot where we can survey the late northern sunsets and the silhouettes of little fishing-boats caught sharply in black against the fragile pink of the western sky.

The dome takes a whole day to put up, and despite our intention to go for a country walk in the evening, we are still working on the trailer, the chairs and so on right up to suppertime. On the first day of concerts we have an 11 a.m. 'Fruehschoppen', or informal concert of light classical pieces, and once again, despite all good resolutions to be quiet and collected before the concert, we are all running around until the very minute of the concert, finding music, ironing clothes, rehearsing new pieces, discussing how to present the concert, etc. etc. The dome is full, and in general we feel that the concert went well, though opinions differ as to how distracting the audience was, coming in late, unfolding chairs, children running in and out, and even a child whose mother instigates a money collection throughout the audience for us during the Bach Suite, which certainly destroys our concentration.

Over lunch we agree that never again must we be so rattled and so unprepared at the last minute before a concert, and resolve to adopt Brook's suggestion of gathering quietly before every show and sitting in silence to generate good group feeling and concentration. This being resolved, we then go into the dome and rehearse for the children's concert right up to ten minutes before it, and then run around like mad things trying to collect all the things we need, finally starting a quarter of an hour late and continuing throughout the concert to discuss in whispers what happens next and who should be where. The children seem to like us, and we agree that all our ideas are good, though our timing is bad, and we have to work on streamlining certain things while elongating others. Michael heroically does all the talking, because of the language problem, but it takes its toll; he is almost cross-eyed with fatigue afterwards and everyone looks a bit as though they are, as Krysia put it, 'victims of saturation nausea'.

Krysia says several times how easy it would be for us all to get very annoyed with one another in these trying circumstances, and she and I agree that we must all make a public vow to be kind to each other, consciously, instead of allowing our tempers to fray, and then panicking when we see tension accumulating. We snap readily at each other and find ourselves being irritated by the small mannerisms which used to provoke affectionate smiles; our imitations of one another are no longer of endearing foibles, but of hard-core characteristics, and there's a big difference. We all have very sharp ears for the timing of each other's speech, the facial mannerisms we use while talking, the pitch and tone of voices, and sometimes when someone does a very accurate imitation of a whole set of these things it feels almost like sticking a pin in a wax image of that person, cursing them with perception.

It puzzles me very much that it doesn't seem to be possible to build domes, cook communal meals, set out chairs for concerts, talk to the audience *and* play music really well. I don't mean just really well; that can be done with perhaps half one's consciousness, and we can all do it, but in the sort of way which creates something that wasn't there before – by being *more* than the sum of the parts. In our concerts today we were just the sum of the parts, maybe less. Only Krysia's playing in the Rumanian dances was on a different level, and the difference was that she has worked on those pieces in quietness, over many years. Leo said after the morning concert that in a way he prefers concerts which are under-rehearsed because it keeps everyone awake; you have to concentrate at every corner. I'm surprised to hear myself disagreeing, saying that the things you concentrate on in such a concert are superficial things; you concentrate simply on survival rather than quality. After the morning concert I feel that our playing was compromised by all our hard work on non-musical labours.

I ask David, 'Would your ideal performing situation with this group be simply to turn up and play at rehearsals and concerts?' David says basically Yes; reminds me that we don't 'simply' turn up at rehearsals and concerts; that we have plenty of new and unusual aims to work at, quite enough original material purely in the music and our approach to it without taking on the responsibility of building, managing, driving, fetching chairs, making the stage. We all want our music to integrate into our lives, and all are reluctant to conclude that music really needs a rarefied and singular consciousness in the performer, but today it really feels that way. We all *have* singular spirits, but they do need protection.

Our third concert in Seedorf, an evening one, is a mixed experience. It's a cold, windy evening and although we complain about the temperature ourselves, we are naturally outraged that the audience shows sensitivity to the elements, and we glare at anyone who is weak enough to shiver publicly. Nevertheless it *is* hard to concentrate on something warm and intimate like the Mozart piano concerto in a chilly draught, and in our white summer clothes we are vulnerable figures, almost slightly ridiculous as we brave the wind for the sake of Art. At the start of the interval, the festival director, without consulting us, stands up and asks the audience whether it would like to sit in comfort and warmth for the second half. It is depressing to see the alacrity with which the audience accepts his invitation to move to the music room in the *Herrenhaus* where he lives. We are furious; we feel we're being treated like foolish children not wise enough to know when we have gone too far with our joke, and we resist every step of the way. But, once inside the beautiful grey-green and white manorhouse room with the Furtwängler piano, I (who am listening) certainly appreciate the peaceful warm surroundings, and find that I can concentrate on a superb performance without being distracted by cold, noise, movement and any of the other sensory nuisances one has to get used to in the dome. I feel guilty about enjoying the comfort, and so do we all, it transpires later; nevertheless it is true that Michael and I found we could listen somehow more purely, without having to spend at least part of our energy and concentration on bracing ourselves against the cold, or not hearing the children playing outside, or not noticing the many flies.

The Schubert is a great success; great enough, I think, to make everyone renew their faith in each other. It's just sad that the success was not allied to the dome, which would have renewed our faith in the whole project; as it was, we left the dome conscious that the whole audience (stuffy as it was) had voted not to hear another hour of music in it, and we vowed to do something about the heating so that that could never happen again.

Travelling onwards to Hamburg

Our next site is a public park in a pleasant area of Hamburg. Michael has heroically wrested permission from the town authorities to put up our dome in the park for a week. The site is slightly sloping, which leads to crucial problems at the final stage wherein the dome is suspended on tripods for the last time, and the whole weight is swinging in the air. We can't work out the tripod angles necessary to counteract the slope, and at least an hour is spent in exhausting trial and error before we realise that the downward side should have been lifted before the upward side, to minimise the slope factor. These new problems at a late stage are very debilitating, and most of the group begins to mutter about responsibility to themselves as well as to the dome; almost everyone says that their hands, or fingers, or arms, are stiff and sore from a day of carrying heavy tubes and hubs around. We feel a sense of real achievement, but all retire to bed pondering intensely the extent of our involvement in practical dome problems and their resolutions.

On the following morning Robin and Felix have to get up early to set up the stage, and both say that they looked at each other with disbelief when they woke up and realised there were two concerts to do. On the dome site everyone is mildly frazzled; it being Sunday, nothing is open and there is no source of coffee or water, let alone changing rooms or places to sit quietly before playing. At the last minute before the concert, two officials of the civic authority turn up to forbid us to park the van on the grass near the dome, which does nothing to improve tempers, and it is with a real effort of will that we collect ourselves at the door of the dome and vow to think about nothing but the music.

The concert, an informal one made up of Bartók's *Rumanian Dances*, Bridge *Miniatures*, a song by David, and Fauré's *Après Un Rêve*, the Kodály *Intermezzo*, a Bach Suite, Mozart *Kontretänze* and Stockhausen's *Tierkreis*, produces rather the same effect as we produced in Cheltenham last year; the audience claps and shouts for an encore. People stay around afterwards without having been asked; someone offers a room in their house for one of the group, and we feel surrounded by affection.

Later in the day we pool impressions and discover that everyone in the audience thought we were a bunch of students, and most of us were asked questions like 'What will you do when you go into the profession?', 'Are you doing this in the summer holidays from your orchestra?', 'What would be your ideal way to play chamber music?', 'Do you hope to make chamber music your profession?' and so on. But most of us feel that the misleading impression of studentness is given by our zeal and earnestness, our sense of fun, which certainly they would be excused for concluding were not the usual distinguishing marks of professional musicians.

A lady from the British Council takes my breath away by spotting that I was not playing the 'right' zodiac sign in Stockhausen's *Tierkreis*, a series of tiny melodies (one for each zodiac sign) which we have expanded by improvisation into a discursive piece. All of us play the melody linked to our own birth sign, but I play my 'opposite', Sagittarius, because at rehearsal everyone pounced upon it as being much more 'right' for me than my real one, Gemini. This lady asks me to identify who played which sign and I go through the order slowly, with her nodding slowly and saying '. . . Yes, that seemed right' until I get to me, when she says, 'Now that was the only one which didn't seem right. It was more like an Aries; anyway it didn't seem like a Sagittarius.' We are all humbled by this small proof of Stockhausen's intuitive delineation of zodiac qualities, and I feel I have been reproved by the gods for this little piece of musical deceit.

A small but attentive audience comes to the evening concert of Bartók *Rumanian Dances*, Mozart piano concerto (with string quartet instead of orchestra) and Schubert string quintet. Before the concert we try, for the first time, to sit quietly together at one side of the stage, but of course the quietness soon degenerates into the usual to-and-fro of imitations, jokes, Groucho Marx voices and the like, and Robin (who is fixing the main door) says that he is aware of the audience watching this display, fascinated by our high spirits and at the same time a little disapproving. This, Robin thinks, is what makes us seem like students.

The concert is a success, but physical tiredness begins to show and makes the edges ragged, especially in the Schubert. My hands are so cold that semiquaver passages almost don't work in the Mozart, and a motherly listener tells me afterwards that if I don't get a warmer concert outfit I will be ill by the end of the week. The Schubert has all its spirit from the last performance, but the ensemble is much more scrappy and the sound curiously unfocused, perhaps just because of the new acoustic. In the park, we are more or less playing outdoors, and are sometimes competing with all kinds of park noises immediately around us. The five players are very divided in their opinion of how the Schubert went; Krysia says she didn't enjoy it much, while Leo was thrilled by it, and the others agree that basically the spirit was willing but the flesh was weak. Several people comment privately that when they are tired they are more than usually sensitive to each other's annoying mannerisms in performance, and that when they look up and see certain facial expressions of leering intensity, or buccaneering swagger, or 'ham' emotion, they are distracted to the point of hostility. It is a real problem; we have to open ourselves to one another to open the telepathic channels, but when we *are* open we risk overloading our nerves with the strong flavours of each other's concentration. Krysia says she doesn't wish to be withheld while playing, and making her face open to the feelings wrought in her by the music, she sometimes sees other players looking at her with a personal responsiveness which makes it clear they didn't realise the distinction between musical intensity, and personal intensity directed at them alone.

Chamber music at this level is like other very intimate relationships; you must try not to mock your partner for anything they say when they are absorbed. And you must try not to be offended by facial expressions which go out of control; it's a sign of openness, of course. Concentrating on 'going with' the mannerisms of one person is difficult enough in this sort of situation; concentrating on four other people is like being force-fed with rich sauces, and I personally find that in the end I have to find a way to be open without bringing my personal style of openness into it. It's something like Brook's description of ideal acting as being not the person who tries to *be* the role and feel its emotions, but the one who takes the role in, digests in, absorbs it and then gives it out again. Once again I'm reminded of his story of teaching three actors to perform the same role with identical gestures; all three came across quite differently because of their physical appearance, voice, timing etc. Their personalities did not have to be imprinted on the role; it was the other way round.

Angus Brown, the designer of our hub system for the dome, once quoted to us an inscription placed by a Buddhist on a stone monument on a Scottish island: 'He who seeks the inner through the outer goes deeper than he who seeks the outer through the inner.'

The tuning ritual which we devised in Finemere now works well, and at the start of a performance the other day, just as the 'A' was resonating all around the circle, a stray listener put his head inside the tent from outside and withdrew it again immediately, as though he had perceived the concentration of the atmosphere; the 'A' ringing the dome like one of the tension ropes which rings it during assembly.

Our third concert, consisting of French music, attracts a much younger audience and the dome feels fresh and open. David and I play the Saint-Saëns *Allegro Appassionato*, and Fauré's *Après Un Rêve*; Robin and I play the Ravel *Habanera*, Liat sings the *Chansons Madécasses* of Ravel, and Krysia, David and I do the Ravel Trio, which is very enthusiastically received. People in the audience magically say all the right things afterwards; one says he liked the trio because we didn't have to demonstrate 'playing together', we simply *were* together. Another says that she loves the unified atmosphere that results from our doing everything ourselves with such a small number of people. There is an archetypal Domus concert-goer who says that she never goes to classical concerts, but had read that we were supposed to be friendly, had come along as an experiment to the first concert, and had come back to every concert since. Several people again comment how exciting it is to be at such close quarters to live performers, and how they feel touched by the physical effort and communication, as though by a live current.

We have a lovely review of the French Music concert in the newspaper *Die Welt*; the critic says that one hears so often of 'more contact with the audience' and so often it turns out to be just foolish dilettantism, whereas we really know what we're doing and we can really do it. He says the atmosphere of the dome is incomparable, and the playing flawless, with wonderful temperament. 'It was fun to listen,' the review ends; a nice simple Domus-like statement which gladdens us greatly.

The next day's evening concert proves to be one of the best. It begins with the Beethoven Serenade played in the middle of the dome with the three musicians standing more or less amongst the audience, and Krysia later says that although it disoriented her because she didn't know where to try to project her sound to, it pleased her too because she could hear chuckles coming from the audience all around her. Then we do the Stockhausen again; this time the audience, whose average age is a good ten or twenty years older than on the last occasion, is less enthusiastic but no less intent during the performance. In the second half we try out Felix's idea of having everyone in place on the stage for the various small French pieces which have to be played. Three people sit on the edge of the stage facing the audience and play from their sitting positions; David sits on one side of the piano and Leo comes on from the side. Thus there is no getting on and off the platform, bowing, scene-shifting, moving of stands and so on, and the result is delightful, like a tableau of which the various parts come to life at different times.

David's *Allegro Appassionato* by Saint-Saëns is followed by Robin's *Habanera* and Krysia's Blues movement from the Ravel Sonata; Michael plays the Poulenc Sonata, David the Fauré 'Après Un Rêve' (all these with me playing the piano); I play Francaix's solo piano piece *In case of delirium*, and Leo and I play Ravel's *Tzigane*. The audience is rapt throughout, and follows the amusing juxtapositions with delight – for example the quiet G major ending of the Ravel *Habanera* and the quiet G major beginning of the Blues immediately after it, with no distracting applause; then the end of the Fauré and the delirious Francaix which follows it. By the time we get to *Tzigane* the audience is completely with, us, and Leo makes the most of this by exaggerating every episode and change of character in the piece. The audience gasps and laughs at every new idea as though it were watching a clever comedy sketch, and 1 am astonished at how closely they follow the progress of the piece, and how free they evidently feel to laugh aloud. Of course Leo's comedic skills are a crucial factor.

Our Coffee Concert two mornings later, though it contains all the pieces which drove the audience wild a couple of nights before, and though we play with the same kind of panache, is received with polite appreciation. Robin later says that perhaps the programme contained too many jazzy pieces, making it inappropriate for a type of morning concert which in Germany traditionally follows the Sunday church service. Whatever the reason, it sets us musing on how extraordinary it is that each audience has a definite 'feel' to it, something we have all been disinclined to believe when theatre people talk about the phenomenon, but which we are forced to acknowledge when we have played the same piece three times in a week to three different audiences.

It seems incredible that a totally random collection of people should at once acquire a collective mood, but that's what happens. It would be understandable if both listeners and players demonstrated the same mood, but this is rarely the case, and therefore it can't be explained as collective participation in the electricity of the aether, or anything like that. The players in fact often discern the 'mood' of the audience as being different to their own. Each audience has its own collective soul, even if those people have never seen one another before.

The evening concert (our closing concert in Hamburg) is another example, but this time a delightful one. For the first time in Germany the dome is packed; twenty minutes before the concert every seat is taken, and by 8 p.m. people are packed into every available space, and are standing behind the back row as well as sitting on the edge of the stage. The atmosphere is elating, and we all feel the adrenalin which has been missing from many of our concerts here. Everything goes well; the Poulenc flute sonata, dignified by Michael's sorrow at parting from an old girlfriend in the afternoon, is more than usually meaningful. Then the Mozart concerto goes beautifully; I feel the concentration of the audience surrounding me and the string quartet as the white of egg surrounds and protects the yolk.

The Schubert after the interval is an even more striking example of this feeling; they play it in the middle of the dome, sitting directly under the five points of the topmost pentagon, and I am very struck by how antiphonal things in the music really seem antiphonal, not experienced flatly, or on one plane as they are when you watch the players on the stage, going 'tick-tock' from side to side like a pendulum, but passing in 'deep' space from one part to another of the dome, north–south and east–west. I notice that the audience is fascinated by the player nearest them; for example, people follow the viola part all the way through, which they never have a chance to do if the viola is in its usual position on the stage, and people are obviously fascinated too by the nearness of physical exertion – not only that, but the nearness of such graceful movements too. I notice too that, with the audience sitting in a complete circle, it's nice to be able to watch other people listening. You look past the players to a quarter-circle of attentive faces, and it feels much less lonely than being in the concert hall, where you all look in the same direction and you can't see anyone else's face. Far from being distracting to see other listening faces, it feels supportive, and Warren Stewart, a cellist friend who had come along to help us, says it's nice that no-one is further back than the third row; you always listen better when you're that close to the musicians.

The quality of the whole evening, of the playing and of the listening, is what we've been striving towards and we all feel, having experienced it, that no finer reward could come our way. It feels as though all the effort is justified, and in fact the whole evening is a rather moving experience especially for those of us who have seen a lot of the rough, and who therefore respond emotionally to the smooth. Felix and Warren, 'high' with good humour at the end of the concert, start packing up the stage while the rest of us go off to the British Council for a drink, and they continue until 2 a.m., when a technical problem with the tripods restrains them.

The next morning we take down the dome after a breakfast gathering. As soon as we begin, rain clouds amass like magic above the dome site, and with a revolting sense of *déja vu* we all work soaked to the skin and once again with no proper rain-gear. Meanwhile the van is delayed at a garage, Michael is delayed in getting back to Schnelsen to pack, and – surprise, surprise – our departure from the dome site is several hours later than planned – not so serious for those in Michael's van which is reasonably fast, but a disappointment for those in Felix's van, which is expected to take ten hours getting to our next destination halfway between Cologne and Bonn.

To Cologne and disaster, 23 July

Three weeks after the last entry, writing this in the middle of the break between two halves of the Domus season, I've been struggling for days with the thought of describing what has happened, and feeling totally unequal to the task. My last entry, worrying about the van's journey from Hamburg to Cologne, has been mocking me with its apparent presentiment of something wrong, and it seems almost trite to set down the fact that something *did* go wrong. But it did.

Midway between Hamburg and Cologne we all stopped in a layby to say hallo: Felix, David and Krysia in Felix's van, and the rest of us in Michael's new van, a much faster vehicle. By this stage it was clear just how arduous a journey the people in Felix's van were going to have, and Krysia was debating whether to change into our van to spare herself the long hours on the road. We switched some luggage into Felix's van to give ourselves more passenger room; Warren's cello and Leo's suitcase went in the trailer.

There was a strange sorrowful atmosphere amongst us as we said goodbye, knowing that it would take the others till about 3 a.m. to arrive in Cologne; easy to exaggerate that atmosphere with hindsight, of course, but nonetheless I have to record how strange we all felt as we sat, half an hour later, in the motorway cafe stretching high above the road and saw Felix's van creeping by in the slow lane with the three tiny figures waving, somehow spotting us despite the reflection of the evening sun across the plate glass.

We arrived at Michael's parents' house in Cologne, and went immediately to bed. Krysia was to share a room with me, and I went to bed with the door ajar so that she could come in quietly during the night, but instead of Krysia it was Warren who came in and woke me up to say that they had just had a phone call to say that the others had had an accident. Michael and Robin were setting off immediately to the hospital from which they had called, 200 km away. In my half-sleep I thought at first that it was an absurd practical joke such as David had been perpetrating amongst us frequently, a fantastic story designed to test the sharpness of one's wits, and I felt irritated before I realised that it was serious. Then I dashed into the living-room. Robin and Michael, already dressed, were gathering what they needed for the journey; Robin was shaking, clearly upset, and he kept saying that we had been idiots not to insure the trailer. What little we knew at this stage was that all three were 'all right', but Krysia's voice on the other end of the telephone had been shocked, and we were anyway shocked that Felix had not phoned himself. That convinced us that something must be wrong. Robin and Michael departed at about 3 a.m. and the rest of us sat up for a while trying not to let our minds run riot with the awful possibilities.

The next morning the news filtered through in dramatic coin-box phone calls, and gradually we got to know that David had broken several bones in his spine and was badly burned on shoulder, arm, shin and foot by a tin of acid cleaning fluid which spilled on him; Felix had broken both feet and/or ankles, and Krysia was relatively unscathed except for shock, and a bump on the head. The trailer had been smashed to pieces, and over a 50-yard radius on the motorway were spread bits of the Kawai piano, two cellos (Warren's and Felix's) and most of our equipment. David and Felix, it seemed, would be in hospital for some while.

The three of us in Cologne wanted to come to the hospital at once, but we stayed behind to oversee the first obvious tasks in the wake of the accident; cancelling our week at the Bonn Festival, phoning the families of the injured people. It was incredibly strange to be doing this without having seen the people in hospital; we were all numb from the shock and numb from the distance of it; almost light-hearted at first with the sensationalism of the facts, we didn't know how to comport ourselves. We went out for a walk and, suddenly beginning to be struck by the loneliness of our out-post position and by the misery of being healthy while our best friends were in pain, we all held hands along the riverbank.

That evening we had to go to the British Council in Cologne to play at a function at which several of the guests were our potential patrons. Michael arrived back from the hospital exhausted, and displaying again that curious elation of horror which sets in before actual sorrow does, rather turned our concert into a ghoulish recital of what he had seen in the hospital, and what he saw on the motorway. Nobody felt like playing a concert, but we did our best and seemed to win their hearts; we were all dead tired after no sleep the previous night and a day of intermittent long-distance drama, and I remember Leo sprawled between two German ladies on the sofa, chain-smoking, chain-drinking, his eyes red and glazed, his legs splayed dramatically. I remember the ladies seemed to be charmed by the spectacle.

On the next day the three of us went by train to the hospital, and after a quick look at David, painted all over with some red liquid to cool his burns, and looking as though he had just been flayed alive, I chickened out and went to talk to Krysia in a different ward. The bump on her head had made her nose swell slightly and it seemed to have pushed her eyes apart, making her look slightly cross-eyed but somehow outlandishly beautiful. She told me what she remembered of the accident, which happened in the dark. The most extraordinary thing about it was David's behaviour; not only was he completely relaxed, but as he lay with his injured back in the grass after being thrown through the window, it was he who took in the most information and tried to prevent Felix from running out into the road to save the cellos, which he imagined were in the path of the traffic.

The driver of the lorry which had hit them from behind came up to them shining his torch and asking in German, 'How many dead?' The tin of cleaning fluid, which nobody realised was acid, had spilled on David and he began to complain that he was on fire, but of course no-one thought what the matter might be until they got in the ambulance, when suddenly the smell was everywhere and Krysia realised that something had soaked through David's jacket onto his skin. By that time the damage was done, and he was badly burned. They arrived in the tiny religious hospital in Greven in the middle of the night, and (as we later found out) there was very little proper night staffing; Krysia said she was ready to create a huge fuss on behalf of her injured friends but was unable to do so until the morning, when a platoon of doctors appeared and took charge.

Felix had been the most depressed of the three, and still seemed to be when we arrived. Pale, with a cut beside one eye and bruises all over his face, he looked more than ever like a wicked pirate, and was as restless as hell. Beside him David lay with saintlike patience and closed his eyes when his back hurt too much; otherwise he tried to join in cheerfully with the conversation, and we were all very touched by his composure. At tea-time his father arrived from England and was obviously shocked by David's appearance. We left them alone together.

Meanwhile it was becoming clear just how much damage had been done to the equipment, and Robin had begun to take charge of the depressing pile of remains which were now at a lorry park in the town. We went down to have a look at them. The trailer had been destroyed and the borrowed piano was a pile of hammers and strings. Warren's cello was so completely smashed that it was difficult to believe it had ever been a cello before, and we were surprised to find how little wood there actually is in a cello, which always seems so stout an instrument. Felix's cello had several pieces missing from it, though compared to Warren's it looked immaculate. Felix's beloved van was a write-off. We took photos of ourselves beside it, with its stove-in rear doors, holding such items as the broken fan, the mashed toolbox, the fragments of signboards. The hubs of the dome seemed all to be present, though Robin thought that over a hundred tubes of the dome's frame had been destroyed.

Michael, our only native German speaker, was dealing with the police. What had happened, it seemed, was that the trailer was hit from behind by a 40-ton truck at about 11.45 p.m.; the driver of the truck told the police that our trailer was unlit. The van had veered into the crash barrier and had landed eventually in the grass just where the barrier ended. The police took away the light bulbs to test them and could give us no idea whether the truck driver's assertion was true. The matter taxed us very much because of the insurance position; if the accident was the truck driver's fault, it would not matter that we were not insured, but if the fault were shared, the costs and damages could finish us. The van was insured, and the piano and cellos were individually insured by their owners, but nothing else. The trailer, the dome, and the equipment were not insured, and it seemed that although David had American health insurance, Felix might have none. Michael, Robin and I went to see a German traffic lawyer in Münster. The lawyer was young, cold and impervious to Michael's jokes. After an unpleasant hour trying to sort out such questions as Who owns the dome? Who is legally responsible for it? Who owns the equipment? Who officially *is* Domus? Are you a business, or are you seven individuals? (all of which made Robin and I exchange miserable glances) the lawyer told us that it could under no circumstances be *entirely* our fault. At worst the fault would be shared and the damages shared, probably with the weighting in our favour.

Legal fees, it seemed, would be paid by the insurance companies concerned, or whichever of them lost the case. But the lawyer reckoned it would take at least a year to clear up, with the damages involved. The cellos alone would represent £20,000;

the piano about £2000, the trailer about £2000, the dome and equipment several thousands more. This of course without the immense costs that we would face *because* of the accident, which immediately became the bane of our lives. Felix later said that lying in bed with two broken feet was the simplest role to play, and indeed it did begin to seem that way. We began to tackle the great labour of how to get back to England with the remains of the dome and the equipment. For this kind of task we were cruelly ill-equipped in all sorts of ways.

In London, preparing for our second visit to the Cheltenham Festival

Back in London we set about the catalogue of tasks which had to be done in order for us to fulfil our week at the Cheltenham Festival. Not only were we on the phone to the hospital about once an hour (keeping in touch with Felix who, meanwhile, had had a tendon operation) and to Michael about German legal matters twice a day, but we were hiring pianos, borrowing stages, buying equipment, lights, borrowing chairs, hiring guest players, writing to newspapers and magazines to exhort them to help us with sympathetic publicity about the accident; we made a hundred new tubes of the dome and flattened the damaged ends of the old ones.

Robin and Warren drove the German van to Cheltenham and unloaded the dome into a shed outside the Town Hall, and the next morning Robin had to drive the van to Sheerness to put it on the ferry back to the Netherlands, where Michael (meanwhile having caught a train from Cologne to Vlissingen) would pick it up. There was a train strike in England, so Robin had to hitch back from Sheerness to London.

We were held up by hundreds of totally unnecessary setbacks; unnecessary, we thought, because we personally felt as though the accident was like an immense thunderstorm which purges the air of any lingering malaise, and we felt that we too were purged of bad luck for ever, but it didn't work like that. Almost every little thing that could go wrong went wrong – and it was this feeling of being dogged with misfortune even in these urgent circumstances that nearly broke our nerve. Even things like the hiring of the piano were oddly fraught with trouble; Kawai in London suddenly refused to lend us the Kawai again 'because it came back from your rehearsal week with scratches on it'. This hardly seemed the moment to tell them that their piano was now strewn all over a German motorway. The Kawai headquarters itself, when we eventually confessed all to them, said that they 'didn't want to lend another new piano to a group which smashed up pianos'. Once again the monstrous sense of unfairness descended; 'I think you should know', I said miserably, 'that the accident was entirely the fault of the other driver', but we still felt cursed for being the harbingers of bad news to Kawai, who had after all been amazingly generous in lending us a piano at all.

Hiring a piano for Cheltenham proved oddly, bafflingly difficult; those firms which had pianos couldn't transport them, or the firms which had transport had no suitable pianos, or the firms which had both were out of our price range. Several tantalising chances came and went; SouthWest Arts considered lending us their grand piano for a week, but it transpired that they had only considered it because they didn't realise we would be playing it outdoors, and when the truth was revealed they snatched the offer away. Several kind people offered their own domestic pianos, but no transport could be found. Robin and I spent almost two days in endless pursuit of a piano through firms in Cheltenham, Stroud, Gloucester, Bath, Bristol, Oxford, and London, and when we left for Cheltenham we still didn't have one.

We all converged on Cheltenham at the same time; Michael drove from Germany with David and Felix lying in the back of his van, and one unexpected bonus of this arrangement was that Felix was spared the trouble he had anticipated at Immigration; they just waved the van through. They stopped in London to deliver David to a hospital near his home, and then came on to Cheltenham, where Felix was being wheeled about on a trolley with both legs in plaster when we arrived. He was therefore able to preside over the most difficult dome assembly ever – a less-than-ideal convalescent gift from us. It turned out that in fact all the hubs were damaged; they had all been twisted out of their 'memory' positions, and therefore when we started to put them together we had no way of remembering the alignment. If the tubes were not lying at the correct angle to the hubs, the hemisphere of the dome could not be created, and it was horrendously difficult trying to create the right shape by pushing and pulling.

When we got back from Germany, I asked the *I Ching* what it thought was the cause of the accident. It replied 'Youthful Folly', with a 'moving line' which read 'Childlike folly brings good fortune.' This linked to another hexagram, which said that although our intentions were good, nevertheless we must find a teacher or guru to help us through this difficult time. 'Youthful Folly' we all found an irritating answer, but we all believed the advice about teachers, even if it only related to finding an administrator for next year. We decided to put an advert in *The Guardian* and *Time Out* when Cheltenham was finished.

Mentally what I found very hard in the wake of the accident was that, while previously I had been able to persuade myself that the role of chance in life was a force for good, a force for balance, and that the universe was fundamentally beneficent, the accident made me revert (and I think several of us did) to more primitive thoughts of life containing a blind fury which lashed out randomly at the undeserving as well as the deserving. I, who usually can see the logic in events if I think about them in terms of karma, or in terms of Yin and Yang, could not see any possible logic to this particular event – particularly where David was concerned. It seemed monstrous that he, a guest player in the group, who had come all the way from America to play with us, should be the one to suffer the worst injury, and I quite understood the resentment his father was unable to conceal in our presence. We felt that if there were injuries to sustain, it would have been much easier for the hard-core Domus people to sustain them, since we had the greatest emotional faith in the group and therefore the greatest reason not to blame it. But David – though he never did blame us for anything that had happened – gave us all much heartache because we felt him so innocent, so undeserving of any rebuke the universe might have stored up for Domus. His bravery was poignant for us.

In the winter of 2002, twenty years later, David told me that he holds no resentment about the accident. The period of convalescence had enabled him to think hard about what he wanted from his life, and to plan some important changes. These changes led in a very short time to his meeting the woman he was to marry, Dylana Jensen. On a professional level they led to a new interest in conducting. So he, now a successful conductor with four children, says he looks back on the accident as the catalyst for the best period of his life. He even said that his injuries led to his having to develop better posture, and a healthier diet and lifestyle. I can't think of many people who could turn such a disaster to such positive effect, and am still grateful to him for being able to do so.

Cheltenham Festival 1982

Since I wrote so much about the atmosphere of the town last year, I should perhaps just summarise our visit in '82. We did seven concerts there, four of which were packed out: the opening serenade (a free late-night concert), the children's concert, and the two closing concerts, one at lunchtime and one in the evening. The weather was fairly unkind to us throughout the week, and on one occasion a thunderstorm obliterated a lunchtime concert and almost stopped the show because of flooding which crept under the sides of the dome and made its way in deep puddles towards the centre. We leapt around rescuing electric cable and cellos from the water, and the audience moved more and more into the centre of the dome; the Beethoven Serenade was like watching a silent movie through the hiss and crackle of old equipment – we could see their bows and instruments moving, but for much of the time we could hear nothing at all above the downpour.

The most heartwarming thing about Cheltenham this year was the number of people in the audience who had been at our concerts last year, and who came back like old friends, trying to catch our eyes and wave in the opening concert. Over and above this there was a large new contingent of the audience who came to every concert this year, and it was delightful to see a larger and larger proportion of the audience composed of newly familiar faces. People kept coming back with their children and friends, and many people behaved towards us with extraordinary affection.

It was nice for us, too, to be able to speak in English to the audiences after our three tongue-tied weeks in Germany, and the audience in any case needed little encouragement to stay behind and talk to us after concerts, particularly with the stimulus of Ione's (a friend of Robin's) superb food such as the sushi (fish, egg, cheese and avocado rolled inside leaves of seaweed) which alarmed the first audiences, but quickly became popular.

A necessary innovation which pleased us was the stage. Without our trailer we had to make do with what was at hand, and after experimenting with a box stage, we decided on flat boards covered with a red patterned carpet we found in the Town Hall shed. After a couple of days we decided we liked this arrangement better that our old raised stage, and when we found a red standard lamp to put on the carpet we were even more pleased. We continued to experiment with playing in the middle of the dome but found it less satisfying than we had done in Hamburg. The acoustic seemed deader, which may simply have been the length of grass, or may have been objective fact.

Several members of the audiences commented that they much preferred the pure sound quality when we were playing at the far end of the dome and eventually we did most things there, compromising between the flat performing position in the centre and the raised platform position at the far end of the dome by having a flat stage approximately at the Golden Section of the dome. The piano, a Lechleiter upright which we hired in Cheltenham, was a disappointment, and its feebleness spoiled both performances of the Ravel Trio for me who had to play it. But it looked solid and dignified, as befitted the new drawing-room atmosphere of the dome with its carpet and standard lamp.

We got a wheelchair for Felix from the Local Health Authority, and he bowled around the dome like a hyper-active child, but in the house he was reduced to crawling around on hands and knees, dragging his plastered legs behind him. It was heartrending to see him crawling into the kitchen to make his breakfast, or to meet him crawling to the loo as one was sprinting past. One day a lady member of the audience dropped by the dome to remonstrate with us about the way we were neglecting him; 'You haven't even put a rug over his knees', she accused. It's true that his was hardly a conventional period of recovery. He was no conventional patient, and we were useless as nurses.

Steven Isserlis came for the last three days, and arrived to find himself the butt of multiple imitations of him by Leo, Felix and others. Leo's imitation of Steven, whetted in Steven's absence during the entire German tour, was by this time so wellknown that the slightest hint of the Original Edition from Steven had everyone in fits of mirth, and Leo lost no chance of imitating Steven while the latter's back was turned. But although Leo's version of the squeaky voice, the tilted head and wagging finger was sillier than the real thing, he had not caught the strength of Steven's obscene imagery nor the potency of his dirty looks, which remained inimitable.

On Steven's first evening with us we happened to be doing a performance of *Tierkreis*, without his participation as he very snootily refused to have anything to do with it. Unlike the German audiences, however, the Cheltenham audience was embarrassed and annoyed by the piece, and after the concert Steven began a litany of complaint about our interpretation of it which became more and more insistent until he was all but insisting that we take the piece out of the Final Concert on the grounds that we would drive away any possible audience if we left it in.

This made us all feel insecure right up to the final concert, when moral fibre impelled us to leave the piece in the programme if only to demonstrate our resistance to tyranny. But on the second occasion I introduced the piece with a much longer explanation of why we liked it, the various odd coincidences which had accompanied our learning of it, and the unfolding process which the audience would hear in it. This time the reception was completely different, and the audience seemed to be enthralled. Steven gave me a filthy look as we were taking our bows, so I knew it had been a success, and later I said to him, 'I hope you've eaten your words.' 'I have *not*,' he replied in the original squeaky voice. 'If I hadn't given you all such a bollocking about it, you would never have taken the trouble to get it so good.'

Despite Krysia's initial superstition about playing the Schubert Quintet without

David, they did play it in the last concert, and it was fascinatingly different with Steven playing the second cello part and acting as the rhythmical powerhouse of the group. The last movement in particular was ten times as good as it had ever been in Germany with Steven chiselling away all its soft edges, and Krysia's violin suddenly began to sound like its old self after the trauma it had clearly experienced during the accident.

We ended the week very happy with the results of our concerts, and happy too on the last evening to have sold seven of Greg's (Greg Warren Wilson, multi-talented friend) cartoons which he had hung around the dome. John Manduell said he hoped we would return to Cheltenham next year; Sir William Glock confirmed our invitation to the Bath Festival for 1983, and David Glass wanted to discuss touring with us. Members of the audience donated several hundred pounds to our Appeal Fund following the accident, and several more people offered generous interest-free loans. We were glowingly previewed, described and reviewed in the local papers.

Following Cheltenham, we spent a rehearsal week in the West Country and returned to London for the second half of our summer. We were joined by several new guest players: Gabi Lester, Eva Tomasi (both violinists) and Chi Chi Nwanoku (double bass). Krysia and I no longer had to feel guilty about being the only girls in the group, and indeed, it was noticeable that the male ego flourished in the company of these new glamorous ladies.

Wormwood Scrubs, Thamesmead and Battersea

Wormwood Scrubs, 4–8 August 1982

The dome went up quite smoothly in Wormwood Scrubs, on a site crammed improbably between the West London Stadium and the prison, with a vast bare piece of land behind the dome. As in Hamburg, we discovered that the Scrubs had a definite 'park life' of their own; the sports stadium had a certain shape to its day, which always witnessed, and late at night there was a sort of 'happy hour' in the prison from which noises of raucous self-expression would suddenly burst at about 11 p.m. and continue for an hour unabated and then would suddenly cease.

In the mornings there were gangs of trainee vandals and hooligans who hung around the Scrubs looking for people to molest and hinder. Of course we were a prime target for them, and we didn't really know how to cope. One small boy of eight adopted us and became our 'assistant'. He was a sad figure, playing on his own from early morning till late in the evening, and he told us that he had written down all about us in a book which he said was 'like a bible'. I asked him what he had written, but it turned out to be mainly a catalogue of the various biscuits and sweets we had given him. We were supposed to be a focus of activity for the local community, but it was hard to see where the local community was, and for the most part we felt and looked like visitors from outer space, puzzling the local people and amusing the regular joggers and dog-walkers.

The balance of the group changed in this week and was mildly disorienting.

Suddenly there seemed to be a lot of younger people around; they were all lively and goodhumoured, and got on well with each other, but as a group we were not so integrated as we had been in Germany and personally I missed David's positive sanity. Also there were more people around, and though adding three people to a group of eight would not seem to be an enormous addition, it seemed to convert us socially into an unmanageable number which tended to split into groups of threes and fours. In Germany I remember thinking that we had never split the basic group into smaller units, but in the Scrubs we definitely split into subsets (though not always the same ones) and my perception of it was that the new people initiated the splitting, perhaps in self-defence against what *they* perceived as unassailable closeness amongst the hard-core members.

All our programmes were designed with a first half of varied, lighter pieces and a second half consisting of one big chamber work. Presenting the first halves was quite a problem but we capitalised on our experience in Germany and insisted on 'walking through' the programme before every concert, as well as deciding who was going to introduce each piece, and exactly who was going to move the chairs and stands into their appropriate positions while others were speaking. It really seemed that fifty per cent of the success of these first halves depended on the skill with which we stage-managed them, and we noticed that the audience responded much better to the music if it was presented with flair and smooth timing; a banal thing to comment on, perhaps, but still a slight surprise to us who have in the past relied on the quality of our playing to endear the work to the audience. Here we did not rely on it because we were not sure that the Scrubs audience would be sensitive to it, and we were right, not only about the Scrubs audience but about audiences in general, all of whom perked up when they felt they were in the presence of skilled programme architects.

We had quite a lot of publicity; LBC Radio came and interviewed us and recorded a little of a rehearsal which they played that evening on 'London Life'; Hugo Cole wrote an article about our accident in *The Guardian* on 7 August; *The Times* mentioned us in their Preview section; *Time Out* carried a photo of the dome and a nice paragraph about us, as well as two weeks of individual mentions of concerts, and *City Limits* also mentioned our concerts. Hugo Cole also reviewed our last concert in *The Guardian*, flatteringly, and we were relieved that he treated us just as seriously as he would have done any South Bank concert, not disparaging us by references to our enterprise or youthfulness instead of to the quality of our playing. The review said, 'This invigorating concert . . . the physical closeness of sounds and performers added hugely to our involvement – almost participation – in a strongly expressive performance.'

The most strenuous part of the week was the children's concerts. The first one, the Trip to the Zoo, proved much too elegant and innocent for the ruffians who came determined to heckle and disrupt. We kept going manfully, but the kids got more and more out of control, and finally at the appearance of the bear (Warren dressed in a hired bear suit) the older children got close to him under cover of the little children dancing to the String Boogie and started to kick and punch him quite violently, which he tried to evade by getting out of the dome, only to be followed to the bus (which was locked) and assaulted quite painfully. His contact lenses were knocked into the upper eyelids by someone pulling on the bear head, and poor

Warren was temporarily blind amidst a sea of hostile teenagers until someone came to rescue him with the bus key. I found myself hitting one of four boys who had been pestering us all morning, and who sat throwing things at me during the concert.

After the show we were all tired with that kind of bad tiredness that comes when you pit yourself against odds that are too great. On the second occasion, a few days later, we used up a tremendous amount of energy in the morning by worrying about what would happen during the afternoon children's concert, and trying to visualise all opportunities for heckling so that we could devise ways of preventing and blocking them. We cut most of the concert music from the programme because on the earlier occasion it was the concert pieces which seemed to act as a signal for the kids to get out of control; therefore on the second occasion we composed the programme of participation pieces: African chants with percussion, the Geographical Fugue and other hearty items.

In the event, of course, a perfectly docile audience of small children and willing parents turned up and enjoyed every minute of it, and such was the smoothness of transition from one item to another that the show was actually too short – the first such occasion ever in the dome. Krysia's parents were there, and said that there was not enough concert music, so it seemed that our compromise had been too radical.

Before the show Felix said to me, 'Let's not get ourselves into the position of taking on too many new items of this kind again, shall we?' and we agreed that having cut down our sphere of activity from 93 kinds of music to a basic chamber music format, as Peter Brook suggested, had definitely been a Good Thing. At the same time we always seem to be learning things the hard way, and they're always new things – which I suppose just proves that we're always trying new things. We had, for example, a Press Conference in the dome on the final Saturday, to which not a single member of the press turned up despite having been sent printed invitations and despite the lure of wine and cocktail food which we could ill afford to provide. Once again it seemed painfully clear that we needed administrative help.

This week we started for the first time to record our concerts, and were generally pleased with the results. John McDowell, who was also doing the video filming, rigged up the microphones with invisible wires which we kept detaching by walking into them on the stage. The tapes proved, as I guess they do to all musicians, that what we thought were enormous liberties with the timing and dynamics of the music sounded like coy modifications when one listened back to the tape.

Thamesmead, 10–15 August 1982

We were invited by the Greater London Council to put the dome up in a new development where concerts had never been tried. Birchmere Park was in the middle of a vast housing estate so new that it did not appear on the London A to Z maps, and even when we arrived in Thamesmead itself we could not track down a local resident who had even heard of the park, which was not an auspicious start.

The park turned out to be a new park amidst a lot of newness. There was a new lake, new grass, a new sports hall and a lot of young children and wind-surfers, a curious kind of sportsman to find in London. We had been warned about the violence of the area and the need for security, but in fact the park was much more peaceful than Wormwood Scrubs, and the whole area seemed slightly cowed by its new suburban virtue, as did most of the residents. We attracted a large crowd of children during the building of the dome which went very smoothly, and thereafter they formed a large section of every audience, which pleased some of us and irritated others, because the children were always fidgeting and coming in and out of the tent.

The first concert in Thamesmead, with the Trout Quintet, was about half-full, and we all felt the weariness of the knowledge that it would be uphill work to fill the dome by the end of the week. This process, of starting with nothing and building up to a loving and numerous audience five days later, was one that we were very familiar with, and we didn't always have the energy to plunge willingly into the week's crescendo when once again we experienced the coldness of the first night.

I wanted to find some way of asking the audience how many of them listen to classical music on a regular basis, but we couldn't really think of a way of asking them without implying that something was amiss if they didn't.

One idea that emerged was that of setting it up so that the audience knew they would be asked what they felt about classical music and would have the first half of the concert to consider their response, after which we could take our interval with them, not away from them, and chat to them about their reactions. Some were in favour of trying this out; others felt that it would ruin their own concentration on the second half.

I personally felt sad that the group was splitting ever more noticeably into subsets, and on this particular occasion, when five of us were debating intensely the manner of concert presentation, five others were dancing and drinking in the dome. They came out to enquire whether we were talking about anything interesting? And, on hearing that we were discussing concert presentation, said 'Oh', and went off back to the dome with another can of beer. Perfectly understandable in a way, but it depressed me because this kind of thing never happened in the first half of the summer. I did not like the feeling of suddenly being one of the 'intellectuals', where before it felt as though we were all equally interested in discussing ideas.

The first children's concert in Thamesmead was scheduled as the 'Trip to the Zoo' which got so out of control in the Scrubs. The others wanted to do the Circles and Triangles programme and repeat it on Sunday, but as the author of the script of 'A Trip to the Zoo' I was loudly indignant, and in the end the others agreed to give it a second try, but to amend it so that it contained more audience participation. Thus we worked out a programme which was basically the same script, but which included at the introduction of each animal a contest for the children to imitate that animal and come in from the back of the dome in a sort of Animal Fashion Parade.

Felix narrated the show dressed in a kind of respectable-gipsy outfit and was far more extrovert with his reading. The dome was packed with kids, mostly little ones, and mostly quite docile and co-operative. The new formula of story plus shouting and participation worked very well indeed, and at the end they hugged and danced with the bear, this time with Leo inside the bear costume. But Leo, like Warren last week, was mildly traumatised by being inside the bear suit which he said was a nightmare sauna, with such a deadweight of bear-head between his own mouth and the outside world that he could not make himself heard even if he had needed to. The atmosphere of the show, however, was very 'high', not at all menacing as it had been on the Scrubs, and we retired feeling cheerful that we now had two children's concert programmes, both original in tone.

The following morning I was at home practising Mozart for the piano concerto in the evening when Krysia phoned to say that the dome's cover had torn itself away from the frame in a high wind, and that they had had to cut it down to prevent the tears from extending right across the cover. They had cut the platform out of the cover with knives, and meanwhile the cover, billowing inside the dome, had knocked the piano right over onto its keyboard, breaking several pieces off it. Krysia phoned just ten minutes after this had happened, and at that stage Felix was running around directing operations from inside his plaster casts, and was saying 'this is the end of our season, chaps'. The cover, it seemed, had torn away at almost every point where the strings were attached to the frame, and Krysia's first impression was that it was irreparable.

Robin had already phoned the company which made the cover and suggested that on Monday he hire a van and drive the cover down to them for repairs, which we would pay for. Feeling that this was not the right approach, I phoned straight afterwards and told the Technical Director of the company that we were very upset. He was obviously taken aback at the quick succession of mild and fierce telephone conversations, and said that he had never wanted to hang the cover inside the frame because the material wasn't strong enough to take the weight, and the reason it wasn't strong enough was that our budget was too small to allow us to have the cover made from a good enough material. He was frustrated and so was I. After a polite exchange of hostilities, however, he offered to bring a trailer up to London, to which he was anyway driving that afternoon, and collect our cover so that he could drive it back to Dorset and start working on it on Monday morning in the hope of having it ready for Battersea a few days later.

Meanwhile it seemed that mild hysteria had set in at the dome, where they had opened Robin's birthday bottle of champagne to celebrate the fact that this new disaster could under no circumstances be ascribed to Fate, and that therefore we didn't have to get depressed about it; it was just something that had happened. In a more sober frame of mind, we then cancelled the rest of the week at Thamesmead and asked the authorities to inform all the other groups involved.

David Waterman reminded me that morning that we were active in an awful lot of different fields, and that the catalogue of misfortunes this summer might simply be multiple random wrongness in all the areas which formed part of the project: music, dome equipment, old vehicles, bad weather, difficult audiences, volatile personalities. It only needed minor wrongness to occur in each of those fields for the total effect to be one of unmitigated and frightening Mass Wrongness, but he thought we should try to see each misfortune in context – the tearing away of the dome cover, for example, as.a simple design fault, not a reproof from the gods – and not fall victim to the cumulative effect.

Thus we decided that we just had to go ahead with the Battersea concerts even if it meant doing them in a dome without a cover, or in a frame with a parachute over it, or in someone's house if it came to that. There was now twice as much reason for our Benefit Concert, one of the Battersea concerts designed to make money for the Domus Accident Appeal, as there was when we thought it up.

The following morning I went down to Thamesmead to help, and found everyone having tea and French toast by the skeleton of the dome. The false euphoria of the drama had drained away, and we were all subdued by the notions which now began to creep into our minds of legal action against us by the Greater London Council, possible refusal on their part to let us put up the dome in Battersea, possible battles about who was responsible for the failure of the cover. We very much hoped that the company could be proved negligent; after all, *we* had not designed or chosen the rubber washers from which the strings ran to the frame, and the fact that the washers were too weak, and the whole system inept, should surely be the fault of the designer.

Unfortunately it was a Saturday, and therefore everywhere was closed when we tried to contact all these people to find out where we stood on such questions as paying the fees of the groups who were unable to perform in the dome because of the collapse of the cover. We were condemned to a day of stasis – not a good feeling.

We took the dome down, working with rather less will than we usually do when we're taking it down at the right time, and Krysia, John and I went off for lunch at Krysia's parents' house in Ilford. There was more disquieting news, passed on by John, that the guest players and the helpers had been complaining of the 'closed' circle of the hard-core members, and had been saying that they didn't feel as welcome as they used to feel.

This led to a long analysis of how the group has developed, and we concluded that the balance had changed very much from the early days when Domus was one long party with a bit of music thrown in, and when I went off and stayed in a pensione in Assisi because there was hardly room for me on the dome-site – so full was it of people's friends passing through and staying on for the party. Now, it seemed we had changed the emphasis almost too much in the opposite direction; the tightness of musical ensemble came first, and the rehearsals took priority over socialising; the players had gradually found that they had to isolate themselves from *some* social activity if they were going to play well.

I pointed out that no-one would expect be able to turn up in the place where a string quartet was giving concerts and be welcomed, fed and housed at the expense of the group like people seem to expect to be with us, as though we were a sort of hippy commune. I really felt that we had no duty to open our arms to such visitors when we were trying to work, and everyone agreed that they could not think of another well-known music group whose intactness would be expected to yield to the requirements of visitors.

But we also agreed that it must be confusing for people who got to know us in the carefree days before we became aware of our responsibility to the public, our obligations to fulfil rules of safety, finance, punctuality and so on. We regretted that we had collided so hard with the real world, but felt that in the life of every group which begins as a madly impossible dream there must be a 'coming of age' when the dream has to come to terms with reality.

John McDowell had been puzzled that morning by his camera jamming when he tried to film the taking down of the dome, and Krysia reminded us of that episode in Laurens van der Post's *The Lost World of the Kalahari* where they try to film the interior of a sacred Bushman cave, and the gods prevent them from doing so by interfering with the camera in a dramatic way. To John this theory makes sense, and he still felt that the collapse of the dome cover – apparently in the middle of an unpleasant disagreement between him and Felix – was symbolic of more than sloppy design. We agreed that this was a difficult moment in the life of Domus, and that we had to steer ourselves wisely through the troubles which seemed about to multiply.

In the following few days, while waiting for the cover to be repaired, we interviewed two would-be administrators, and were ourselves interviewed by a concert agent. The first would-be administrator, Sheelagh Barnard, won our confidence with a blend of shrewdness, idealism and intellectual poise, and after our evening with her we all felt that we could quite happily hand over much of the administration to her. The second candidate was more difficult to appraise, and we were divided in our reactions to what he proposed. He was a public relations man who had happened more or less by accident upon the music world and had discovered it to be full of agreeable bumbling artists with their heads in the clouds, and he thought that Domus was a potentially commercial idea, which he would undertake to make into a big success with concerts not only in the dome but in all sorts of new venues such as hotels and cruise ships.

He took the view that concerts in the dome would never be really successful because too many factors worked against them – not only with weather and background noise, but with a built-in limit to the financial success because of the necessarily small audiences. Of course as soon as he spoke slightingly of the dome itself he lost the affection of most of the people at the table, but some were drawn to his ideas of expansion and were tempted to give him a try, on the grounds that he would have ideas we wouldn't have ourselves, whereas Sheelagh, coming from very much the same idealistic background as we did, would probably have just the sort of ideas that we would have ourselves – both qualifying her and disqualifying her for the job of leading us into new pastures. Ultimately, however, we felt that the public relations man was pulling too strongly in a direction which was ideologically painful to us, and we rejected his candidacy.

My sister Nils came to visit at around this time and reported a conversation with a friend doing research into the sociology of organisations – which he said usually developed along a pattern identical to ours. First, he said, all idealistic groups begin by reinventing the wheel. They isolate themselves from the corrupting influence of other groups, and they begin with painful slowness to discover how to do things by themselves. They become a co-operative, with everyone doing a bit of everything, and being paid equal amounts.

Then they discover that this method is inefficient, and they divide up the tasks, giving areas of responsibility to individuals, but they still pay everyone the same. Then they find that some tasks are much harder, more skilled and more time-consuming than others, and the people who are doing them say that they want this fact to be reflected in the reward. Then they start to have a structure of Power and Responsibility with certain people acknowledged as the leaders or pillars of the group, with everyone still being paid the same. Eventually the leaders demand that their work be paid more, and so the group comes to be indistinguishable from any other hierarchical organisation such as a business corporation.

The researcher had experienced all these things himself as the member of an idealistic whole-food cooperative, but he said it seemed absolutely common to organisations all over the world. It certainly seemed to parallel our experience, and reminded me of a similar process described by Mark Vonnegut in his *Eden Express* book. We wondered if such a thing would happen in a cross-cultural group.

Battersea Park

At the end of the week we put the dome up in Battersea Park, much the nicest of the three parks this summer, and much the best-advertised venue, with notices pinned to trees all around the park, 400 leaflets sent to people on the mailing list, leaflets through doors in the area and adverts in three national newspapers as well as in *Time Out*.

Then it transpired that the cover of the dome, which arrived back from repair during the morning, had been patched in unsightly fashion, each node now reinforced with black straps which showed through on the inside of the dome and broke its uninterrupted whiteness with spangles of black tape. Furthermore the straps were set into the cover by means of slits cut rather too wide in the white PVC, and the slits would, of course, let the rain through. We were disappointed and furious, and Felix said there should be no question of our paying for the repair, which the repairers had said would cost £160 – a sum we could hardly scrape together.

The dome building was delayed at several stages by all sorts of modifications which had to be done while the non-experts amongst us lounged around on the grass and group morale sunk low. The wind sprung up, the Brahms rehearsal in the evening was transferred to Cloudesley Square, Dickie lost his cello part and had to go to Hampstead to borrow another, and the day finished in the same atmosphere of mild distress which had characterised its progress.

On the Saturday we went down to prepare for the two concerts of the day, but minor setbacks appeared as though on cue, making it necessary for Robin to drive back across London instead of rehearsing Brahms as planned; making us rehearse the Mozart without a viola.

The weather careered selfishly in and out of the park; sunshine reigned for five minutes and then suddenly we were buckling all the doors shut against the wind. Meanwhile all the ingredients for lunch had been forgotten, Krysia's parents didn't turn up with her concert uniform and I couldn't find a place to put the piano for the Mozart concerto that didn't seem to be half a mile away from the rest of the players, and with my back to the audience.

But suddenly, at 2.50 p.m. a large audience materialised for the free opening concert, and professionalism took over. It is hard, somehow, to make an afternoon concert be as magical as an evening one; daylight is too practical to allow people to forget themselves, and although the Mozart and the Brahms Sextet were as well-crafted as they had ever been, nevertheless they merged too easily into the ongoing afternoon in which people had to go home and get things done, and something of the highly-spiced atmosphere of the late evening was missing.

During the late afternoon the wind became quite biting and the eight cellists arrived for their Villa-Lobos rehearsal with expressions of distaste as though wondering how on earth we could stomach such adverse weather conditions during a whole season. They rehearsed with the stage ingeniously distributed so that they could sit in a big semi-circle; they sounded less good than the ensemble which did the same piece last year, I thought, but on the other hand it was colder, and the cold really does affect people's playing.

The evening concert was the so-called Gala Concert, a benefit for the Domus Accident Appeal Fund. Tickets were £10, and only about 25 people had bought them at that price. Each cellist had been given a couple of complimentary tickets, and at the last minute we had more or less gone out into the hedgerows and besought passing strangers to come in for nothing, so there was a very mixed audience of friends, wealthy patrons and impoverished members of the public who had come in for nothing.

We had made several savoury dishes – Japanese sushi, exciting salads and little pies as well as desserts – and at the interval, after the piece for multiple celli, people ate and drank while Steven Isserlis and I played Beatles songs. The long interval certainly made a difference to the atmosphere; the second half of the concert was noticeably warmer in tone, as Krysia found when she made a delightful introductory speech to the Trout Quintet. 'This piece is based on a song about a trout,' she said, 'and I was interested to find out what the song was about, so I looked it up in a dictionary and I found that it was about a trout.'

Actually this performance of the Trout Quintet, helped no doubt by the warm ambience, was one of the highlights of the whole summer, and several friends in the audience said the next day that they would never forget it. I thought about this on the following day when we performed the piece again with no less spirit and no less objective flair but *in the afternoon*, when tradition converted it into a divertissement instead of an elating experience. At any rate the evening performance was judged to be one of the absolute high points of the summer: absolute in the sense that it transcended any personal cavils which could have been made against it.

The other high points all seemed to be agreed upon: the whole of the last concert in Hamburg; the Mozart concerto in Wormwood Scrubs. Sadly the Brahms Sextet did not figure on anyone's list of high points, but only, I think, because it did not have enough time to 'gel', and was anyway deprived of one of its performances because of the cancellation of Thamesmead. The Gala Concert in Battersea ended with a wonderful feeling of rapport between players and audience. It was only at the end that I really felt it: I had been so worried about the success of the whole evening that I couldn't tell whether it was going well or not, and I spent most of the evening averting my eyes from the cold faces of the cellists, or trying not to hear their disparaging comments as they changed into their white frocks in the sordid public loo.

The Sunday was our last concert day of the season and everyone tried to feel either sorrow or relief, but was too tired to do so. Little problems of a tediously familiar kind kept happening throughout the whole day; I spent the morning at home, practising – where every fifteen minutes the telephone rang with some new example of something that someone had forgotten and wanted to have brought down to the dome. Warren forgot that Felix had phoned to ask him to bring the stereo system for our last-night party, and when we got down to Battersea he was so mortified that he secretly went back to Islington on the tube and collected it, somehow manhandling its several large units back on public transport.

I personally felt that I had switched on to automatic pilot; I had no real idea of how well the afternoon concert went, and even the last concert, which by all accounts was a great success, passed by on another wavelength.

But the Schubert Quintet in the second half was the best-balanced performance I had heard all summer, and therefore the most moving. It did not have the high colour of some of the other performances; it did not have the dramatic personality of the performance in Cheltenham with Steven Isserlis, but it was the most finely blended with Dickie as the second cellist, and for the first time this summer I felt that everyone was so intent upon the music that their personal egos were set aside; no-one tried to draw attention to his or her own playing by disproportionate physical gestures.

David Waterman commented on the same improvement after the concert, though he thought it was a general improvement since last year, which it was not really; it was a product of the last night, when everyone felt more humble about the wonderful music we were about to stop playing for the winter. But his comments were cheering – he felt that most of us were more confident, therefore less 'ham' or less wooden, than we were last year and that (more importantly) we were now a very good group by any standards, rather than a patchily good group whose fine ideas compensated for any sloppiness in the ensemble.

After the concert we tried to have a party, which went in fits and starts as people had bursts of energy or suddenly lost momentum. Robin, on the strength of half a glass of wine, executed a wild acrobatic dance in the middle of a circle of cheering friends, after which he became subdued; John McDowell and I played jazz piano duets, and Greg and Ione danced to them, Suddenly we all felt so tired we could barely speak. We tried to hang on to the sense of occasion, the 'last night' elation, but it slipped away.

This summer had been a dreadful strain; that was clear. But the strain was not of an everyday kind; it may have been the product of very unusual circumstances, or it may have been the inflammatory mix of the people involved. If the latter, of course, it would happen again, and I did not know if I could take it. I resolved that I would work as constructively and cheerfully as I could during the whole of next year – Canada and the summer tour – disregarding problems and trying to make everything run smoothly. If, after that, it seemed to me that strain was an unavoidable part of the group, if next summer produced anything like the anguish of this one, I would probably leave.

I spoke about this to the others, and it seemed clear that we were all wondering how long our stamina would hold out. We were shy of voicing the thought that there was something inherently unstable, explosive, about the mixture of our personalities. We wanted the evil to be external – as Anthony Burgess describes in *Earthly Powers*. But we ended the season unsure of whether our alchemy was a force for good or a force for disruption.

Banff, Canada, January 1983

After discussing the possibility for some time, four of us finally managed to win scholar-
ships to spend one semester at the Banff Centre in Canada. This college, specialising in
inter-arts projects, had offered us a chance to rehearse, perform and try things out – in a
beautiful winter landscape – with the aid of visiting musicians of international stature
who would be there for periods of one or two weeks each. As it happened, there was a
process of paring-down when the members of Domus had to commit themselves to
spending three months in Canada. The four people who eventually committed themselves
turned out to be a violinist (Krysia), a violist (Robin), a cellist (Felix) and a pianist (me).
By default, Domus had suddenly become a piano quartet. This pleased Krysia, who said
that she had always particularly liked piano quartets and wanted to belong to one. But it
was a strangely random start to a piano quartet which in fact continued in that format
for another twelve years.

The winter in Banff was a very happy time for me (partly because we were free to
think about music and ideas, and had no heavy boxes to cart around), and I wrote a lot
about the interesting artists we met there. Our experimental work, however, was not
focused on performance, so I have not included my recollections here. One of Banff's best
gifts to us, our meeting with the Hungarian pianist György Sebök, is described in the
chapter about him and Sandor Végh in Part Two.

When we returned to London in April 1983 we had learned more piano quartets and
were looking forward to our projects in Bath and Berlin. Little did we know it was to be
our last whole summer with the dome.

Serious disagreements, London, 1983

17 May

I keep meaning to write something about the state of mind within Domus, but
putting it off because it is so complex. Of course we all have our private versions of
reality, but in the past it has been easy for me, as the scribe, to see what constitutes
collective truth, a description we'd all agree on. Here, however, it is not at all easy. I
notice that, whenever one of us explains to an outsider what the current situation is,
another usually interrupts to say, 'That's not really how it was,' or 'I didn't see it like
that.'

It's so hard to know what I ought to do. Playing with Domus is intermittently
very rewarding. Sometimes it feels, however, like being a living ingredient in a piece
of process music like Steve Reich's, glued to the fabric by the fact that I saw the
process begin and want to see its end, want to see how it all evolves.

The end sometimes feels as though it might be near. Felix has been increasingly
restless and un-cooperative, and because of his crucial role in the group, this affects

us all. We've agreed to work together as happily as possible until the end of the summer tour, at which point we will review the situation. It already seems clear that Felix will not be in England next autumn and winter; he speaks of going back to Canada to do a film course, or to form an improvising group.

One thing is certain: Felix has changed very much. Instead of being the driving spirit of the group, his energy and enthusiasm have vanished. He seems to resent meetings, finds it hard to control his temper, says he doesn't see the need for rehearsals, is unwilling to help with any administrative tasks and generally seems (as he said of himself the other day) to be 'on a very short rein as far as patience is concerned'. His interest in classical music is dwindling, and his mind turns on other, newer projects such as video, African drumming and improvised music.

In addition, he is fed up with England, its weather, and the problems it represents; being far away from loved ones, and because he is American, not being allowed to work outside of Domus, as well as the very real difficulty for the whole group of earning a living here. He is out of sympathy with the current policy of 'professionalism', trying to get fees, and to base our reputation purely on music this year. It goes very much against the grain with him to be bound to any conservative policy, as he sees this to be, and he blames me for instigating it, though without being able to offer a viable alternative. He is miserable in rehearsals, especially when he thinks we are being 'subtle' rather than 'spontaneous'. His state of mind makes us all feel low because we were so used to his energy: 'Come on, you guys, let's make this piece *jump!*' Everyone is struck by the irony of his losing interest in the group which he began with such white-hot enthusiasm.

For a while in Banff, both Robin and Krysia felt that if Felix were to leave Domus, it would be a death-blow to the group. Robin passed through a sort of crisis with his feelings on this point, and came to believe that we could indeed carry on with a different cellist and a different group spirit, but perhaps just as enjoyably. Later Krysia, too, reluctantly came to the same conclusion. Meanwhile Felix speaks of collecting a band of like-minded people to explore and travel and improvise and make films, but pointedly hasn't asked any of us to be in it. This is very hurtful to the people who have embraced his ideas whole-heartedly, especially Krysia and Robin. Krysia is, of course, still very interested in improvisation and workshops, but not as a lifestyle, and not at the expense of classical music which she reveres probably more than any of us, and derives great pleasure and satisfaction from rehearsing.

It's heartening to see how Robin pulled himself through his crisis of confidence, first believing that without Felix he would not be strong enough to continue, and then gradually seeing that he was. The other day I said to him, 'It was Felix's enthusiasm which magnetised you into this group, but his current enthusiasm for a new kind of group doesn't seem to be magnetising you into that', and he said, 'No. He magnetised me into feeling enthusiastic about Domus, and I still haven't lost my pleasure in it at all.'

I'm not sure, and I don't think any of us are, whether Felix has actually decided to leave at the end of the tour or not. The other day, when our planned visit to Greece was cancelled, he said he was pleased because it would allow him to go off and do other things with other people. He even suggested that, if more dates came in for August, we were welcome to look for another cellist to replace him.

In the end came to a compromise wherein we said that we, too, would go to Italy and do experimental things with him and his friends, during our newly quiet month in August. He accepted the suggestion, but with a certain lack of enthusiasm which made us wonder if maybe he would have preferred to be there without us.

Felix seems to feel that our tedious preoccupation with programmes, fees and dates is squashing his creativity. He mourns the passing of spontaneous, unplanned events and serendipitous encounters. Unfortunately it has proved impossible to show that we are more than an experimental outfit without tackling these utterly practical issues, which are after all just as tedious for us as they are for him. Certainly we'd never have been able to build the dome in its fully functional form, or buy a Mercedes van, a specially built trailer, and so on, without the patient spade-work put into money-raising by the rest of us, Robin and me especially. Yet such efforts have never been regarded as 'creative' although they enable the creativity to continue.

Even as I write all this, I can hear the others looking over my shoulder and saying 'Oh, no, it wasn't like that.' But perhaps now there *is* a consensus on this. The other day I was writing an article on Domus for *The Strad*, and asked Krysia what it should be about. 'You could write it', she said, 'about what it feels like to have everyone else think you're on the crest of a wave, while actually you feel as though everything is collapsing around you.'

23 May

An extraordinary day, a bad day. We met at Camberwell to rehearse all day. We were all on edge because the lady in whose house we were rehearsing had returned unexpectedly, and we felt like intruders.

In the afternoon we sat down to discuss how, why, and when we could do the final things in preparation for the tour. Suddenly we found ourselves plunged, for perhaps the fourth time in a few months, into a deeply unpleasant argument about concert clothes. This was the subject of our bitterest argument in Canada, and of one or two more since then. Three of us want to make a unified impression on the stage, and are prepared to agree on style or colour of clothes. Felix, however, is not. He dislikes formal clothes, and his attitude to informal clothes has become more and more hard-line since we first 'discussed' it. His argument is that people do not look good if they compromise their own personal taste. Therefore wearing unified clothes is a stupid idea if it results in no-one wearing garments they particularly like. He insists (and *insists* is an understatement) on wearing clothes he feels comfortable in. What he means by 'comfortable' is his pink and green Camden Lock jumper, his old grey boots, his baggy striped trousers and so on. This afternoon he said that we could wear what we liked if we wanted to conform, but that he was going to follow his own style sense. Suddenly Krysia could not bear it any longer, and with a furious cry, burst into tears and wept brokenly. Not because Felix wants to wear different colours, but because she could not believe (as none of us could) that he was willing to plunge for the fourth time into exactly the same argument which had almost split us up in Canada. 'The good of the group versus the rights of the individual.'

Robin told me later that while I was outside the room comforting Krysia, Felix shocked him by saying that Robin in any case knew nothing about clothes, and how dare Robin lecture him on what looks good when Robin has no dress sense himself.

Robin said he summoned all his powers of communication in an effort to break through the hostility, but failed. He, too, was deeply upset.

Later in the evening, during a rehearsal, Robin also broke down and cried. We abandoned the rehearsal and went home. Robin was more upset than I have seen him for a long time. We wondered, in the car, if Felix has any notion of the extent to which his behaviour is upsetting his colleagues.

The issue of concert clothes, which has proved one of our touchiest, is of course symbolic. In itself it is not so grave; nobody's enjoyment of the concert would be ruined if someone was wearing the wrong colour. But everyone else wants to dress in a special way for concerts, and outsiders know that the unified appearance of group members proclaims their cooperation. Felix would say that cooperation over clothes is a trivial matter compared to other, more meaningful kinds of cooperation. Alas, if only clothes were the sole focus of our disunity. But the clothes issue is representative of many others, less easy to pinpoint. This is why the three of us respond so acutely to his refusal to wear the colours the group had agreed on. I, personally, have never felt that white particularly suits me, but I accepted it as a unifying visual motif: everyone thought it would be nice for us to wear white, matching the colour of the dome.

Thinking back on all our disagreements since Canada I realise that, in every one, Felix has maintained that to follow one's inner voice is the only way to behave with integrity. In other words, if he's involved in a group which needs him to be responsible for something or other, and he doesn't feel like it, then the most honest thing to do is to say so, and not to do that thing, If he doesn't feel like rehearsing, he makes it perfectly clear. If he doesn't feel like being civil to visitors, he isn't. If he wants to wear grey boots on stage, he does. To him all this is the badge of courage. To us it is selfish. Perhaps it is simply best to agree that he is not suited to long-term participation in a group, and to part company amicably. Yet he was really our original motivating force. Moreover, his visions of 'how life could be' have always had potent allure for us. Is he leaving us, or are we leaving him? Do we have the right?

Sometimes I think how like a divorce this must be. Normally, in the past, when any of us have had a relationship go sour, it has been easy to leave it, and not to see the person again. Here, external circumstances and promises given to outside persons force Felix to stay with us even when his emotional commitment has been withdrawn. I now realise a little what it must be like in a marriage when one party wants to leave, but is constrained by external pressures to stay. I'm not sure for whom it is worse. Yes, I am. It's worse for the party who still wants the relationship to work and still hopes that the partner will return with a light heart. This is our position with Felix, or at any rate it is Robin's and Krysia's. My own situation is slightly different. As a non-technical person, I was always slightly surprised to find myself in Domus, and always struggled to come to terms with the huge quantity of practical challenges it added to an already demanding musical life. Although I have tried as hard as anyone to make it a success, the prospect of it breaking up sometimes brings me a tiny source of relief.

1. The original Domus team. From left: Robin Ireland, Krysia Osostowicz, Richard Lester, Susan Tomes, Felix Wurman (and a guest, Ruth Ehrlich).

2. Building the geodesic dome for a rehearsal week in Finemere, 1981 [photo: Susan Tomes].

3. The frame assembled.

4. The dome ready for use in Finemere, 1981 [photo: Robin Ireland].

5. The dome outside the Kunsthaus Bethanien in Berlin, 1983.

6. The illuminated dome at night on Wormwood Scrubs.

7. The Florestan trio. From left: Richard Lester, Anthony Marwood, Susan Tomes. [photo: Richard Lewisohn]

Bath Festival, May 1983

27 May

In Bath we were fortunate to be given another spectacular site for the dome – on the gardens of the Royal Terrace. Here, as in Cheltenham, the futuristic shape of the dome fitted beautifully into the backdrop of Georgian buildings, though the effect was even better in Bath because the Royal Crescent itself describes a curve, and seemed to echo the dome's outline.

Sometimes the dome feels like the big kiln described by the Japanese potter Shoji Hamada. He says that man's own self is a small thing after all, and that he tires easily of the extent of his own control over the pots he makes. With a big kiln, he says, he can't control it and the power beyond himself is necessary. He wants to be a potter whose pots combine human skill and divine intervention, or at any rate some further dimension outwith his understanding. The dome feels like a big kiln into which we invite spectacular powers to supplement our own skills. What puzzles us is that these powers do not always seem to be beneficent.

Our tour begins with the usual array of foreseen and unforeseen problems. It's strange that unforeseen problems can still arise, given the time we spend trying to foresee them. But on the first day of our tour we still do not have a van, and the trailer is not yet finished. The new grand piano, a little Blüthner found by Mr Glazebrook of Steinway's, travels down to Bath in the Steinway van and is then found not to be equipped with a 'shoe', the professional device for moving it onto a trailer. All manner of delays then ensue.

Meanwhile Gerry, our roadie, hires a van, drives to Bath and later has to drive back to London with it and return in his own van because we can't afford to hire a big van for more than a day, while Robin, over the Bank Holiday weekend, tries to sort out finance for the purchase of a Mercedes van. As usual there is little time to think about music.

One noticeable thing on the first day is how little energy anyone has for things which go wrong. When we finally get the dome up, we merely note the fact with relief, and fail to dance round like we did last year, exclaiming how lovely it is and greeting it like an old friend. We get on with the next thing, which as usual takes three times as long and is three times as complicated as we envisaged. Nevertheless it is nice to have Gerry, whose presence feels symbolically like a weight taken off our shoulders even if it simply means an extra pair of hands. In his presence, because he is an outsider, we don't bicker as much as we do when left to ourselves.

Our day begins at 8.30 a.m. when Robin and I leave Bradford on Avon, and we finish at 7 p.m. I notice how resentful I feel, this year, of anything which prevents me from thinking about music and preparing mentally and physically for it. In previous years by an effort of willpower and the charm of novelty, I have been gladly immersed in the welfare of the dome itself. Now any dome problem causes me real irritation. I tolerate it when its assembly goes smoothly, but when it doesn't I start to question the wisdom of the whole project and lament the distraction from artistic focus.

The next day is even worse. The weather is cold and it rains dismally, a constant demoralising downpour. We collect the trailer from its overnight storage and bring it down to the dome, where it reveals several (would you believe) unforeseen problems, such as not having grease in the screws, and wheels that can't be unscrewed. During an entire morning the chaps labour at it with hammers and jacks and spanners, finally breaking off for a quick bite before the first concert at 3 p.m.

We are in a very poor state psychologically for this first event, which ironically is sold out, and contains several critics and important festival people in the audience. After the arduous and problematic days of preparation, and the last-minute conversion of the dome to a viable concert hall, the sudden exposure to the audience and critics feels premature, and we realise that the concert has burst upon us with our nerves slightly ragged. Nevertheless the concert runs fairly smoothly. Krysia and I don't enjoy it very much, feeling the lack of unity amongst the group, which is expressed in the usual symbolic way: Felix is wearing grey trousers and a pink and green jumper while the rest of us are in dark red and white, and at the last moment he also declines to introduce any of the pieces. This kind of mutiny, which Robin insists we make light of and disregard, affects both Krysia and me emotionally and we feel that our differences are cruelly exposed to the public.

In the evening we have the clarinettist Janet Hilton as a guest. This concert is not quite typical of Domus concerts, as the afternoon one also was not; long substantial pieces instead of a compilation of little ones. But the audience transforms itself rapidly into a typical Domus audience; though perhaps older than our usual audiences, and consisting partly of people who couldn't get tickets for an official festival concert, they respond almost instantly to whatever it is in that dome audiences respond to and become beaming and kindly listeners, smiling benevolently when we catch their eyes as we bow and so on. At the end of the day Robin feels that it has all been worthwhile, and says he feels completely happy. Felix says nothing, so I don't know what he feels and don't particularly want to know at this juncture. Krysia and I feel a modified rapture cloaked by fatigue. We all sleep heavily and dream heavy dreams.

The next day is a more typical Domus concert, with a first half composed of Eastern European pieces – Janácek, Bartók, Penderecki, Chopin, Dohnányi – lent sudden gravity in the middle by a quietly emotional speech by Krysia about freedom of action in Poland and how impossible it would be to build a geodesic dome there and give concerts in it. The audience, once again middle-aged to elderly, suffers this political speech in tolerant silence, and afterwards comment that it was perhaps 'slightly out of place in a concert'. Nevertheless we are all touched by it, and pleased that she did it.

The second half is the Mendelssohn Trio, unrehearsed because the rugby pavilion, where Felix's cello was stored overnight, was locked until an hour before the concert. We have not played the piece since our rather unsuccessful and aggressive performance of it in Canada, and the memory of this, too, makes us reluctant to confront it before we absolutely have to. But when we do, it becomes pliant in our hands. It is one of those strange occasions where the character of a piece changes without any particular intention on the part of the players. We surprise ourselves with our capacity to be mellow at a time when we are all in fact feeling brittle.

On the third day in Bath we have our first children's show of the season, always an ordeal. It's a story about a disc jockey who suffers an accident in his studio and, as a result, is wandering around in a dazed state, exhibiting an antipathy to silence and insisting on playing his loud radio, which he carries on his shoulder. The moral of the tale is that he learns how to turn off his radio, listen to music and finally learn to play an instrument himself so that he learns that it is pleasant to control the amount of sound in his life, and learns to enjoy silence too. The depiction of this tale is not quite so Victorian as the outline sounds. It begins with a cameo performance by Krysia and me of two charladies cleaning up the dome and discussing the dirty habits of musicians in the hearing of the audience. Then the 'concert' begins and Robin, attired in ludicrous wig and assortment of freakish clothes, interrupts it as the dazed disc jockey wielding ghetto-blaster radio.

Various amusing episodes lead up to the conversion of the whole audience into a human radio with different groups of kids representing different stations on the dial with their characteristic kind of music and in the background I provide all the sound cues for this music at the piano. Felix compères with his usual flair. The Bath children respond perfectly, picking up all their cues correctly and generally failing to demonstrate the cynicism which made our London shows so difficult last year. It is pretty much a success, though a great deal more tiring than our adult concerts because we are not used to acting.

We have a long, late and overindulgent lunch at the Hole in the Wall with Sir William Glock, the director of the Festival, who invites us back to Bath for next year, and, over-glad and over-tired, we lurch into the final concert, which sadly is the only one not sold out, because we clash with several other important concerts. This concert contains half a programme of Scherzi, which we do not manage quite slickly enough, although the raw material seems to be fine. After the interval the Fauré Quartet passes for me in a kind of dream. Everyone assures me it was fine, but suddenly disorientation grips me and I do not know how to judge any longer the effect of dome, music, people, anything. This is an unpleasant feeling because I associate it with 'normal' concerts where I sometimes feel that a bell-jar has descended over me, cutting me off from the audience. I don't want to feel like that in the dome, but I think the stress and anxiety of the last days have shut down my reactions.

In Berlin, Summer 1983

Perhaps the most ideal site yet devised for the dome; visually and atmospherically, the Kunsthaus Bethanien with its circular front lawn and setting amid the pink and red houses of the toppling Kreuzberg district is exactly right. The local community is largely Turkish. Thus large numbers of Turkish children swarm around the dome all day and it is hard to believe that these children will ever grow into adults, so little does their world seem to link with the adult world. They are at every door of the dome simultaneously, and keeping them outside is like trying to keep a flood at bay with a broom.

Here, as in the last two concerts in Hamburg, we feel a powerful sense of significance, and this is not because we play better, but because the audience has a collective concentration that inspires us. Of course we play better as a result of it, and wonder why or how it happens that an audience has first to create its identity and push it across the footlights in order for the artists to respond.

It cannot in fact be that way, or at least from the audience's point of view it would seem to be the other way round, but as artists we certainly distinguish between an audience which 'gives' nothing and is therefore hard to play to, and an audience like the ones in Hamburg and Berlin which sends waves of sympathetic concentration across the dome and revitalises our playing. Certain pieces which have always been a little bit taken for granted in our repertoire, or have become jaded or banal, like the Mendelssohn Trio or the Schumann Quartet, suddenly seem to become mines full of glittering unsuspected prizes, and we discover an affectionate involvement in them because the audience educates us into doing so, with their benevolent listening. It's a mysterious thing and of course from the listeners' side it must seem that we 'give' and they simply measure what we give.

After the first concert, which isn't full but is very gratifying for the reasons just stated, we go out for supper with the British Council people, and say we sometimes regret that our experiment with the dome has classical music as its vehicle. They all disagree, and say that there is no point in presenting a kind of music less congenial to *us* just because it fits better ideologically with the notion of taking music to the people. We have to play music we feel strongly about.

We are all still smarting a bit from our roadie Gerry's remark, casually made while we were putting up the dome here, that Domus was built on a basic flaw, the flaw being that 'people' do not specially want to have classical music taken to them, and would prefer some other kind. Certainly we always feel apologetic when we arrive in a place and start putting up the dome and onlookers arrive to ask whether we are a circus or a rock band or a theatre, and seem disappointed when we say that we're classical musicians. I say this to Klaus Henning of the British Council but he replies that it's merely a matter of education, and we can't expect to change things overnight. Three or four years are very little against the inertia of popular opinion. There may still be a basic flaw, but perhaps it's too early to know.

One other good thing about Berlin is that Felix cheers up because of the lively atmosphere, and our association with an Arts Centre which is very much to his taste. In discussion he is a lot more amicable than in all the previous weeks. In concert he still declines to play solo cello pieces, and he still declines to introduce things, but the refusal is now couched more in terms of 'I'd prefer not to', said with a mildly apologetic air. Yesterday there was some disagreement about how many Frank Bridge pieces we should do. He was on one side, and we were on another, but he suddenly backed down and said 'Well, I don't want to cause trouble, so let's do it the way you want to do it', which was very unusual indeed. Robin said that the other night in a restaurant Felix told him he envied our commitment to classical music and wished he felt it himself. Alas, he feels only that he is good at it, but that doesn't forge a commitment to it.

In Berlin we get a long review in the *Tagesspiegel* saying that our introductions were no more illuminating than quotations from textbooks, and that our playing of the 'uncommented' Mendelssohn was much more illuminating than anything we might have said about it. The critic then praised our playing highly, and said that we obviously put the stress on sheer musical quality, and rightly aimed to communicate through that, *not* through spoken introduction. This criticism, which ironically could only have been made this year because this is the first time we have put the stress primarily on the music, sends us scurrying to debate what we could say that would be better, more organic, more personal. Half of the problem, as the critic recognised, was our shyness in German, but it is also true that of late we have trusted the music and our interpretation of it more than our ability to describe it in words. We then try quite hard to make the introductions personally interesting, and are pleased with the result. For example I have to speak about the Stravinsky Duo, and describe how I first heard it in Poland, in a competition where it was played by a Japanese violinist and I thought it an insane choice for a competition, so lacking in personal feeling and so machine-like in its function. Then I said how, in working on it, I had discovered the heart beating under the remorseless exterior and how I formed a respect for its optimistic small voice singing in the midst of mechanisation. This definitely changed the atmosphere in the dome in favour of the piece, and Krysia said it made her look forward to playing it.

In Berlin we also meet a mime artist, Paul Clark, who is part of the Amsterdam Festival. He does a special extra performance of his show for us. It is like one of Italo Calvino's *Invisible Cities*, a world of harmonious objects presided over by the deeply respectful and yet manipulative professor who sometimes threads paths of geometric precision through swinging spheres and sometimes eats the objects of his study. It has a musical quality like the Ravel Duo, a beautiful clockwork with colours all in white and silver and black. Paul is interested in working on a new show with us, and we start to plan things for next year with the tentative plan of coming back to Berlin to work on it in the spring. This leads us to talk generally about next summer. All of us feel that the preparation for this tour was vastly longer and more complex than the tour itself, and that once on tour, the demand of always 'giving' is too great unless there is also an opportunity for taking, by which we mean getting fresh and outside influences. So for next year, instead of simply planning a long summer tour, we want to divide the summer into perhaps three different projects, and administer and finance each one separately.

One might be a festival created around Domus in England. Another might be a tour in England with a small theatre group trying to maximise the potential of the dome. A third might be the 'pure' Domus tour to other countries. We all feel, having concentrated now on the music long enough to secure our basic ensemble, that we are ready to branch out again.

The involvement of Felix in the group still hangs in the balance. He wants to tackle a video project using film to be interspersed with music during the concert, showing aspects of the musicians' lives or rehearsals to complement the live performance. His interest in the cello is clearly dwindling, and consequently our interest in him as a cellist. Everyone wants to retain him in some capacity, perhaps as the experimental wing of Domus, but it is mutually, if tacitly at this stage, agreed between us all that his participation as a year-round cellist seems pointless. It is very strange that we appear to be parting company with the person who started this all by saying, 'It can't be just any old tent – it has to be a geodesic dome!'

Here the diary broke off with a brief description of a riot in multi-ethnic Kreuzberg, indeed in the very square where the dome was situated. I described our distress at being suddenly surrounded by rioters and police with tear gas. Obviously our activities were interrupted, and afterwards I was too busy to write more for a while.

This was also because I had a sense that my narrative had become a sustained catalogue of problems, and I lost the will to keep it going.

This wasn't the end of Domus, of course – just the end of the beginning: the end of Domus as a larger experimental ensemble with guests joining and leaving as they wished. Felix left the group and was replaced by the cellist Tim Hugh. We continued to use the dome in the summer, and eventually summoned up the energy to take it to Australia. By this stage we were once again doing all the administration ourselves. The overwhelming practical problems we encountered on that trip – such as the dome being impounded by customs on both ends of the journey because the formalities had not been properly observed – were the last straw. After that, we decided that music had to regain priority, and we decided to spend at least part of the year playing 'normal' concerts in ordinary concert halls. This 'part of the year' rapidly became all the year. The dome was packed away and remained so, in fact, until some years later when Felix decided to take it back to America with him. It is still used there by him and his friends and colleagues for occasional concerts and celebrations.

When I look back on this period, I realise that our disagreements at the end of the diary period were debilitating because we were all so close. In particular, I now find it extraordinary that so much bad feeling was engendered by the topic of what clothes to wear in concerts. I've since discovered, by the way, that other music organisations have experienced these arguments too; the leader of an American symphony orchestra told me that concert dress was the subject of the players' bitterest debates. Yet I feel ashamed that we spent so much energy on it. Looking back, it seems to me that the clothes topic was symptomatic of a move from idealism to practicality. I could say that we had been in very deep, and were now coming up for air.

For a long time we had been spending both working time and social time with one another, and sharing all our hopes and fears. Therefore there was no private zone into which anyone could withdraw. Being in Domus was a full-time occupation, especially for Robin and myself who were doing all the administration as well. Actually, it was meant to be a full-time occupation, a way of life as well as a way of work. So when we started to have serious arguments, there was nowhere to hide. I think this gives a peculiarly intense flavour to the final pages of the diary.

I would not wish, however, to give the impression that this was the end of the personal friendships between Felix and other members of the group, or indeed that our difficulties at the end of his Domus years caused us to forget how important he had been. After a fairly turbulent period in his life, Felix returned to the USA, gradually regained his interest in classical music and the cello, and now enjoys a successful professional life with fingers in both classical and non-classical pies. He remained a close friend of David Lockington who chose to live in North America as well. It's clear that without Felix's unbounded enthusiasm and charisma, his enterprise and inspiration, the whole project would never have come into being, and we would never have achieved much of what we did with the dome.

Though neither of us meant it to be so, Felix and I probably polarised the group. We were both thoroughly committed to the idea of communicating with new audiences, but we felt differently about how best to do it. He was always pushing forward with new and adventurous ideas; I was always trying to make sense of what we were doing and make it last. Both approaches were essential, but they came to seem like opposing forces. The other members of the group sometimes felt close to Felix and sometimes to me. Everyone loved his ideas and longed for them to be attainable, but they also wanted stability. There was a precious period, which lasted for a few years, when we all faced in the same direction. Felix and I tried wholeheartedly to embrace one another's point of view. He was happy to throw himself into rehearsal and performance, just as I was happy to run about hillsides carrying boxes of metal hubs in the rain. But ultimately, a nomadic life of spontaneous festivals was not my ideal, just as trying to see how deep one could go into classical music was not his. Slowly and gradually we each reverted to our natural characters, unwittingly pulling the group apart as we did so. The fact that I stayed and he left may seem an unjust ending to this process, but when it happened I think it made emotional sense to us all.

After Felix left, Domus based itself on its British members. As it was now clear that we wanted to concentrate on building our reputation as players in the traditional concert hall, it became much simpler to recruit new members. Because there were few professional piano quartets, we decided to continue in that format. Almost immediately we attracted the interest of Ted Perry of Hyperion Records, who invited us to make our first disc, of Fauré piano quartets. This was a lucky choice for us, as this first record won a Gramophone Award in 1985, and has won many other awards and accolades since (listed in the discography). We were very grateful to Ted Perry, who died in February 2003, for taking a chance on us when we were largely unknown. We went on to a long and fruitful collaboration with Hyperion Records which continues to this day.

In due course, Robin was invited to join the Lindsay String Quartet, where he remains very happily, and he was replaced in the group by violist Tim Boulton. Krysia and I were then the only original members of Domus. The piano quartet started to build an international reputation and to undertake tours which eventually took us all over the world. The name Domus, which now had no immediate point of reference, sustained interest in the original project, and wherever we went, people constantly asked us about the dome and our adventures with it. We still considered ourselves to be doing the same sort of concerts, and playing in the same way, as we did in the dome. But inevitably, with the constraints of the traditional concert hall (such as the audience being too far away to hear any conversational comments made to them by the players) our presentation became more traditional too. To be honest this didn't worry us for a while, as we were enjoying the focus on quality of playing above all. We did, however, continue to introduce concerts wherever it seemed right, and in fact it seemed right more and more often.

After several good years with Tim (I think he himself estimated that he had played over 200 concerts with Domus) he was invited to become the principal cellist of the BBC Symphony Orchestra. At this point Richard Lester, who had been so important in the early days of Domus, re-joined the group as its cellist. For the last few years of Domus's career the members were therefore Krysia Osostowicz, violin, Tim Boulton, viola, Richard Lester, cello and Susan Tomes, piano. This was probably the version of the group which was most successful in the eyes of the outside world. During these years I didn't keep a diary; 'the happiest women, like the happiest nations, have no history', as George Eliot says in The Mill on the Floss.

It's strange looking back now to think that Domus had only five or six years with the dome, but ten years together after we stopped using it. The impact of our years with the dome – even though these were restricted to the summer months – was so enormous that in a sense it dominated all the rest, and continues to reverberate long after the group disbanded. Those members of the group who joined after the dome was no longer in use must have got very fed up with people constantly wanting to hear all about it. They good-naturedly went along with it because they, too, had always been interested in building new bridges to our audiences.

Domus was pioneering in several ways. At the time of writing I don't think that any other classical group has made such a major attempt to create its own conditions in its own portable venue. Also, our decision to speak about the music to our listeners, to explain what it meant to us, was very unusual when we began to do it in 1980. We encountered surprise and even resistance when we started to do this in the ordinary concert hall, and were indeed sometimes requested not to do it by concert organisers. In recent years, however, I notice that more and more musicians are incorporating spoken introductions into their programmes, and it is currently considered ungenerous if one doesn't do it. All this is connected to the new interest in educational projects and 'outreach work', but when Domus started doing it, we were breaking new ground in the classical field.

Alas, the piano quartet repertoire is fairly small. The core repertoire is two Mozart piano quartets, three by Brahms, one by Schumann, two by Fauré, and two by Dvořák. These were the pieces everyone wanted to hear, and though we commissioned excellent new works from composers such as Judith Weir and John Casken, built up an extensive repertoire of rarely heard piano quartets by Romantic composers, and branched out into duos, trios and quintets, the core piano quartets remained by far the most popular. Many concert promoters took the view that, as it was so rare to hear a 'dedicated' piano quartet, they didn't want to dilute the programme with non-quartet works, and they always requested the same ones. Gradually it became hard to retain a sense of freshness and commitment to these pieces when we had performed them so many times – and perhaps particularly so for Krysia and me, who had to re-learn and re-rehearse the whole reper-toire every time a new person joined the group. Though our involvement in chamber music never wavered, we eventually concluded that Domus as a piano quartet had run *its course. The group disbanded in 1995, ironically just before the announcement that we had won our second* Gramophone Award *for our disc of Fauré piano quintets.*

'*Something between a lunar module and a wigwam, the geodesic dome in which Domus started giving concerts ten years ago enshrined a kind of cultural evangelism. The very idea of four young players quitting the concert platform for a circus life, pitching their tent (they put it up and took it down themselves) and taking their music anywhere, was crazily attractive, and it brought them into an unusually close contact with their audience – physically as well as ideologically*', wrote The Independent *at one of our tenth anniversary concerts in 1989. 'Ten years on, and after several changes of personnel, Domus have retired the dome. Apart from one last al fresco next year, the group will only play now in conventional halls. But the name lives on, and it is not redundant. To hear them is to understand what the domestic immediacy of chamber music can achieve, and they seemed to have absorbed that quality so deeply into their playing that it ought to survive in almost any context.*'

From Domus to Florestan

Domus disbanded in 1995 after a long period of heart-searching about its future. When we finally stopped, there was a painful feeling of fatigue and dissent. I think we all felt that we'd probably never play in a group with one another again. A period of silence followed, in which we all licked our wounds and considered new projects. Then I had a call from Richard Lester and our old friend the violinist Anthony Marwood, who had joined Domus for its final recording, the *Gramophone Award*-winning disc of Fauré piano quintets. Anthony and Richard were interested in playing piano trios, and they asked me if I would join them. We agreed to have a 'reading session' to play through some piano trios and see how it felt. On the day of the trial session I think all three of us had a strong sense that we were musically very compatible, and that such a trio could be very rewarding. Rather surprisingly, it felt quite natural to talk of starting a new group.

For Richard and me this felt at least partly like a continuation of Domus, especially as Anthony had worked with us on our final project. Therefore, when we came to think about finding a name for the new trio, we wondered whether we should use the word 'Domus' in some form. 'The New Domus Trio'? 'The Domus Trio'? Clearly the reference to the dome was obsolete, but on the other hand the group had successfully existed for a decade since the dome was last used, and with personnel different from the original Domus members. So the relevance of the dome seemed less important than the opportunity to use what advertisers would call 'brand loyalty' to the name, and 'customer goodwill' associated with Domus. Richard and I were, after all, half of Domus, and since the piano quartet had disbanded, it felt quite natural to pick up the name and continue with it. Everyone on the business side of the profession told us that it would, in fact, be commercial suicide not to use the name, especially as it was otherwise lying dormant. 'If you start with a new name it will take ten years before people understand the link with Domus', we were told by agents. (This was pessimistic, but they certainly had a point.)

Nobody owned the name – we had never 'wised up' in that sort of way – so we were at liberty to use it, but when we consulted our former Domus colleagues, we found that they were deeply upset by the idea. To use the name against their will seemed too high a price to pay. So we took a deep breath and decided to start with a different name.

To search for one, we sat down with a list of favourite names, artists and words, but found that most of them were already in use by other groups or by other musical or non-musical ventures. A recurring idea was to find a name which was something to do with Schumann, whom we all loved. As Schumann himself was a writer and left abundant evidence of his own favourite words and names, we started looking through those. In his diaries he wrote about various sides of his own personality which he experienced as distinct characters. There was Florestan, the impulsive, optimistic man of action; Eusebius, the introvert and pensive dreamer, and Master Raro, the wise teacher. There was his wife Clara, who found her way into many musical works, and the 'Davidsbündler' or Band of David, who protected art against Philistines.

We liked both Florestan and Eusebius, and to be honest, either would have suited us. However, Florestan had immediately positive associations, and it is a beautiful word in itself. In conjunction with the word 'trio' it also had that pleasing 'dactyl-spondee' rhythm, three syllables followed by two – or more importantly, triplet quavers and then duplet quavers, to put it into musical notation – which linguists have identified as an important ingredient in the memorability of famous names, at least in the English-speaking world: Benjamin Franklin, Abraham Lincoln, Oliver Cromwell, Christopher Marlowe, Emily Brontë, Dorothy Parker, and so on. 'Florestan Trio' seemed to roll happily off the tongue. We didn't foresee that most European countries would automatically turn it round to become 'Trio Florestan'!

Playing in a trio was surprisingly different from playing in a quartet. No doubt mathematicians would be able to analyse the properties of a group of three as opposed to a group of four. A quartet is a very flexible grouping, with obvious permutations of two plus two occurring in various different ways within it, and indeed these realignments seem to happen continually. No doubt a quartet can be at least as stable as a trio – indeed it must be so, as the quartet is such a long-standing and beloved format in chamber music – but I personally have found it easier to find my own balance within a trio. A trio seems to have a different dynamic: more stable, more compact, and because each person is the only one who plays that instrument in the group, better balanced. However, a more subtle alignment is that of the two string players against the pianist, though perhaps in our case the fact the two string players are men, and the pianist a woman, emphasises the tendency.

The piano trio repertoire is also far larger than that of the piano quartet. I really don't know why this should be, as the piano quartet is a delightful combination of instruments, and it may be simply a historical accident. It may also be due to the shortage of good viola players, for a piano quartet depends on having a good one. At any rate, we found with relief that there was an enormous new repertoire to learn – so much so that we wondered how we would ever find time to tackle, for example, all forty-five trios by Haydn.

Mozart wrote only two piano quartets, but eight piano trios; Beethoven wrote only one piano quartet (itself an arrangement of a piano and wind quintet) but seven great trios plus variation movements for trio, trio arrangements of other works, and rarely-played early trios. Schubert wrote only one piano quartet, which is really a disguised piano virtuoso work (the *Adagio and Rondo Concertante*), but he wrote two masterpieces in trio form, as well as other trio works, and Schumann wrote only one piano quartet, but three great piano trios as well as the *Fantasiestücke* for trio. Dvořák wrote two piano quartets and four trios. Then, of course, there were some composers who wrote no piano quartets at all, but did write trios – Ravel, Tchaikovsky, Rachmaninov, Shostakovich, for example. In short, there was very little danger of our looking miserably at one another as we launched into a performance of one of our half-dozen 'core pieces' for the 547th time.

I'm writing as though these considerations of repertoire, name and stability were the most important factors in the founding of the new trio. But actually the most important motivating factor was the sense of musical compatibility between us. We are very different in personality, and in some respects we stand quite far apart from one another on the emotional spectrum, but the combination seems to work. We found from the beginning that we think alike musically, have the same kind of priorities, and approach musical analysis in very similar ways. Thus our arguments in rehearsal are never because we're ideologically opposed to one another, or can't see each other's point of view. We always seem to be driving instinctively at the same kind of result. It may seem superfluous to point this out, but there are many groups whose disagreements are much more fundamental. I can also think of chamber groups who are very compatible socially, but not very coherent musically. In the trio I think we always feel that, whatever our personal differences, we add up to something musically, and it may even be that our differences are the safeguard of our survival.

One thing that has changed since the early days of Domus is how much we share the stories of our personal lives with one another. When Domus started we all considered this sharing of our preoccupations an essential part of togetherness. Indeed, it seemed to feed directly into our closeness as musical colleagues. We would have hated it if anyone was suffering a personal problem in silence. Discussing one another's problems and plans was one of things that I enjoyed most – both listening and telling. We all relished the chance to talk things over constantly with one another. At the time we probably thought it would go on for ever. Later, it seemed that that kind of sharing was characteristic of 'early years'. None of us had partners or children at the time. In fact, when I remember how I used voluntarily to type late into the night after Domus concerts, recording our conversations, I realise how much things have changed.

At any rate, people now seem to find it essential to be able to retreat into their private lives. We're now responsible for other people, for children and for houses. There are instruments to be paid for. The income from chamber concerts is a great deal less than most music-lovers imagine. Pressure of work, of earning a living, has increased greatly and our diaries have filled up with things that don't permit much sitting around and chatting. So talking things over late into the night is far less common than it was. This is not to say that we are any less close musically, for in a mysterious way one's sense of musical intimacy proceeds unaffected by external factors – which is why one can sometimes so successfully play together with people from other cultures and languages, or with complete strangers. You may know nothing about a person, but find that, for example, your views of Beethoven are in tandem.

The focus of the trio has always been on its *musical* togetherness. This seems somehow appropriate to our age and stage in life, but when I look back to the early years of Domus, I realise how different it was then. Sharing our private thoughts knitted us together; today, our private thoughts find their way into our musical selves, and have been diverted from a social channel into a musical one. These days we meet to rehearse, and hurry home afterwards. I haven't kept regular diaries about the trio's discussions as I did with Domus – partly because I haven't had time, and partly because the trio has never been deliberately woven into the whole fabric of my life as Domus was. For Florestan it is our working time that counts. Perhaps this simply shows that we have learned to focus and concentrate more, to use our emotional selves judiciously. For although we often don't know much about what's going on in one another's personal lives, we get straight on each other's wavelengths as soon as we start to play. This is mysterious, but perhaps shouldn't be analysed.

August 2001

Touring Japan with Florestan, October 2000

Japanese English, with its mysterious word combinations, is a joy throughout our visit. On the first day, Richard sees a sign at the airport café: 'Live Coffee'. Its paper cups bear the slogan, 'The Art of Hot'. My hairdryer in the hotel has two settings: 'Normal' and 'Healthy'. Our first restaurant offers 'Shell Ligament in Batter'.

Because I haven't much been looking forward to this tour, I haven't given much thought to being in Japan, and so the sight of Tokyo is like a pot of shocking pink paint flung on to the white canvas of my mind.

Day One

I have been booked a practice studio at the Yamaha shop in Tokyo's Shinjuku area, where many of the skyscrapers, flashing neon signs, nightclubs and electrical goods shops are located, along with what appears to be the most fashionable crowd of young people in the world. My practice room is a very Japanese affair: a cubicle lodged in a corridor, with windows in it so that every passer-by can stare at me in my goldfish bowl, which has just enough room for a grand piano and space to walk around it. The noises from the kitchen shop below are clearly audible, so I assume that my playing is the same for them.

I'm practising Schumann trios slowly, with big finger movements and good articulation. This is partly because the long flight on the day before has left me with the usual feeling of swollen joints. Trying out a new fingering for a complex melodic line, I suddenly 'see' my hand folding in on itself like a piece of origami. Why this image should occur to me at that moment I don't know, except that I'm in Japan. I look down at my right hand, folding and unfolding, wondering what shape it might unfold to reveal . . . a swan? . . . a flower? . . . *a hand?*

Later on, I practise Schumann's *Kreisleriana*. Interestingly, this piece, which I first learned in detail when I was a student, still suggests new phrasings and timings to me. I wonder if this means that it is an inexhaustible store of material, or that it's inherently unstable, always changing its centres of gravity? Today I suddenly see how a certain series of modulating phrases, in the Intermezzo of no. 2, just after the first double bar, cannot be properly heard (or understood) unless each 'cadence' is clearly delineated, with a fraction of time after each to let it register. Again, I don't know why I was conscious of the danger that it was incomprehensible, except that I was in a foreign country, where one thinks along these lines automatically.

After hearing some inner parts better than before, and finding new 'voicings' to bring them out, I feel that I've achieved something, and go off to a side-street to eat noodle soup and vegetables (which can only be achieved by beckoning the cook out into the street, and pointing at the 'mock-up' models of soup bowls displayed in the window). The cooks are amused by my request for a spoon, and in fact I find it easier in the end to use chopsticks, though my poor technique clearly intrigues them.

In the evening the trio goes to rehearse in the 'Music Joy' building. Again, we are shown into a small 'soundproofed' studio into which the sounds of a jazz band are blasting from next door. As often happens – or happens to us – on these occasions, which are supposed to be more or less perfunctory rehearsals of pieces we know extremely well, we suddenly start going into details of phrasing, vibrato, tuning, dynamics, tempo, bowings, and 'elan'. This has often intrigued me – not so much what is said, as the timing of our saying it. It's like a respectful admission of the seriousness of the task before us – making an impression on a new foreign audience. We don't want them to feel that there is anything routine in our playing. Curiously, I have the impression that all three of us are privately a tiny bit bored with this detailed spring-cleaning, yet tacitly we all accept that there's a good psychological reason behind it.

After the rehearsal it's already 10 p.m., but because of jetlag, we're confused about eating times anyway. We explore a tiny area of narrow lanes (Shomben Yokocho) packed with minuscule restaurants, each seating no more than half a dozen people at a counter, with the cooks working a few feet away. This is a welcome change from the neon-lit brashness of Shinjuku proper. Taking our cue from the packed clientele, we wait for seats at a Taiwanese establishment which serves delicious fried dumplings, beansprouts with liver and green cabbage, etc. Eating tasty noodles and drinking Kirin beer is a strange accompaniment to our conversation about how parental behaviour has affected us – and how we either pass it on to our children, or try to counteract it. The writings of the psychologist Alice Miller have scared us all at various times.

On the way home, walking among the hordes of ultra-cool Japanese with their mobile phones, spiky hennaed hair, snappy suits and sunglasses, Schumann seems very . . . remote? irrelevant? Yet when I say so to Anthony, he tells me that a friend had specifically mentioned that the Japanese used constantly to play Schumann on their classical radio programmes. 'An Artist of the Floating World', indeed.

Day Two

Signs seen in Japanese shops:
'Freshness Burger'
'Rice Dog'
'Be in Creation'
A chocolate bar is called 'Crunky', a powdered milk 'Creap', a drink 'Pokari Sweat'.

Our first concert is in a new and impressive 500-seat concert hall in Musashino, a suburb of Tokyo. This is the first time we've played all three Schumann trios in one programme. Surprisingly, the Japanese audience follows in total silence. Are they gripped, or are they just well-behaved? At the end of the first half we realise that they are gripped. Several people behave in an un-Japanese way, clapping with their hands above their heads, shouting 'Bravo' – and this is only the interval! It's good to play pieces we know so well. There is no distracting mental effort of the wrong kind. We don't have to expend energy on 'getting inside' the music, or remembering previous instructions once we get there. Instead, I think we all feel free to be struck by new ideas, safe in the knowledge that the others will be open to them, not preoccupied with surface thoughts.

Day Three

Seen on a huge billboard: 'Basic and New!'
On a toolbox, the label 'Tool and Hard'.
Sign on grocery store: 'Lifegoods'.
On sports store: 'Encyclopedia of Life Entertainment'.

I have now worked out how to say in Japanese to my page-turners, 'It was very good – thank you.' For some reason this makes them burst into giggles. I'm reminded that on our last visit (with Domus, in 1993) I thought that Japanese page-turners are possibly the best in the world: alert, quick, quiet, polite, smiling, unobtrusive. Also, they dress beautifully, and observe closely during the concert. In fact, I have often wondered whether the page-turners (mostly pianists themselves) go home and write my fingering in to their scores!

After saying that we know the Schumann programme very well, I have to eat my words at the Osaka concert, or at least in the rehearsal, where, in perverse reaction to yesterday's feeling of security and stability, everybody starts complaining about things they didn't like yesterday. Tempi have got lazy, some are too fast for no good reason; requests are made for others to stop doing little characteristic things which have suddenly become annoying, like playing 'descant' phrases with exaggerated rhythmic freedom, or too loudly, or without due regard to someone else's overlapping phrase. Suddenly I'm sitting there thinking, 'I can't believe it was only this morning that I wrote about how secure this programme feels!'

I wonder about the psychological mechanism that makes us do this. Instead of building on our strengths, we seem to yearn for insecurities – as if it's only through these 'holes in the fabric' that new ideas will emerge. And in a way I suppose it is after all a mark of security that we can dare to stay these destabilising things right before an important concert, and profit from the experience.

In fact we do: the needling of one another in rehearsal results in new things being tried and new things being felt in the concert, with happy results – though even as I'm thinking so, I simultaneously wonder whether an outsider would notice any difference from last night's concert. Is it a bit like the story of the princess and the pea – oversensitivity to some minuscule change?

After the Osaka concert, we're asked to do a CD signing in the foyer. A long queue of about 50 people awaits us. We sign CDs, sleevenotes, programmes, pieces of music, gold-framed cards, and even postcards which one fan has made from xeroxed photos of us stuck onto card (and presumably prepared before the concert). In the middle of signing, I glance up and see my page-turner humbly waiting in line with her programme, along with everyone else. How typically Japanese that she didn't take the chance to ask me for this backstage!

In the sushi bar afterwards, I ask Mr N. (our guide) how to compliment a page-turner in Japanese. He replies that 'one does not say such things to such a person'. 'Thank you' would be the most that is required, it seems. This is a rather shocking cultural insight. It leads to more questioning and lots of embarrassed laughter from him. Eventually I ask him how one would compliment an artist on a fine performance. He replies in Japanese, and then says, 'I translate straightly: You had a hard work.' To me this is not, or would not be, either a compliment or a comment on the artistry. Clearly Japanese social customs are hard to learn. We find the audience's applause puzzling too. They seem to clap using just the tips of their fingers, and this makes frail and uncommitted sound, compared to Western audiences who use muscles and whole arm movements when they clap enthusiastically. At the end of the concert the applause sounds merely polite, yet it goes on for ages, and after many curtain calls we realise that they have really liked us. After an encore, they clap on and on (still sounding somewhat timid to Western ears) and can only be stopped in the end by a decisive single bow followed by a swift exit.

Thinking about this afterwards, I reflect that clapping is in fact a strange convention. I wonder how people first hit on this method of showing their appreciation? I used to think that its main advantage was that it is a universal form of expression, crossing all language barriers, but the Japanese experience shows that it does have regional variations, and that one can't gauge the warmth of the response from the sound of the clapping. In this regard I remember talking to a friend who had given a concert at a New Age community in Scotland where the audience, instead of clapping, waved their hands silently in the air 'to avoid disturbing the beautiful vibrations left in the room by the music'. This is a lovely idea, though in the event my friend told me it was disconcertingly silent for the players as they bowed and left the stage. Perhaps bowing and leaving the stage is the wrong action in such circumstances.

During the CD signing we realise how enthusiastic they really were: people grasp our hands and say, 'You touched my heart', 'You moved me', and 'Your wonderful performance was like an intimate talk.' In view of Mr N's comments earlier, these must be great compliments. Surely they would not say such things just to be polite – or would they?

Ant tells me that he and Richard went back to the lane of yakitori cafés in Tokyo late the other night after our concert. The clientele was noticeably rougher, and they had the feeling that they were amongst gangsters. Suddenly, one of the gangsters got up to leave, and in the press of people his jacket was pulled backwards off his shoulders, revealing a T-shirt with the words 'Prunella Scales' on it. This is especially funny because Prunella Scales and her family are friends and supporters of our trio. I tell Ant I don't believe his story, and quiz him thoroughly as to whether it is really true. Eventually he says, 'Well, to be honest, what I actually saw was, 'runella Scales.' For some reason this is even more convincing than his first version.

Day Four – Kyoto

Seen above the ticket booth at a national shrine (Sanjusangen-do):
'Your admission is used for your smoothly and safty visiting.'
Seen inside a café, a sign offering 'Liquid Coffee'.
A children's clothes shop: 'Hysteric Mini.'
A man's clothes shop: 'Grand-Back Big and Tall'.
Kyoto surprises us with its modernity and size. The new train station is certainly

the most unusual I've seen – vast, intimidating, daring and bizarre. The ancient temples and teahouses – when we eventually find them – are just as magnificent as I remember. All of us are struck by the contrast between them, with their sense of space, dignity, quiet and timelessness, and the garish fluorescent Japanese cities with their 'We never sleep' atmosphere. Last night I looked out of my hotel window, on the 34th floor, at 4 a.m. and saw that all the major roads were buzzing with cars. Whatever happened to the culture which made those secretive, fastidious teahouses in Kyoto? When did the scale change from the little two-storey wooden houses with their sliding bamboo doors and paper screens, to the uncompromising skyscrapers of Tokyo and Osaka, and the messy urban sprawl of the preceding decades? I realise I've turned into one of these people who only identifies with Japan of the Edo period (1603–1867 – my favourite period of Japanese art), and feels alienated by the Japan of my own day.

In the Sanjusangen-do we view with amazement the 1001 golden statues of Kannon, Buddhist goddess of mercy. As the statues are arranged in rows on steps receding from us towards the roof, only the front row is really visible, yet each figure is said to be different. I think how sad it must have been for the sculptors to see that their works were destined to be placed in the back row and to remain there for centuries, never to have their details appreciated. And yet each statue had to be just as good as all the rest. 'Like being a member of an orchestra', I say to my colleagues.

Lunch in Kyoto with Ernst Seiler and his Japanese wife Kazuko, both pianists. Somehow they have managed to get three grand pianos into two small living-rooms in their home. Today is a special day because Ernst has persuaded the local council to let him stage a Hallowe'en pumpkin-carving exhibition and fancy dress parade. All the pumpkins – which range in size from the usual supermarket variety to fruits the size of a tractor wheel – are displayed on the steps of a building in the high street. Some have 'hair' made of branches stuck in their heads. Some have carved eyelashes and blonde hair made by scraping away the orange rind to reveal the white pith. All the pumpkins were grown by Ernst on his farm, a place to which he has also transported an old temple which they use as a concert hall seating 300. For this, and other eccentric activities, he has clearly become a local celebrity. I ask him what Hallowe'en means to Japanese children, apart from pumpkins. 'We haven't got that far yet', he replies.

The whole visit to Kyoto is enlivened by a running joke about our Japanese fans' intention (at least, this is how our fantasy goes) to make us into deities. I think this was started by the attitudes displayed towards us at the CD signing yesterday. It reaches a satisfying conclusion at the end of the day, when we visit a huge temple where dozens of workmen and gardeners are engaged in some massive project of renovation and preparation. As we can't read the signs, and are not hampered by knowing the truth, we conclude that work is already in hand to prepare new lodgings for us when we become deities. On our way out of the temple complex in the dusk, Ant and I lose Richard for a few minutes, during which we visualise him being detained by monks and installed on a platform, cross-legged, covered in gold leaf, and glaring crossly down on his worshippers.

Perhaps the most memorable sight in Kyoto is the narrow street in the Gion district, just after dusk, where red lanterns are lit outside the little wooden houses, and geisha girls start arriving for evening appointments at teahouses. From this beautiful area, to the bizarre new train station a couple of miles away, is a journey too vast to be comprehended.

Day Five – Osaka

Sign in shop: 'Coffee Maker – Tasty Time since 1924'.
A high-quality tailor's shop in Osaka, obviously trying to evoke the ones in London, was called 'Sevile Road'.

The others have gone off to Hakone, and I am to practise in a rented studio in downtown Osaka. Mr N. has described its location and also drawn me a map, but when I emerge from the tube station I find I've left the map in my hotel room. So I try to find the place from its description. The streets are full of office buildings, each with many floors of completely unrelated companies. All the signs are in Japanese, and I can see no reference to my 'Lesson Hall'. So I start asking people in coffee shops and foyers, but nobody speaks English, or not enough to understand my question. One lady even leaves her desk to take me across to the Fire Station, where she says the firemen keep a detailed map of the area. But the map only shows the numbers of buildings (wildly complicated in Japan) and the firemen have never heard of a piano studio nearby. Finally, after wandering about in the rain for quite a while, I decide that there's nothing for it but to go back to the hotel and get the map. Of course, by the time I've done this, I've lost the majority of my practice time, but I don't dare to tell Mr N. that I didn't use the studio, as he had already delicately conveyed his feelings about my not using the studio he had booked for me yesterday.

When I get back with the map and the address written in Japanese, it's a simple matter to get directions, and of course it turns out that the studio is in a multi-storey office building outside which I had been walking up and down earlier. The 'Lesson Hall' turns out to be yet another little studio somehow wedged into the space between the caretaker's office and the stairwell, well set back from the street, and completely unguessable from the outside of the building. Hearing my steps, the caretaker rushes in smiling and bowing, though I am over an hour late. After she's gone, I notice a bunch of white flowers wrapped up, with bows, on a table by the piano. They can't be meant for me, surely? I have no idea whether to take them or leave them – either could cause offence. Eventually I leave them, hoping that she will retrieve them. At the end of the practice my hands are hurting again like they did in the Yamaha shop, I don't know why. Could this still be the effect of jet lag?

In the evening, I attend a 'twilight concert' in the Hilton Plaza, a vast gleaming atrium with marble floors, glass and steel walls with cylindrical lifts whizzing up and down in them. In the midst of all this space-age chic, two Japanese girls dressed like 1930s film stars are playing duets on a Steinway grand piano. Their ballgowns are sugar pink and lime green, with lots of sticking-out petticoats. They play Grieg's *Peer Gynt* Suite and Faure's *Dolly* Suite, and one of them also plays solo Debussy. Once again I'm struck by how Japanese pianists manage to make Western music sound Japanese. How do they do it? They play so well, and yet there's a hint of robotics about the way each phrase goes on to the next, as though they feel it would be too self-indulgent to let the music (or themselves) breathe. The two girls are thrilled to be complimented after their concert by a pianist from 'Rondon'.

Day Six – Osaka

Back in the rented studio to practise. The white flowers are still wrapped, but now in a vase by the piano. I'm practising the Haydn F minor variations for a recital back in England. Clearly my surroundings are getting to me, because the intricate dove-tailed phrasing and the precise figures of Haydn suddenly strike me as Japanese. I've been looking at beautiful little lacquered boxes in the shops, and today the Haydn variations seem like one of these, a musical 'box' (as opposed to 'musical box') with inlaid patterns and secret drawers. I wonder whether this image will now 'stick to' the piece, or fade away again when I am back in Europe.

Afterward, I visit the Museum of Oriental Ceramics. As usual, the loveliest things are the ancient pieces, specifically the Chinese of the Sung Dynasty (12th century). Looking at bowls has always fascinated me. There's something about their different shapes and the fact that whatever is contained in them has to take the shape of the bowl's interior. Inspired by the Haydn/lacquered box musings of this morning, I start to wonder if pieces of music could be compared to bowls – but which is the form, and which the content? You might say that sonata form, for example, is the bowl. So what sort of bowl does Schumann make? I have some images in my mind, but am not sure if I could put them into words.

In Osaka I have been lost several times in the subway stations and on the street. Each time I have stood still in the midst of the crowd, looking patently lost and European, in my pale blue raincoat, map in hand. Yet nobody has ever offered to help me. The odd thing is, I have the feeling that any individual would be very helpful if I asked them directly, but they never proffer information. Perhaps they think that I would suffer 'loss of face' if I had to ask. The only person who has offered to help me, after a week in Japan, was an American on the bridge in down-town Osaka. I must remember to help Japanese tourists who look lost in London.

Sitting in my hotel room on the 34th floor, watching the lights come on as darkness falls over the city, I think I'll never again feel I am doing something useful by switching off unnecessary lights in my little house in London. When I see the blaze of electric light and neon that covers this enormous East Asian city, office buildings with every window lit, all the big buildings with lighted names and adverts with winking and flashing displays of orange, red and blue, it's hard to believe that the oriental pottery I saw this afternoon was made by ancestors of the people who designed Osaka. And yet I am sure that if I could talk to those twelfth-century potters, they would say that their work was an attempt to create something enduring and timeless against a backdrop of change, hurry, uncertainty, the bad behaviour of the young, and so on.

In the museum today there was a sign explaining that oriental celadon ware should ideally be viewed 'at ten o'clock in the morning, on a sunny autumn day, in a room facing north, with one "shoji" sliding paper door'. The museum explains how it has tried to capture this type of light with a complex series of light ducts and reflecting mirrors. I don't think I recall any Western art being placed so specifically in an ideal viewing context. When, I wonder, would be the ideal time to hear the Ravel Trio? At 9 o'clock in the evening in an elegant drawing-room in the south of France, with champagne being served by Malaysian poetesses?

It strikes me that the problem with this hypersensitivity to context is that

99.9 per cent of viewing opportunities are therefore not ideal – since ten o'clock in the morning, in a north-facing room etc., doesn't last very long. Surely it is better to try to get into the right receptive mood at the time that you're looking (or listening)? Or am I missing something about the mystical process of working from the outside in? If a 'thing', like a piece of pottery, has an ideal set of circumstances in which one culture considers it should be seen, what does this indicate? Obviously – well, I say 'obviously' but perhaps that's just my Western upbringing – the 'thing' itself isn't 'demanding' the viewing circumstances. The viewer – let's say the museum curator – is imposing his perception on the object, yet describing the situation as though the object has laid down the rules for its ideal conditions. Clearly the sensation felt at 10 a.m. in the ideal room is one felt by the observer, not one emanating from the object. So why don't they say, 'I like to see pottery in the mid-morning', and so on? Why do they speak as thought the object only gathers all its qualities together in a brief moment *of its own choosing*?

I'm writing scornfully but I do, in fact, know what they mean. A piece of music isn't an object, but I do often feel that the music itself – or what Sandor Végh would call the 'materia sonore' (a typical mishmash of languages) – sends messages about its ideal treatment. I don't mean that the player does – I mean that the music does. And yet it doesn't send these messages impartially, or to everyone, since there are clearly lots of people who don't receive them. I suppose in that sense a piece of music could be likened to a bowl that 'wants' to be seen in a certain light. The music doesn't exist until someone plays it, but even then, they might play it with their inner ear closed to its call for a certain light, season, weather. This is the kind of thing I feel unable to communicate to students – I mean students who don't intuit things very easily. And of course, when I try to tell them what I think the music itself is demanding (as opposed to what they want to put into it), I wonder how I can be sure that my perceptions are absolute, independent of myself?

You might say that the museum curator is laying his own demands on the object by saying that it should be viewed in this or that way, but I fear it isn't as simple as that. An art object does interact with space and light and time in a way which is independent of our analysis of it. This may even be a good thing – after all, the pot lasts longer than the potter!

I remember my pottery teacher making that comment: 'Now you've made something that could endure for many years – longer than you, perhaps!' The idea was disconcerting – after all, the pot meant very little, it was just an experiment, it reflected nothing of me except my incompetence – and yet here it was, threatening to outlive me! A future observer, holding my amateur pot and trying to guess what I was like, would (I hope) guess quite wrongly. Of course my silly pot only showed me as a beginner. Thinking about this makes me realise how difficult it must be to produce a pot which actually shows the potter at his best – and isn't that what the oriental potters have been on about, all this time? That any single pot should be a snapshot of their whole nature? I can see that it would take *years* to achieve that.

Often one gets the impression that with a 'straightforward' Western remark, one is crashing through Japanese cultural boundaries. This constantly happens with Mr N., our guide. Perhaps it is worse because I am a woman. This morning he saw me writing down examples of 'Japanese English'. I explained that the word combinations are often amusing for us. This provoked a shocked gasp following by high-pitched giggling, but then a pause and a respectful little bow, as if to say, 'Of course, you are right.' All this left me feeling clumsy and ill-mannered.

Day Seven – Shizuoka

On the train, the trash bin is mysteriously labelled with the word 'Others'.
In the hotel, the safety instructions leaflet was headed 'Grime Prevention'.
A bag for sale in the station was emblazoned with the words, 'Come up and see me anytime. I'm getting along and in good health.'
A paper cup in the concert hall read: 'Comfortable time in natural gentleness . . . feeling the seasonal fragrance.'

Meeting up with Anthony and Richard again in Shizuoka, they tell me they have been discussing the matter of how to raise sponsorship. I ask whether this has anything to do with our imminent installation as Deities – if we were gods, it would certainly make the whole fundraising issue a pushover. But Richard points out that if we become deities, we would lose the support of the Jewish community, who would immediately boycott our concerts. The loss of Jewish support seems serious enough to relinquish the idea of becoming divine.

The concert hall in Shizuoka is another impressive one, with a gorgeous Steinway. Here the audience reaction is noticeably more provincial, however. The concert goes really well (by which I mean that we play well) but the audience response is formulaic, well-mannered. Two friends in the audience tell us afterwards that our programme of Fauré, Schumann and Ravel trios was too esoteric for 'an uneducated audience'. Strangely, this programme was a request of the Japanese promoter. We attend another CD signing, at which a long line of people waits meekly beside a silken guide-rope. Afterwards, we are invited out to eat for the first time – not by the organisers, but by the Seilers, who with great perspicacity order fried potatoes for us as a starter, knowing that our diet will have been lacking in Western comfort food.

Global communications: Ant's friend Kyoko, living in Amsterdam, e-mails him to say that she reads a Japanese classical music 'net forum' on the Internet and that a fan has written a really wonderful review of our Musashino concert. This amazes us: that someone should write a review of our concert in a Tokyo suburb and that it should be read that same day by a Japanese pianist in Amsterdam and translated for our benefit while we are still in Osaka. Soon it won't matter if the newspapers come to review our concerts or not – the Internet will reach more people, and reputations will spread like that.

Day Eight – Tokyo

Checking into the Keio Plaza, a tall fair American man is checking in beside me. He's asking in American English for a non-smoking room, etc. When the girl brings him his registration form, however, he starts to complete it in Japanese. At this, the girl gives a start and says to him, 'You can speak Japanese!' He looks up and replies, 'I *am* Japanese.' The girl reacts to this with surprise and a charming smile, and she catches my eye, whereupon the two of us burst out laughing. It's just so unexpected that this tall fair man should 'be Japanese'. But the man himself is not amused by our reaction, and he turns to me with a severe look, saying, 'Excuse me?' as if to reproach me for my levity. He then turns and speaks in fluent Japanese to the check-in girl, and I can see her mastering her surprise. The funny thing is that his name turns out to be 'Blab', or so I understand it. It is certainly 'Blab' or 'Blad'. He spells it out for her with a completely straight face. Afterwards, my colleagues have fun with this name, which in full they maintain is probably 'Brad Blab'. The thought of what the Japanese (who find it difficult to distinguish between 'r' and 'l') will make of this name – 'Blad Brab? Blad Blab?' reduces us to helpless mirth in the back of a taxi.

My room on the 19th floor looks out on to Kenzo Tange's vast Tokyo Metropolitan Government Building, which must be 45 stories high. Inspired by Notre Dame in Paris, it's like a terrifying Japanese version of that building altered on a computer to be twice the size and oriental in its details. The transformation of cathedral to office seems to raise all sorts of troubling questions – is this the glorification of administration? Why else take a religious building as the model for something ultra-secular? It's odd, as if the architect only saw the form of Notre Dame, but disregarded its content.

Day Nine – Tokyo

Our concert is in Toppan Hall, a brand-new hall opened earlier this month. It's beautifully built with many details of design and workmanship one would not find in Britain. As in other Japanese halls, the backstage staff (all impeccably dressed in suits) literally *run* to fulfil our requests. In each dressing-room is a shower, a loo with various accoutrements like warm seat, spray function, etc., a grand piano, slippers, flatscreen TV, video link to the concert hall, sofa.

As I described on an earlier occasion, the rehearsal before this important concert is full of remarks that any outsider would construe as negative. This bit has been too slow, this slowing-down has got out of hand, the tension is missing here, that lead is hard to follow, the bowing is uncoordinated, this bit is always out of tune, the feeling is wrong. None of these remarks are personal or intended to hurt, but are expressed as concerns for the way the music comes across, so in that sense they are not destabilising. There's a section in the slow movement of the Schumann F major trio (the transition to Lebhaft) which is suddenly declared to be 'not working', and we rehearse it for a while, trying louder bass trill in the piano, different timing, different momentum, a different person leading, and a new impetus on the first chord of the 'Lebhaft' section. All this leads me to say that if we are going to make conceptual changes to our Schumann trios, we shall have to hand back the Gramophone Award, as our Schumann recording no longer represents what we believe. Some jocular debate follows about the publicity that would be generated by our handing back an award on the grounds that we had changed our view of the music.

Our concert in Toppan Hall is the biggest success yet. The audience is completely silent while we're playing, as if they are utterly absorbed. At the end, they clap so much and for so long that we have to run to the dressing-rooms to get a second piece of music to use as a second encore. Even after that, they clap on and on. All the Japanese staff of Hyperion's Japanese distribution have come to the concert, and they tell us afterwards how pleased they are with our CD sales – 50 or 60 at each concert, if I understand them. Small fry for pop musicians, but pleasing for us. After the concert I comment to Ant that the audience gave me the feeling that they were not used to sitting together in that new hall, and didn't quite feel an identity as an audience. Ant says that he knows exactly what I mean, but wonders how on earth we could pick up on that feeling from the stage.

In the Mainichi News there's an article by a top Japanese businessman about the importance of loving your native land, but also being able to see it in perspective. His text contains the marvellous lines, 'I have always believed that Mount Fuji is the ultimate mountain. But to believe that it is the ultimate mountain is not to say that it is the greatest mountain in the world.' This strikes me as a wonderfully fine and Japanese distinction to make.

Later in the evening we find our way back to the alleys of Shomben Yokocho and the steam and woks of a Taiwanese café, where our tour manager would be very unhappy to find us, sitting alongside smartly-dressed Japanese businessmen who have had too much to drink and keep sliding off their seats onto the floor. The cooks are still working flat out at midnight. It's amusing how they seem to invent the bill each time. Without writing anything down during the entire meal, they simply scribble a figure on a piece of paper and hold it up to us, and we can't dispute it anyway.

On the walk home, a strange thing happens: a young British woman walking towards us in the crowds outside Shinjuku Station suddenly comes up to me and embraces me, saying that I look exhausted, and asking if I am all right. For some reason this does not surprise me, as I've had frequent exchanges of sympathetic looks with other Western women in Tokyo, as if we are saying to each other, 'Are you having a funny experience? I'm having a funny experience too!' But it does surprise my colleagues, and when I tell them that I often find myself exchanging looks with European women here, they are quite envious, and say that men are far more likely to avoid eye contact and to swagger past, trying to give the impression that they are completely masters of the situation.

An interesting discussion about the art of saying 'No', with my Japanese page-turner who speaks good English. She explains that it is considered vulgar to say an outright no. We explain that in Europe it is almost the reverse: if No is the answer, then any prevarication can be confusing, evasive, even insulting. There's clearly plenty of room here for mutual misunderstanding. I admit I find it hard to understand our guide when he answers 'Maybe not' to questions. I know now that this is the closest he can come to saying No, but I still feel that the question has been left unresolved. It gives one a glimpse into the intricacies of Japanese politeness.

Day Ten – Tokyo

For some reason, on this 'free day', I feel very tired and Anthony feels the same. Over coffee in Starbucks, of all places (where even the Starbucks style of customer care suddenly seems much less polite than the prevailing Japanese standard), we agree that our senses feel continually assaulted by urban Shinjuku with its noise and crowds – and by the fact that we don't understand either the written or spoken language all around us. Our feet have been sore nearly all the time in Japan – and yet surely we walk around on concrete just as much in London? It is very puzzling and we agree that being in a very foreign country is more tiring than one would expect.

In the afternoon, we are interviewed for the Japanese version of *Gramophone* magazine. Disconcertingly, the interviewer seems to think that we are obsessed with Schumann and don't want to stray outside of his era. When we tell her that our next disc is to be Schubert, she demurs, saying that surely Schubert is 'too modest' for our 'wild and free' style of playing. We explain that we've played Schubert at least as much as Schumann, and esteem his music just as highly. Afterwards, we disagree about the benefits of being typecast as Schumann experts. Anthony and I dislike it and are cross about it, but Richard feels it's helpful to be identified with something – anything – as it marks us out from the crowd.

This evening, after what is by my standards a very expensive meal, I feel demoralised and disconsolate. Being 'on tour' like this is anathema to me, and I wonder what I ought to conclude from this feeling. As I write this, police sirens wail in the street below, people are shouting, loudspeakers advertise electronic wares just a street away, motorbikes roar, and I feel a million miles (well, about six thousand miles) from where I want to be.

Day Eleven – Tokyo

I've arranged to spend the day with Noriko, a Japanese woman who's the friend of a friend in London. She lives in Ueno, the park and museum district, where she has offered to meet me at the subway station.

Ueno is a huge relief after Shinjuku, and I realise that some of my demoralisation last night was fuelled by an overdose of neon and loudspeakers. The park district is laid out like a spacious Parisian area of broad avenues and symmetrical gardens. It's raining, and throngs of people hurry through the park with their characteristic transparent umbrellas. I don't know what it is about Japanese people that makes them look so appealing with umbrellas.

We visit the National Museum, which holds a stunning collection of Japanese pottery, kimonos, theatre costumes, masks, swords, netsuke (often humorous little carved figures designed to dangle from a belt) and so on. Afterwards, we visit a special exhibition of Chinese art uncovered in archaeological excavations. This is even more impressive. Immediately noticeable is the peaceful, smiling – sometimes positively merry – expressions of the Buddha figures. In two weeks I've become used to the fierce, combative expressions of Japanese deities, who look quite stern even in meditation. But the Chinese statues, made of a cream-coloured limestone with pink colouring and gold leaf, are serene and welcoming. Some of the most striking statues are from many centuries B.C. – and of course these look the most modern of the lot.

We spend a very Japanese afternoon in the rain, walking from gallery to teahouse, to temple and artist's home, to pottery shops, incense shops, and exhibitions of calligraphy where they serve us frothy green tea in beautiful bowls. I'm amazed at how it is possible to talk all day about personal, cultural and deep matters with a complete stranger and to feel that we have so much in common. This gives me a great feeling of satisfaction and of bridges built between our two cultures.

Day Twelve – Tokyo

In a music shop, a velvet bag designed to hold a folded-up music stand is called 'Stand Bra'.

Our last concert is in Maebashi. On paper this town seems to be an hour away, but in practice it turns out to be: half an hour in a taxi to Tokyo Station, plus the obligatory waiting time on the platform; an hour on the train, and then another half hour in a taxi from Takasaki Station to Maebashi. The hall is nice, as all the Japanese halls have been, but the backstage area is drab and depressing, making us feel as if we've been transported back to a typical British music club. This prompts Richard to say, 'I could murder a pineapple quiche' – this being a reference to the kind of food one is always offered at British music clubs. Then he recants; 'Actually, no – there are no circumstances in which I could *ever* murder a pineapple quiche.' Luckily the backstage staff here have quite different notions of food, and have brought us fresh chunks of persimmon (a pear-like fruit), packets of peanuts, bitter chocolate and cups of green tea.

As before, our rehearsal is full of 'This hasn't been right, this is too slow, I feel uncomfortable here or there.' So we do slow practice, and take the first movement of the Ravel to pieces – with good results. The closing bars have always been a problem because of the cello harmonics which sometimes fail to 'speak' when they should, making it impossible to guess how to play together with the cello notes as they move. We also discuss the timing of the final cello 'pizzicato' chord, which Richard claims to be 'placing' in a dramatic way, but which Anthony claims is simply late, and unrhythmical. When Richard plays this in the concert it is perfect.

I am pleased in the concert because I've been able to control my posture – making it five concerts in a row. Very often I feel that stress and adrenalin cause me to lose touch with the solar plexus, the balance of the spine, the free breathing from the abdomen. I've often noticed that to play a whole concert with off-centre balance is strangely exhausting. But in Japan I haven't lost touch with the 'centre'. If this is right, many technical aspects of playing, and indeed many others, seem to fall into place.

The Ravel Trio goes particularly well tonight, and afterwards Richard says it's the best performance he has ever given, especially of the last movement. Once again we are whisked off to sign records for apparently awestruck people.

The end of our tour is anti-climactic. Our tour organiser not only doesn't say anything about the concert (as indeed he hasn't about any concert) but hasn't organised any kind of celebratory drink or meal. We simply set off and do the whole taxi-train-taxi sequence in reverse. This we find strange. From my last tour, some years ago, I remember Japan as a place where concert organisers like – indeed, feel obliged – to give gifts and flowers, and to entertain and take out to dinner. But there has been none of that on this trip. We haven't been taken out once or given any gifts, even though we ourselves gave gifts at the start of our tour. Is this economic change in Japan, or something about the way this particular tour has been organised? I've seen businessmen in our hotel receiving lovely gifts, and flowers are constantly being delivered at reception – but not for us. This gives a forlorn tone to our visit – for me, at least. And it leads indirectly to an acrimonious discuss on the train from Maebashi about whether we were right to come to Japan for 'budget' fees.

Day Thirteen

Seen on the side of a bakery van: 'Better product quality through higher bakery's bakery spirit.'

Mr N. comes to the hotel at 7.30 a.m. to say goodbye. Polite, smiling and bowing, he nevertheless refrains from saying a single word about what he thought of the tour. So I ask him if he was happy with the concerts. 'So happy', he replies with a bow, but of course one can't tell if this is really just what he thinks I want to hear. And then we are off on the two-hour bus journey to the airport, the two-hour check-in, and the 14-hour flight back to Britain.

On the way, we have a diary session to put in rehearsals for next year. Things have got so complicated that we find ourselves arguing about rehearsals a year from now – 'I can't manage that day in December 2001.' It's all a bit like that Polish joke about the man who orders a new car, and is told that it cannot be delivered for three years, as there are such industrial problems. They tell him he can collect his new car on the 14th March three years hence. 'Morning or afternoon?' he asks. 'What difference does that make to you?' they want to know. 'Because I have the plumber coming in the morning', he replies.

Arriving back in Heathrow Airport is always a shock, and particularly jarring today, as there is a combination of road, rail and weather problems which hit all of us in different ways on our journey home. I often wonder if people who work at Heathrow and on the tube system there are aware that they form a first impression of Britain for foreign visitors, and a reminder of British attitudes for Britons who have been abroad. Perhaps it would be hypocritical of the authorities to fill Heathrow with smiling milkmaids and genial professors with pipes, but I have often felt that they don't give enough thought to the impact made on travellers by disgruntled and unhelpful staff. Today, since we know what it's going to be like, we start lamenting the loss of Japanese courtesy and helpfulness while we are still in the air.

Because of the storms this week, which have caused many road closures, it takes two and a half hours to drive home from Heathrow to Wimbledon, and when I get there, I find that part of the garden fence has collapsed in the storm, and that rain has seeped in to discolour the bathroom wall. Anthony finds that his car has been broken into, and has to drive to East Sussex with a broken window – only to find that his TV aerial has blown down, severing the power lines. His house is in total darkness, with not even the cooker or the telephone working, so after this immense journey he has to grope about in the dark to find a few candles, and go to bed in the cold. It's an unpleasant 're-entry into the atmosphere'.

The following morning, as we compare notes on the phone, we wonder aloud whether we ought just to turn around and go back to Japan. We agree that we are terribly glad to be home, but can't help shuddering at the reality. And soon our tour won't be spoken about any more, as everyday life takes over. This is one of the oddest aspects of the professional performer's life – a trip like ours, which might form the basis of weeks of dinner party conversations for an independent traveller, is erased from the agenda almost as soon as it is over, and may hardly even be discussed with people at home.

Home now from Japan
Nobody asks me questions
No answers to give

October 2000

Visiting Ireland: West Cork Chamber Music Festival, Bantry, June 2001

Saturday 23 June, Bantry House

This remote spot in rural Ireland turns out to be full of international residents, especially Dutch, who have moved here to escape the stress of city life. Thus the influx of musicians from around the world doesn't create an exotic layer, but merely adds to the prevailing rich mixture.

It's delightful to be at a festival celebrating committed chamber groups. Most festivals produce chamber music by inviting impromptu collections of soloists to rehearse something while they're there. If the individual players have good intuition, this can have wonderful results, but for me such performances will never reach the depths attained by dedicated groups who live with and focus their collective minds on this repertoire.

We attend the opening concert, with the Octuor Paris-Bastille (a wind octet) playing Gounod, a Russian all-girl string quartet playing Gubaidulina, and an Irish string quartet playing Brahms. For most players it's unusual to play only one item in a concert for which normally they would expect to be thoroughly responsible. In this format, which I guess is designed to provide the audience with a full palette of impressions, each group has only one chance to bond with the audience, and how they do so will inevitably be compared with how other groups do it in the same concert.

Once again it strikes me that wind players have a more pragmatic approach than string players. This is partly to do with their repertoire. Which comes first, the chicken or the egg? Do composers write more superficially for wind players because they know what they're like, or do wind players merely respond to the repertoire? Why do composers appear to focus their deeper feelings on string and piano music? I don't think this is a prejudiced view, since I've often heard wind players complain about the relative shallowness of the works written for them.

One might think that because the wind instrument is held in the mouth and played with the breath, it would be an extension of the soul and personality, a more human amalgam of person and instrument, but in fact it generally seems that string players are far more concerned with plumbing depths on their instruments. Maybe, because wind instruments are obviously linked with the human voice, the connection is assumed to be innate, not in need of expression, whereas string players – and pianists – have to find a way to sing and speak on an instrument which is independent of them. They have to exercise mind over matter to a great extent – often with good artistic results.

I know from experience that wind players in rehearsal tend to talk about the mechanics of timing and perfect ensemble, whereas string players talk about what is to be expressed. Why are people drawn to choose the instruments they play? Do they choose them because they are a certain type of person, or does playing the instrument make them into a certain type of musician?

Sitting at the back of the Library, a beautiful 18th-century room, we gaze out of the large windows across a formal Italianate garden to an improbably steep flight of 105 stone steps leading to an observation point overlooking Bantry Bay. From time to time during the concert people slowly ascend the steps, pause at the top and then turn and return to earth. Somehow this looks poignant and symbolic to the accompaniment of great music.

Sunday

'Ceaseless activity in every comb.' This line from the Spanish film *Spirit of the Beehive* comes back to me as I walk through the hallway of Bantry House with musicians practising around me in every available room, even offices, billiard rooms and attics. This morning I too am a worker bee and must practise Beethoven. For some reason, the aged Blüthner piano I'm given has no pedals. No pedals! To practise with no pedals, within earshot of some of Europe's best musicians, is like appearing at a dinner party without make-up. I shall practise everything slowly and clearly, and with luck anyone pausing to listen will think that my dry sound is deliberate.

At midday, Anthony Marwood gives a solo recital of entrancing virtuosity, including the Six Caprices by the Italian contemporary composer Salvatore Sciarrino. As Anthony says, these are like the 'air from another planet' which Schoenberg referred to in the sung text that accompanies his Second String Quartet. Almost entirely played in harmonics, and executed at top speed, with flying glissades of icy feathers, they're like passing through a musical hailstorm in the stratosphere. Alas, despite their technical wizardry, these are pieces that have more visual than emotional appeal.

After lunch we rehearse Beethoven's 'Archduke' Trio. It's a relief to be moving towards our first appearance as artists in the festival, the moment when for the audience we will spring into relief instead of merely being part of that scruffy group who sit on the stairs at the back of other people's concerts.

Our method of preparing for concerts would be outlawed by today's morale-building team-management gurus. Although we have performed this piece many times, even ten days ago at the Aldeburgh Festival, we now start to complain mercilessly about our own interpretation. Anything which sounds routine, or predictable in the wrong way, is attacked. This is now traditional, though we've never discussed why we do it, or its psychological point and effect. I suppose it's a way of restoring our conscious idealism about the task before us. All the same, it takes strong nerves to be heaped with negative criticism just a few hours before our first public appearance. It's so obviously insane psychologically to do this (just the opposite of what a sports coach would be doing before an important match) that I wonder what curious love of adversity motivates us.

Our Beethoven is the last item in a programme whose first half consists of contemporary music. After the searching, dislocated quality of the modern music,

Beethoven suddenly seems a) old, and b) new. One becomes aware of the modernity of his radical ideas, and yet also of his deep affirmative embrace of the style of his own time. He rests in it and affirms it. How diverse everything is now! National styles, post-modernism, pop, club, world music, minimalism, ethnic links and so on. Certainly Beethoven wasn't asking himself the plethora of questions that today's composers are asking: Shall I write in a key or not? Can I have tunes? Should I use the instruments in an unexpected way? And yet he seems to have out-thought most 20th-century musical inventors.

The audience sits to our left and right as well as in front of us. This creates an eccentric acoustic as well as psychological effect. The sound is dry and exposed, and we don't know to where we should project. Yet despite the curious layout of the hall, the atmosphere is wonderfully quiet and concentrated. It proves once again that we must think of drawing the audience in, being a magnet – not spreading ourselves thinly over the hall.

Monday

We perform Beethoven's E flat Trio opus 1, and Schumann's first trio in D minor, in an afternoon concert. Both go really well, but somehow 5 p.m. is a subdued time for the audience. They've been at a morning masterclass, a midday concert, our afternoon concert, and they still have a huge evening concert at 8.30 p.m. and a late night concert at 11 p.m. ahead of them. Consequently you can almost feel them saving themselves up, leaving space in their hearts for more impressions and reactions later in the day.

After this, we go down with viola player James Boyd to Vickery's Inn in Bantry where a grand piano has been stationed in the back bar during the festival. We spend the evening rehearsing the new piano quartet by Latvian composer Peteris Vasks which has been commissioned for us by the festival. The new quartet is unusually long, has six movements, and is a crazy mixture of Baltic dance music with strong manic and mechanistic components, alternating with movement of deep religious fervour, in rapt contemplation and very slow.

The notation and structure are a lot easier than the other new works we've learned recently – just as well, as we have only a few days to rehearse it before the world premiere, on radio, on Saturday. Yet it has plenty of its own difficulties. The composer doesn't exactly provide us with the substance to fill the long, slow movements, though somehow it's clear that he means them to have a devotional atmosphere. We have to find a sound which sustains the slow tempo without sounding thin, a sound which carries the right kind of meditative force without recourse to cheap vibrato and other technical effects.

There's a hilarious moment when, after playing the long slow movement with intense involvement, we come to a stop with pulses racing and perspiration flowing. There's a short silence, and then Anthony says '. . . Cigarette, anyone?' None of us smokes, so we all collapse with merriment at his implied comparison.

The day ends with a splendid performance of Beethoven's C sharp minor quartet opus 131, by the Vanbrugh Quartet from Ireland. After working all evening on new music, Beethoven manages to seem even newer and more inventive. How does he do it? He seems to have thought of every gesture, every sonority, every layering process, every shocking contrast. And yet he does it all within a tonal language. As ever, the most touching things are the simplest, though their simplicity has a complex effect. There are still passages where, although I've known this work for twenty years, tears spring into my eyes.

Tuesday

I have to teach a public masterclass in which three terrific Irish girls hurl themselves at Tchaikovsky's piano trio. I always feel a fraud in teaching situations until I hear the students play, and then suddenly I realise that some cumulative knowledge has been acquired after all, that I do actually know more about the music and how to perform it than they do. A musician's life doesn't often feel cumulative. You enter and exit from many different situations, interpretations, attitudes, with everything constantly shifting and changing. But sometimes – as when teaching – you do feel that you've travelled quite a long way down the road.

These three girls are good players, but while playing they each seem cocooned in their own thoughts and technical preoccupations. So I see my task as trying to open up their consciousness of one another. I tell them about individual moments where one or both of the other players need their compassion, because of difficult things they have to do. And I tell them when it's their turn to listen, and when they have to dive from the foreground to the background. As the lesson goes on, I see that they begin to look at one another more while playing. Instead of seeing their parts as parallel lines, they've started to see that they are constantly intertwined.

I also talk to them about the importance of understanding the whole structure and psychology of these big movements, and of creating a shape which makes narrative sense across the whole movement. We talk about how physical attitudes, and physical approaches to the instrument, are perceived by the audience, and may convey other messages than the players would like to transmit. We discuss places where, for example, it is no good looking heroic if you are playing something intimate and confiding. Similarly, it is no good looking like the back desk player in an orchestra when you are about to play a sublime and crucial melody. I ask the girls if they can conceive of a space in the air between the three of them, a kind of magic circle into which they can all place their awareness, so that there's a place where 'concentration' in its literal sense occurs. Despite these ideas being new to them (as the cellist later tells me), they make remarkable progress, and I see the audience starting to smile and nod silently as they enjoy the changes.

After the class, a man is waiting to tell me that he and his friends still feel 'transported' by our performance of the 'Archduke' Trio the other day. His description of their feelings ('We couldn't even find words to speak to one another for a while after the concert') is humbling. However, as I thank him and turn to cross the hallway, my eye falls on a review from the *Irish Times* (about whose critic I've been warned) pinned up on the public noticeboard. In it, the critic dismisses this same performance with the words 'sadly rough-hewn'. This is a slap in the face. Anthony has already seen it and is equally surprised. What on earth can the critic mean? Our outraged feelings are only slightly soothed during the day by members of the audience coming up to us to commiserate, and to say that the critic's views are complete nonsense. Sometimes negative criticism evokes an admission in oneself that there was some grain of truth in it. But in this case I have no idea what he meant.

Two singers talk about working with the Hungarian composer György Kurtág. They describe the terror and depression they have suffered because of his insistence on rehearsing and criticising far past the point where most people's instinct would tell them to stop. To one British singer who announced he wanted to learn a certain work, Kurtág said 'Only if he's prepared to give up everything else and spend two years of his life to studying my music.' Yet everyone agrees that Kurtág is a sincere and delightful man, that his music is fascinating and worth a certain amount of sacrifice. The question is: can one person impose sacrifice on another? Surely sacrifice is something you have to make yourself? One singer recalls an occasion where Kurtág got furious with her for going swimming at the end of a long day of rehearsal. He said, 'How dare you go swimming when you're supposed to be learning my music?' This to me shows a profound misunderstanding of the way people learn things. Speaking for myself, I often find that things get digested during swimming, walking and other 'vacant' activities. The notion that the composer is 'full' and the performer 'empty', or the composer 'right' and the artist 'wrong', indicates that no good will come of such a collaboration.

In the afternoon we continue rehearsing the Vasks piano quartet. Now that we know it better, we begin to think it's too long. Many passages seem over-extended and repetitive. However, since we know that the piece is 'about' oppression, of the Latvians by the Soviets, it may be that he actually intends a mesmerising, trapped effect. Is the length of the movements deliberate, or has he miscalculated?

The Guardian has invited me to write this week's 'diary' on the back page of the Saturday Review section. I spend part of the day writing, typing and correcting my article. After I've e-mailed it to them, it occurs to me how happy this journalistic assignment has made me. While writing, I'm hardly aware of time passing. This rarely happens to me. Even in rehearsals I find that time passes slowly. But writing puts me in a happy reverie. Perhaps this is because it's a hobby for me.

In the evening, the trio has an admin meeting. It's labour-intensive because we have to analyse the income and expenses of the Peasmarsh Festival – six concerts at the beginning of June – and decide what to pay our guest artists and ourselves. As ever, the money doesn't stretch to all that we need to do with it, and we speak of the need to raise funds and find sponsors. We agree it's likely that nobody realises just what a tiny budget we work with. It's remarkable that for four years we have managed to run a festival on box office takings alone, and even to pay ourselves something each year.

I find this kind of meeting very strenuous, and can feel a stomach cramp coming on. So we bring it to an end, and agree to walk down to Bantry to a pub where Irish traditional music is being played this evening. The scene is fascinating. In the front corner of the pub, facing inwards in a circle as if the music is nothing to do with listeners, is a group of men ranging in age from about ten to eighty years old. They play violins, tin whistles, accordions and an Irish drum, the bodhran. What's surprising is the grim, almost miserable air of the group as their fingers dance around the instruments. Their faces are glum, drugged-looking, but their hands are astonishingly vivacious. This reminds me of the impassive faces and arms of Irish folk dancers as their feet twinkle to and fro.

Everything is played by ear, and my impression is that the youngsters – one of whom is blind – learn by copying the older men. There's no conversation between them; when one reel finishes, there's scarcely a pause before someone takes up another tune and they all join in. The tunes and harmonies are all very simple, but embellished with thousands of grace-notes, trills and mordents which require tremendous agility from the fingers.

I mention their detached air to one of the classical musicians resident in Ireland. He tells me there's a tradition of folk musicians 'talking with the fairies' while they play. So their focus is not on us, but on communication with another realm. There's an element of that in our performances too, but we can never afford to forget the audience, especially as they buy tickets to our concerts, and don't just overhear them in the corner of the bar. So economics do enter into it, alas.

Thursday

Over breakfast we discuss playing from memory versus playing from the score. Some feel it's important to memorise things, to have no barrier between oneself and the audience, whereas others feel that the effort of memorisation is in itself an obstacle to feeling relaxed on stage.

We also discuss the preference of pianists for playing from a full score, and the (to me incomprehensible) preference of string and wind players for playing from a part with only their own notes indicated. This is not just the result of working from the single-line parts supplied by publishers; even when given the opportunity to play from a score, many players reject it, saying that they are not used to reading vertically as well as horizontally. I have tried both (I used to play violin and percussion), and know that I shall never feel comfortable without a full score, for as well as knowing what I must play, I want to know what everyone else plays, and how my part relates to theirs. A violinist says you can do this by ear, and don't have to do it by eye. But my answer is that you can only do it by ear after lots of rehearsal. In other words, you have to subject all the other players to the period in which you don't know what is going on. To me this is unacceptable, especially since I (like most pianists) know what is going on from the first moment of rehearsal. My pianist colleagues confirm that in rehearsals they often feel they are waiting for others to figure out what they have known from the start. There must be something profoundly different about the brain activities involved in these two methods.

Later I listen to a rehearsal of Schoenberg's *Pierrot Lunaire* in which a great deal of trouble and delay is caused by the fact that most of the players are reading from individual parts. Only the conductor, the singer and the pianist have scores, and all three keep trying to indicate helpful things to their colleagues when they come adrift. To an observer this seems like a simple matter of information imbalance, easily rectified. Yet, as I said earlier, there are many players who don't want to play from a score even when offered one.

At lunch, the first violinist of an American string quartet describes how he started to feel that every day his job involved getting up and going off to spend the day being criticised, and criticising his colleagues. Though there's an unspoken agreement in music that you have to be able to give and take criticism, it is actually a very peculiar way to spend one's working life, not matched by many people. No doubt there does come a point when one doesn't want to hear any more how one could change in order to be better. He described the quartet as being like 'a marriage without love'.

The evening concert begins with a superb Mozart wind octet played by the Paris-Bastille octet. Afterwards, when I go to congratulate François Leleux, their marvellous oboist, someone asks him how they play such lovely soft staccato chords. He replies that they try to think like string players and use their breath as a string player would use the bow, preparing for the note with a graceful upbeat which cause the 'attack' to begin with the right sound. He says that in good music, there's natural tension in the phrase, and 'you don't need to put your own tension on top of the tension in the music'. Of course you need a very good player to rise above the physical and technical challenge of making the sound, but these *are* very good players – 'even though French', as Tchaikovsky's correspondent Madame von Meck might have said.

An Israeli violinist tells me how the musical atmosphere in Israel has greatly changed because of the enormous Russian immigration in recent years. He says that on a recent visit to the Tel Aviv Conservatoire, where he studied as a young man, he had the strange experience of walking through the corridors unable to understand the language he heard around him, which was spoken by Russian teachers and players. And, rather disturbingly, the previous focus on Mozart, Beethoven, Schubert, Schumann, Brahms etc has changed. Now they study Tchaikovsky, Prokofiev, Shostakovich and so on. I wonder if this significant social change is being documented by anyone?

Friday

I attend a masterclass given to a group of Irish students by Valentin Berlinsky, cellist of the Borodin Quartet for 55 years, on good terms with Stalin, and a friend of Shostakovich – therefore one of the few people left who can remember what Shostakovich said about his music. He speaks quietly and dogmatically, though from time to time he assures the youngsters that they 'must find their own way'. That doesn't seem like an option, though.

He strictly controls their tempi and their pauses, occasionally delivering a crushing, 'Not very good'. He tells them it's hard for anyone who didn't live through that era in Russian life to interpret Shostakovich correctly. This is evident from the rather liberal, casual way they play the bitter scherzos and machine-like hammering which goes on and on, and which clearly bores rather than frightens them. In the row in front of me sits another young quartet whose turn in the masterclass will come tomorrow. As the scherzo hurtles towards its menacing end, the first violinist sitting in front of me begins to cry. Is it the music, or the thought of being exposed to criticism tomorrow?

In the midday concert, there is more exquisite playing from oboist François Leleux. He seems to have found a way to remove the penetrating 'quacking' sound which so many oboists have. Everything is floating and effortless. At lunch I have a chance to ask him if he invented this technique himself, and I wish I had a tape-recorder to record his reply. He says yes, that his revered teacher Maurice Bourgue plays quite differently. But he says that he, François, has a different approach. For him a concert is not an opportunity to show how much energy you have. He tries to draws energy from various sides of daily life, and then to use that store of energy to release himself into enjoyable playing in a concert. He also says he's trained himself to relish the fine sensations of playing, and to regard them as Enough. He says other artists still seem to be searching for Yet More, something beyond the playing, which makes them incapable of experiencing happiness in the act of playing itself. This extraordinary Zen-like attitude makes everything seem so simple, yet I'm certain you have to be spiritually developed to a high degree to put it into practice. I can think of plenty of musicians who just enjoy the sensation of playing and are not looking for more, but the results are elementary. Francois seems to be able to relax at the same time as retaining access to a sort of Platonic ideal. I hope he will pass on his insights to young oboists.

In the afternoon, we meet Peteris Vasks and play him his piano quartet. This is the first time that he has heard it played by anyone, and the experience is clearly a shock to him, even if a nice kind of shock. He's a lumberjack of a man, big, shy, sad-looking and of few words. Hearing his music become a reality seems to be painful in some way. He can't find anything nice to say, but confines himself to speaking about the two most important movements, the Passacaglia and the Canto Principale. The atmosphere of these is not right yet, he says. The Passacaglia must be 'full of negative, aggressive energy' and the Canto must be 'like a message from another world' – full of 'intense, ecstatic spiritual contemplation'. This indeed is what we had intuited about the movements and were already trying to achieve, but he says that our approach is 'too formal' – a surprising complaint considering the sweat-soaked shirts that bear witness to our involvement.

I think one problem is that the spiritual content he wants is not exactly innate in the music. His writing is quite simple, folk-like, almost sentimental in places. Therefore I have to overlay it with a mental attempt to be spiritual and intense – instead of deriving this from the music itself. Maybe I don't understand Latvian devotional music. It's undoubtedly attractive and melodious, and peaceful and sustained, but the intensity is something I have to add from my own resources.

Peteris Vasks is on record as saying that he hates cities and gets all his inspiration from nature – forests, lakes, birds and so on. During one of his slow movements, a strange thing happens. There's a moment which brings a sudden surge of power and volume along with an emotional outburst. Precisely as we play this, a huge gust of wind from the terrace sends the big doors crashing open and bursts into the room, whirling leaves and dust around and sending all the music flying off the stands. It's like a scene from a film, a choreographed cooperation of music and nature. Somehow this seems apt for a man who says his music all derives from nature – even though he seems more startled than any of us.

During dinner, someone tells me a lovely story about the viol player Jordi Savall introducing a piece in imperfect English. Intending to say that the next piece was written about the moon, what he actually said was, 'This next piece is the only piece I know which was written on the moon.' My informant said he would never forget the bemused expressions on the audience's faces as they digested this.

Saturday

A quick breakfast, and down to Bantry to buy *The Guardian*, which I desperately hope has my article in it. It does, and I immediately puff up with pride at seeing my name in big bold letters on the back page of the Review section. Reverting to primary school behaviour, I immediately insist on showing it to all the staff in the shop, who look from the paper to me with sceptical expressions as if to say, 'Oh yeah – and I wrote all the Harry Potter books.'

After coffee we meet Peteris Vasks for our second and last rehearsal with him. Perhaps he's repented of his critical mood yesterday, or he's recovered from the disorientation of hearing his work for the first time – at any rate, he's now full of thanks and praise, even though we all feel our playing was very much as it was yesterday (though admittedly we're all trying hard to envisage the correct atmosphere). In fact, he's undergone a thorough conversion and is now reduced to wordless gestures of heartfelt pleasure, especially after Richard's cello solo at the start of the slow movement. He makes lots of little changes to things – deleting 'ritardando' markings, inserting little pauses, asking for more pedal on the piano, agreeing that the viola can play an octave down in certain high passages. These are the kind of things one wishes one could discuss with composers of long ago, whose markings we struggle to honour, even though they themselves might give way immediately if asked for a bit of flexibility, just as Vasks does.

Lots of people tell us that our young Irish students gave a terrific performance of the Tchaikovsky Trio in the back room at Vickery's Inn last night. Interestingly, all these people – who were present both at the classes and at the concert – seem to think it's entirely due to us that the students played so well, even though we had only four hours with them in total. This gives me an insight into the power which is held and sometimes wielded by teachers.

In the afternoon, we call an unscheduled Vasks rehearsal to make sure we've digested the changes he has asked for – some of which are going to be hard to remember in tonight's concert after we'd rehearsed them a different way.

In the concert, the performance of the Vasks quartet goes very well, mainly because the string players are on tremendous form. This is maybe the only piano quartet in the whole world where the piano part is easier than the string parts. The work is indeed almost 45 minutes long, making it one of the longest piano quartets. The audience responds with enormous warmth, though I later discover this was as much a sign of their appreciation of the playing as of the piece. Vasks is very happy, though he intimates that he might cut the work before it's printed and published. I mingle with the audience to canvas their reactions. Some of the musicians see the faults in the work – basically the imbalance between substance and length – but many people loved it, and all agree that it is sincere and gripping – an accolade that many contemporary works would not gain from an audience after a premiere.

Vasks' publisher tells me a curious thing about the composer oppressed by the Soviet rule. When the official instructions were to write clear and straightforward 'music for the people', all the avant-garde composers wanted to write in outlandish notation and startling effects. Now that things have relaxed and they may write in any style they wish, they have all reverted to writing in crotchets and quavers, and they don't like to modulate any more. This prompts some wry reflections about creativity and adversity.

Just as I'm on my way to bed, an American couple stop me to say how much they enjoyed my masterclass on Tuesday. The woman says, 'We talked about you after the class and we said, "We wish we'd had her as a teacher when we were young. If we had, we'll all be big-time now, not just playing the piano in Sunday school." ' I thank them for these nice remarks. Then the woman says, 'And what is your instrument, Susan?' I ask, 'Haven't you heard me in any of the concerts?' 'No', they say. 'Have you been playing in the concerts? We haven't been to many. We like going to the masterclasses.' I was already feeling happy, but the fact that they liked my teaching without even having heard me play, or knowing that I am a pianist, makes me even happier.

Sunday

'This is terrible, terrible weather in which to leave', says Richard as we pile in to the minibus taking us to Cork Airport. It's a flawless day and we can already see some of the festival helpers sunbathing on the lawns. As the bus approaches Cork, conversation between the musicians imperceptibly changes in subject. The delights of Ireland fade away, and we all start to talk about agents, finances, problems, and our next bookings. Whereas during the festival nobody has mentioned what happens next, it now seems that our psyches reach outwards and create a map of the world with ourselves as little coloured flags pinned to various far-flung places. By the time we've all checked in and find ourselves upstairs in the lounge, the rapport created by the week in Bantry has almost dissipated, and we all sit in different corners waiting for our flights to be called.

June 2001

With Florestan in Australia and New Zealand, September/October 2001

Our journey begins in sombre mood, because it is only four days after the terrorist attack on the World Trade Center in New York on September 11, 2001. The days between that event and the start of our tour are filled with anxious friends and relatives wondering aloud whether it is wise to spend three weeks travelling around on planes on the other side of the world. I'm always reluctant to leave home for extended periods, and this time is especially hard because we're all aware of the potential problems should the political situation deteriorate in the next three weeks. The Americans are talking about retaliation against Afghanistan, presumed home of the terrorists, and it seems clear that if they do take military action, it will cause many nations to rally behind either them or the victims of any further attacks. There's a sense of destabilisation around the world. All this makes for a very stressful and tearful day of farewells at home, and I wonder for the millionth time why I didn't become a librarian or cake-maker.

Anthony has gone ahead of us, and is already in Australia having a holiday up at the Great Barrier Reef. The knowledge that he's already there, waiting for us thousands of miles away, makes it almost impossible to broach the idea of cancelling the trip. In any case, none of us knows how to assess the political situation in this sudden crisis.

Richard and I fly to Melbourne and then on to Adelaide – a flight of about 20 hours, plus stopovers. By the time we arrive, exhaustion has made us both start to hallucinate slightly about words. On the last flight of the journey, I'm handed a packet of cutlery with the word 'Cutlery' printed on it; this I read as 'Cruelty'. Richard meanwhile kept saying the wrong words when talking to his neighbour on this same flight. My eyes feel dry and swollen, as they always do after long flights. Both in Heathrow and Melbourne we encounter chaotic scenes at the airports – in Heathrow because of increased security measures after the attack on New York; in Melbourne because of the sudden collapse of Ansett Airlines, a development which looks likely to affect us all through the tour, with its corollary that Air New Zealand is also in trouble.

Adelaide

We left London at the start of autumn, and arrive in Adelaide at the start of spring, with a hard, brilliant sunlight. Everyone but us seems to be wearing sunglasses. We keep ourselves awake by walking round the city, and I set off to try to find the spot where in about 1985 our dome was set up in front of the Museum on North Terrace. Seeing the site brings back all sorts of memories about the difficulties we had on that trip. It was the most ambitious foreign trip we ever planned with the dome, and we were unprepared for the complexities of things like customs declarations and freight regulations. I remember travelling back and forth to Adelaide airport day after day to retrieve those boxes of equipment which had finally been released from customs. The administrative nightmare of bringing the dome to Australia was, in fact, the last straw for Domus with the dome, and it was the last foreign trip we undertook with it.

This initial period of a tour, before concerts begin, is always difficult for me. I feel anonymous, in limbo, conscious of everyone going about their busy lives without the least interest in us. But seeing a poster of us pinned up outside the Town Hall – with the headline 'Triple Treat' – presages a day when we will have a public reason to be there.

Anthony arrives from Cairns at the end of our second day, excited by his scuba diving and snorkelling. As soon as he's dropped off his suitcase, we go and rehearse at the Flinders School of Music, most of our pauses being filled with scraps of discussion about the American situation. It's crossed all our minds that developments might prevent us from travelling home as planned.

The next day, though we aren't scheduled to rehearse until the afternoon, I go to the Town Hall in the morning and ask if I can try the piano. I'm glad I did, as it turns out to be a big, heavy, new Steinway perhaps more suited to modern concerto work. Touching the keys gently means that the notes sometimes don't 'speak', and it takes me an hour to adjust my finger and wrist action to the extra weight of the keys. Getting to know new pianos on tour is always a challenge. I have no control over what I'll find, relying on the local organisers to make sure that the quality is adequate. Even so, there is a wide variety of instruments I have to play. I try to find 'my sound' on each of them, but it isn't always possible.

In the evening, the hall is packed for our first concert – over a thousand people are there. The acoustics are splendid, and apart from a slight feeling of struggling with the heavy keys – which, to my chagrin, make me miss a few crucial notes in the opening line of Beethoven's Trio, opus 1 no. 1 – the concert goes very well. We've agreed that I should introduce the Fauré, and before I do so, I tell the audience that it is a pleasure to be playing our very first concert in Australia, though, as they can imagine, this hasn't been the easiest week to jump on a plane and travel to the other side of the world. At this, there's a spontaneous burst of emotional applause from the whole audience, which Anthony later says 'was rather wonderful'.

This Australian audience looks and behaves very much like a British audience – that's to say, predominantly older folk, and reserved though warm in manner. I'm conscious of our style being highly refined and 'European' – how this asserts itself I don't know, but I sense a kind of surprised attentiveness in the audience, who are so focused and silent that we realise they don't often hear this kind of playing. Whether it's the style, the quality or the intimacy that intrigues them, or whether they are simply puzzled by the whole occasion, I can't tell.

After the concert we're invited to the home of a committee member for supper. Conversation revolves largely around the American situation, the difficulty of travel in the future, and how the world situation makes us all reassess our jobs and their relevance. Several people mention how glad they are to be living thousands of miles from the trouble spots and in a country very unlikely ever to be involved[1] – which is of small comfort to us Brits. One woman tells me that during the concert she kept thinking of Yehudi Menuhin giving concerts to boost the morale of the troops during the Second World War – there is some parallel sense of needing to be comforted and sustained by great music at this uncertain time.

Sydney

I was unprepared for the scale and energy of Sydney, which I had somehow imagined as a smaller, more relaxed city. The recital hall in Angel Place is only a year old, a 1200-seat hall of delightful appearance, shoebox shape but with galleries around three sides of it. A bank of lighting has given the technicians scope to design three different 'light settings' for the three pieces in our programme, though their choice seems to be independent of the music – at least so I deduce when I see on the technical sheet that 'bastard amber' is their choice for Schubert.

I've decided to return to my hotel between rehearsal and concert in the hope of having a shower and emerging fresh for the evening. But I've miscalculated the extent of Sydney's traffic. The taxi takes about twenty minutes to get to the hotel, and I have to sprint up to my room, get changed and set straight off again without having time to wash. A similar taxi journey back again gets me back to the hall just ten minutes before the concert and in agitated mood. However, the packed house, the cheerful atmosphere of the hall and the fine piano help me to calm down, and the concert proves very enjoyable. It's my task to introduce the Fauré again, and this time I speak about the first time I heard it played, when I wondered when the 'action' was going to begin, and gradually realised that it wasn't. I describe how I came to see that I had ruined it by having the wrong expectations of the piece, and how one has to give up the idea that a piece of music will be written in narrative form, with contrasting themes, intellectual development, mood changes, reconciliation of contrasting themes at the end, and so on. I say that for me listening to the Fauré trio is like that kind of time-lapse photography that one sees in nature programmes, where you watch a flower unfolding, and see everything in great detail. Nothing 'happens' apart from that process of flowering, which in itself is a beautiful thing to witness. As I speak, I see people gazing at me with deep attention, and I wonder once again whether there is a way to develop this kind of talking about music from the performer's point of view. I do have the impression that it's new to many people. Perhaps Dr Johnson would say, 'It is not done well, but one is surprised that it is done at all.'

---

1 Sadly, their feeling of remoteness from terrorist activity was dispelled a year later on the occasion of the bombing of a Bali nightclub, in which many Australians were killed.

Again, there are almost a thousand people in the audience. Playing the same programme as last night in Adelaide – Fauré, Beethoven opus 1 no. 1, and the Schubert B flat Trio – is surprisingly tiring. Thank goodness we don't have a concert tomorrow! In fact, we now don't even have a flight, thanks to the national work stoppage organised to protest about the collapse of Ansett Airlines, which has left many Australians without a job. So we will now have a whole day in Sydney.

Next morning I meet for breakfast with Roger Dean, a contemporary jazz musician whose professional life is high-powered science research. I know him from the days when he used to be a guest artist in our geodesic dome. Now he runs the Sydney Heart Research Institute. As we sit on the quayside just behind the Opera House, Roger expresses surprise that I'm still a performing musician, and says he expected I would have got fed up with the problems of a travelling British musician's life by now. This makes me feel obscurely guilty that I haven't – or at least, that I haven't succeeded in finding something more peaceful.

Describing the trio's life and prospects to him makes me feel dissatisfied too. He wonders tactfully whether there is anywhere for the trio 'to go'. He's aware of the market forces which keep our fees down, and of the British lack of sponsorship and funding. And he expresses surprise that even on a trip like this we are still expected to travel economy class, and to pay for all our meals and daily expenses out of our modest fees. He asks why we can't insist on going business class, considering that we have to emerge from this long journey and immediately be in top form for our concerts, but this is him speaking as a scientist – as a jazzer, he knows as well as I do the budget constraints that concert organisers are dealing with. The reality is that some artists do succeed in travelling business class, but they are not chamber musicians, who by temperament are always inclined to see the other person's point of view, and are always talked into the financial necessity of travelling cheaply.

I find that after this conversation I have a tantalising sense of thoughts hovering in the back of my mind, thoughts of various shapes waiting for me to assemble them and make up a new picture I haven't seen before. As I walk about the harbourfront afterwards, I feel the bits of the jigsaw floating about, but they won't come together.

Mornington

On the next day, we pay for our free day in Sydney with an early flight to Melbourne, transfer to the city centre and then a drive out to Mornington, where there is a small Music Society. Alas, it reproduces every unpleasant feature of our least favourite British music clubs: a school hall, an inadequate Kawai baby grand piano, a tiny, dirty and freezing cold backstage changing room we all have to share, cold water, etc. The audience is warm and delightful, but I resent having to struggle with the piano, whose stiff keyboard action and thin tone forces me into projecting the sound too much, over-exerting my arm muscles, and making my arms stiffen up throughout the evening.

We sit in the dressing-room and debate whether it would be possible to refuse to play such pianos as this. During my first tour in Australia, with Domus, I played a number of very poor pianos (though admittedly in places rather off the beaten track), and I'll never forget one particular concert where I had to play a half-broken upright that hadn't been tuned for ages. Perhaps this will make me sound ridiculous, but I started crying during the first piece on the programme and wept all the way through it. Because the piano was an upright, my back was to the audience, so ironically the lack of a grand piano gave me some privacy. Since those days we have tried to specify the quality of the piano required, and these days we ask that the piano should be a Steinway concert grand or equivalent. Clearly, however, there's a wide range of interpretations of 'equivalent' by promoters around the world. I've been very disappointed by the piano on many occasions and have considered making a fuss, but have always been able to see the mitigating circumstances and budget constraints that make it hard for certain venues to get hold of better pianos. To make things worse, I am aware that piano hire firms often charge considerably more for an evening's piano hire than I get for playing the concert.

Richard says I am too understanding about this kind of thing, and that many pianists would be much fiercer. He reminds me that promoters have quite often apologised to us for the state of the piano, adding naively that 'we do hire a Steinway grand for solo piano recitals, of course'. Some promoters seem to think that chamber music requires a less good instrument, which is obviously absurd – especially as the piano parts of piano trios are every bit as rich and complex as the piano parts of solo pieces. I take every opportunity to point this out to them, though of course it is usually too late if it happens on the day of a concert, when there is no chance of getting a different piano.

Melbourne

On the following day, a sad honour awaits us: our concert in the huge Melbourne Concert Hall is to be the last in the long-running Sunday afternoon series. Our tour has been organised in conjunction with Musica Viva, a prestigious Australian concert promoter. Its new director, the composer Carl Vine, has come to explain to the devoted audience – many of whom are European émigrés – why this is the last concert in the series. In fact, the Concert Hall is one of the largest venues we've ever played in, and is not really suitable for intimate chamber music. It's considerably larger, to my eye, than the Royal Festival Hall in London. Nevertheless, and despite the gloomy warnings of the promoters, I thoroughly enjoy the concert. Ant is very cheerful after the Beethoven, and says that he only now feels that he understands it, after months of performing it. I feel happier today, because the piano is excellent, and because I seem to be able to fill the hall with sound without straining, even though the hall is so enormous.

After the concert, many people of European extraction (easily spotted by their accents – Hungarian, Viennese, etc) come up to tell us how much they enjoyed the concert and how sad they are that the series is fading away. This theme – that audiences are dwindling – is now sufficiently global to be really unnerving. And it's obvious that young people are missing from the audiences. We keep being told that they'll discover the classics when they are in their forties and fifties, but that will be too late for us.

New Zealand: Christchurch

Next day, a lengthy journey takes us from Melbourne to Sydney and then from Sydney to New Zealand, arriving at midnight in Christchurch. On the plane, Ant and I find ourselves sitting in the midst of a group of music-lovers who've just travelled from their Christchurch homes to see the new production of Wagner's *Parsifal* at the Adelaide Opera House. 'You've just travelled 1500 miles to go to the opera!' I say to my neighbour. 'Well, we're starved of cultural events down here', she tells me.

It's after 1 a.m. by the time we get to the hotel, and I still feel strange from the four-hour flight and can't sleep for ages. At 7 a.m., after only a few hours of sleep, I'm woken by traffic surging past the hotel, and get up for my daily dose of alarming CNN reports about the American situation. There is talk of further terrorist attacks, of military preparations by the Americans, of support in the Arabic countries for the alleged perpetrators of the World Trade Center attacks. There's also news of sudden problems in the airline industry, and the beginning of reports of airlines suspending flights and cutting jobs. It's clear that many things will change in the world as a result of the September 11 attacks on New York, and there's a sense of new coalitions – and opponents of new coalitions – emerging.

Dunedin

A morning flight takes us to Dunedin and to an unexpected oasis of European elegance at Corstorphine House, a small 'stately home' lately converted by a Dutch and Russian couple into a stylish hotel, what the New Zealanders call 'a boutique hotel', though 'boutique' seems to have lost its original meaning and now merely means 'elegant'. Something about the ambience – floral displays, beautiful paintings, blond wood, palest grey linen, Persian rugs – causes us all to relax.

As we sit chatting over lunch in the conservatory, I realise how numb and silent we have all been for days – bludgeoned into anaesthesia by airports and queues and repetitive tasks. Sometimes it feels as if we have nothing to say to one another. And yet here, with the Beaux Arts Trio playing Haydn on CD in the background, we all cheer up and start discussing whether rehearsal is a good thing or not, how to get foreign agents, and other positive topics. One tries to carry all one's resources inside, and to have access to them in any surroundings, but when we find ourselves in congenial surroundings, we open up like flowers.

In Dunedin we change to the second programme of the tour: the little Schubert Trio movement, the Fauré, the Ravel Duo for violin and cello, and Beethoven's E flat Trio, opus 70 no. 2. After rehearsing quite briefly – we know all these works well – I go out for a snack with Dorothy Duthie, the local organiser. Three years ago she baked a cake for us when we played in Dunedin, and remembering that I particularly liked it, she has made me another cake today. Funnily enough, these are the little things that you remember when you look back on a tour. In the restaurant my mood shifts back to a gloomy one, because Dot tells the same tale of woe that we heard in Melbourne – diminishing audiences, lack of local support, unsold tickets for tonight, student indifference. Indeed, the hall – which was packed full for our concert three years ago – is only about two-thirds full, though the audience who do come are delightfully warm and involved, as though they want to make up for their missing friends.

During the night I have a disturbing dream that, instead of travelling on to Christchurch, we catch a plane back to London. All the way back we travel in silence, but when we reach Heathrow, an argument breaks out about whether we should have done it, whether we should go back and attempt to complete the tour. A few sums convince us that the cost of going back, at our own expense, would wipe out any profit from the remaining concerts, so it's a just a question of moral scruple. Miserably we decide that we must go back to New Zealand. Then it turns out that the only flight available is going to Durban in South Africa. I wake up in a panic.

We discuss whether it might be nice, or even good, to play the occasional concert without rehearsal on the day – though only with works we know well. I ask the others whether they think the audience would notice any difference between a rehearsed and unrehearsed concert (given that the preparatory work had been done, of course). 'Almost certainly not', they say, 'but that's not the right question to ask – the comparison would be between what we achieve and what we might have achieved with rehearsal, so we're the ones we'd have to satisfy.'

Though this is true, I sometimes wonder whether the re-thinking of dynamic schemes, articulation, timing that goes on in rehearsals on tour is largely an exercise to prove to ourselves that in the midst of numbing travel our minds are still working. I suppose that even if this is all it does, it's still worth doing. One would think that performing the same programme six times in a row – not our wish, incidentally – the rehearsals would get briefer and briefer, but this is not to be relied upon, as we are all sensitive to the danger of producing that feeling of routine which is anathema to us collectively.

Christchurch

The next day we travel back to Christchurch, which has unpleasant memories for me, because on our last trip here, I lost my footing while climbing out of a high-sided vehicle and fell so badly on my left foot that I had to have physiotherapy for six months afterwards – and my foot still hurts at night sometimes, three years later. When I set eyes on the hotel outside which it happened, a curious psychosomatic link causes my foot to start aching again.

At each concert, I've introduced the Fauré Trio, and set myself the task of doing it differently on each occasion. Tonight I speak about Fauré's rejection of the 'story-telling' mode of composition, and how he was perhaps trying to do something else with his music, something more akin to Oriental music, establishing a meditative mood and drawing the listener in to share it, building up intensity within each movement until a certain pitch of intensity is reached, when the movement burns itself out. One of the music committee tells us afterwards that when I finished speaking, the lady behind her said 'Thank you' in a fervent tone, as though I had been speaking to her personally. This pleases me, as I take the task seriously.

To be honest, our performances out here have been less 'developmental' than in other places. The standard of our playing has been very high throughout, I think, but each concert has been a painstaking attempt to produce something whose recipe we agreed on a while ago. The variations within each concert are slight, perhaps discernible only to us. I think this simply shows the gruelling nature of touring. Spending half of each day being bumped around in an aircraft, in a taxi; finding the concert hall, figuring out when and where to eat – it's all rather numbing, not leaving much surplus energy for re-conceptualising the music together.

New Plymouth

The following morning, it takes two flights – one to Wellington (where Anthony's neighbour on the plane has a panic attack as we start that famously bumpy landing, and sobs and gasps her way to the ground, giving voice to what many people are no doubt thinking), and one from Wellington to New Plymouth – to reach our next venue. New Plymouth is a place we disliked last time, though we enjoyed our audience there. The town itself still makes a bleak impression. However, this time Ant's guidebook reveals the existence of Pukekura Park, a really splendid botanical garden in early spring finery – cherries, azaleas, waterlilies, ducklings, and birds frantically building nests and calling to one another seductively. Ant and I go for an afternoon walk there, and by instinct don't talk about music or work.

The concert is certainly the most depressing of the tour. For a start the new theatre (unfinished in many details because they ran out of money) is bleak and cheerless, very cold backstage, and with a Japanese piano. In theory these Japanese pianos are copies of the best European ones, but they are often disappointing, particularly in their lack of singing tone and projection. The tone seems to 'stop dead' as soon as it is produced, especially in the treble. This problem is often exacerbated by the piano not being properly 'voiced' and regulated, and this in turn is linked to the shortage of really knowledgeable piano tuners and technicians. I have lost count of the number of times I've been dissatisfied with the tuning of a piano, even when it has just been done on the day of a concert, and I have definitely concluded that the world is short of really good tuners. On days like this I envy my colleagues, who always have their own instruments with them, and never have to face the limitations of unsatisfactory pianos as I do. Of course, they have to carry their instruments with them on every journey, and I don't underestimate the burden and nuisance of doing so, especially for Richard. However, on the plus side they always know they'll have their own familiar instrument in the concert, which must be tremendously reassuring. Every piano is different, many of them are not as nice as mine at home, and in every place there's a very limited time to get used to the unknown piano.

Once again there's just one dressing-room for us all to share. Shortly before the concert, when the audience is already filtering in to the hall, a local organiser offers to heat up some mini-pizzas for us in the microwave. As we're getting changed, the microwave suddenly belches forth a cloud of acrid smoke and, when we manage to get the oven door open, far worse billows out from inside. The smoke alarm goes off, triggering a public address system ordering everyone to evacuate the building; staff come surging through our dressing room and out into the cold night air, and then the fire brigade arrives. All the doors have to be opened, causing cold air to rush through and the theatre to become ridiculously cold. Eventually the audience and staff are allowed back, but the stench of acrid smoke hangs over the hall all evening, and the dressing-room is like a fridge.

This coldness somehow affects the whole evening. Though we do our best, there's a sense of blankness from the audience, and this is borne out afterwards by the comments of the committee as they join us in the cold dressing-room for a glass of wine. 'That was a lovely bit of music.' 'Very pleasant evening.' 'You all seemed to enjoy yourselves!' One woman tells me it was the first time she'd heard Beethoven's E flat Trio, opus 70 no. 2. I ask her what she thought of it. 'Well!' she says. 'I thought the third movement had a lovely waltzy feel.' So it does, but somehow this remark sends me home in low spirits.

Auckland

Next day, we fly to Auckland where Nan Gibson, a delightful New Zealander who came to our trio festival in Peasmarsh last year, has invited us to lunch at her Torbay house about half an hour's drive from the city. She picks us up at our hotel, and soon we're sitting on her balcony looking over the sea. After lunch we walk along the impressive beach – no dolphins today, alas – and back through the park. Conversation turns around how hard it is to find concert opportunities, kindred spirits and mental stimulation in Auckland. Against this, Nan admits that the quality of life – clean air, space, beaches, food, nature – would be hard to find elsewhere, certainly at New Zealand prices. We tell her that in London it's the other way round – plenty of stimulation and excellent colleagues, but a diminishing quality of life, and ridiculous prices of things like transport and food. Everyone I know seems to be split between these extremes. Why is it so hard to find a place which reconciles them? I know several people who live in enviably comfortable places with good salaries and a leisurely lifestyle, but they all claim to be bored and lacking in interesting companions.

In the evening, my colleagues want to see a film, and I end up walking around the new harbourfront area, built only last year for the America's Cup, and bursting with chic restaurants crammed with Auckland's glitterati. The weather is so fine that the restaurants have set tables out on the boardwalk with candles glowing on each table. I do a complete circuit of the whole area before feeling bold enough to enter any of the cafés. Then I reflect how disappointed my favourite food writer M.F.K. Fisher would be with me if I fail to have a comfortable meal by myself. So, telling myself that I am old and mature enough to go into a chic restaurant by myself, I select an Indian restaurant and am instantly pleased with my choice, as the kind waiters come solicitously to look after me, and far from being stuck at a corner table for one, they invite me to occupy a prime table for four right out on the patio overlooking the harbour. I have a delicious vegetable biryani, and make it last for a while in between reading sections of the New Zealand *Herald*, disappointing in literary quality as have been all newspapers out here. When I compare the standard of journalism here with the one routinely available to us in broadsheets at home . . .!

Over a thousand people attend the concert, and rather alarmingly, I have to introduce the Fauré through a powerful microphone, but after the concert several people tell me that my words 'made all the difference'. The concert itself goes well, despite Richard's dropping his bow to the floor with a clatter during the Schubert. Yet, though I'm aware it's going well, I feel curiously detached. On the one hand, I feel relaxed and at home in this large handsome venue, but on the other, I feel isolated from everything and everyone.

After the concert there is one of those extended pauses I hate – where people take ages to gather their things, ages to move out of the hall, ages to decide where they want to go, and then ages to get there in various cars. I think my ideal post-concert situation would be to have a group of congenial people and a bottle of wine right next to the Green Room, so that there would be only minutes between the end of the concert and the welcoming feedback and relaxation with friends. Because I suffer from IBS (irritable bowel syndrome) it's often in this kind of limbo that I start to feel unwell. The adrenalin of the concert drains away, my stomach starts to hurt, I feel tense and shaky, and if it goes on too long, I don't recover my equanimity. However, everyone else seems to cope easily with this kind of situation, and I realise that I am the odd one out.

Someone in the audience asks me in the hotel lounge afterwards if I could jot down what I said about the Fauré trio as a memento. I have a go:

'Fauré's piano trio is a piece we've all become immensely fond of – though I admit that we were puzzled by it at first, because it doesn't unlock its secrets at first glance. Fauré was one of a group of French composers who felt that Wagner's influence on French music was too overwhelming, and that they had to find their own way – their own specifically French way – of expressing themselves. During his life, he found various successful ways of departing from Wagner's path, and in his old age he found yet another, which was quite different from other people's solutions. He simplified his style – on the surface – to the point where it became enigmatic, even cryptic for some people, and indeed still is.

'For people who liked Fauré's earlier style, it must have been as if a favourite painter had stopped producing colourful Impressionist oils, and started doing delicate Chinese-style line drawings in black and white. It was a radical change of style, and the surface of Fauré's late music became so smooth that some people feel shut out by it. Yet it's a case of "still waters running deep", for beneath this still surface, when you look down into the depths, you see how much is going on beneath the surface, and how much intense life he stirs up down there. This inner intensity and outer serenity, combined with his exquisite sense of harmony – which is uniquely French – makes a powerful blend.'

Napier

Next day, we fly to Napier, a small town famous for its Art Deco buildings, all of which were built after the disastrous earthquake of the 1930s which flattened the town.

In the evening, out for a walk by myself, I find a café with a live guitarist playing in the background. I go in for a glass of wine, and when he has a break, I go over and introduce myself as a fellow musician. At the next break he comes over and joins me. We chat for a while – about the influence of classical guitar on his jazz playing, about rates of pay, and so on. He tells me that he became interested a few years back in some classical repertoire, and having noticed how much his audiences liked it, he decided to put on a whole recital of such pieces. But the effort of having to practise, of memorisation, of appearing alone in a concert setting, were too daunting and he never tried it again. 'Since then, my respect for classical musicians has gone sky-high,' he tells me. 'You guys cope with that kind of pressure all the time!' He prefers to play in the café, where he is paid just 75 dollars (about £20) for three hours of solo guitar music – a hugely demanding job.

Next morning, we finally manage to have the admin. meeting we've been trying to have in ten-minute bursts in airport lounges. It starts at a pavement café and moves to a grassy spot at the edge of the beach on a brilliant spring morning. Topics range widely over grand expansion plans, the need for major sponsorship, our long-standing wish to do more in Europe, and my equally fervent wish not to do long-haul touring, especially under budget conditions. On this point we're divided: Richard sympathises with me to some extent, whereas Anthony admits he thoroughly enjoys international travel and concerts. Our individual attitudes to touring are very much linked to our domestic situations. We discuss whether it might be possible to limit these kind of long-haul tours to once every few years, and put far more emphasis on mainland Europe.

In the afternoon, instead of rehearsing the same programme, we rehearse Beethoven's 'Ghost' Trio, to take pressure off ourselves when we get back to Britain and have to play it a week after our return.

The Century Theatre in Napier is perhaps the smallest venue on our tour – 300 seats – but the audience is delightfully warm. There's even a busload of folk from Hastings. Here in New Zealand the average age of the audience is like it is in Britain – one looks out over a sea of grey and silver heads. Much as we value and need them, it's disturbing to see so few younger people.

After our concert, the friendly Napier committee whisk the piano aside, carry a table onstage and spread out an impromptu supper – quiche, cheese muffins, chocolate brownies, Sauvignon Blanc. Conversation turns on the difficulty of keeping the series alive in New Zealand. I learn that in addition to the major centres we've now toured twice, there are 26 small societies who don't have the funds to 'buy in' international artists such as us, but which thrive on local artists. Someone tells me, 'You thought Napier was small – you should see some of the places our artists go to!' Thinking of the likely pianos there, I'm glad not to have to confront them.

Wellington

Our last concert is in Wellington, which means landing at that alarming airport again, and because of the wind direction our pilot swings out over the ocean and back in towards the runway from the south, virtually skimming the rocks as we land. Later a Wellingtonian tells me that everyone she knows has gloomy thoughts as their planes fight to land at that airport.

Wellington Town Hall is a handsome old hall, once scheduled for demolition when the inferior Michael Fowler Centre was built next door – and reprieved after a public outcry – and built on the 'shoebox' plan which all the fine old concert halls seem to follow. Often acoustics were better in the days before technicians started making mathematical calculations to get them perfect.

Our final concert is broadcast live on national radio. Whereas in Britain the BBC is very discouraging about artists introducing their own performances, preferring to use their own announcers, the producer here tells us to do exactly what we'd do if the radio weren't there. As the hall is large, the stage staff tell us it's essential to use a powerful microphone, so we practise using theirs. It's always a scary and unfamiliar feeling, but we've all noticed that audiences enjoy hearing our voices, and that it creates another bridge – a different bridge from the one created by our playing – between us and them. We object in principle to using microphones, because all our playing is acoustic – that's to say, unamplified – and we instinctively feel that to speak though a microphone will set up a certain expectation of volume level which will make our playing seem small and far away in comparison. But experience has shown that in large halls, only people at the front can hear us speak, whereas everyone seems to be able to hear us play.

At this last concert, my tenth time on this tour of introducing the Fauré (which Richard has fervently requested we never play again!) I talk about its simple exterior and how different that is to the simple exterior of the little Schubert movement which preceded it in the programme – the Schubert simple because he hadn't yet matured, and the Fauré simple because he had transcended complexity in his old age. I explain that clearly this music is to be played, and therefore heard; but it's not at all clear how it is to be *performed*. I say that for me, performing the Fauré is like showing a partly-closed oyster to someone in such a way that they can see there is a pearl inside.

In this last concert I have the feeling that, while we were able to lock into a high level of ensemble playing, our interpretations have been more or less stable throughout this trip. For me that's because great reserves of energy – mental and physical – have been used up simply in enduring the huge quantity of travel and all its attendant tasks – keeping up with laundry and ironing, keeping in touch with people at home by finding internet cafes everywhere, sorting out problems at home from a long distance away, figuring out the layout of each new town and how to get around it.

Although we've been here for almost three weeks, I've spent most of the time in a fog of jetlag which has been incredibly slow to clear, and I still don't feel adjusted to the time zone and the season. I still feel dizzy many times each day. My sleep pattern has been disturbed throughout, and I think there was only one night – interestingly, the one day on which we had neither a flight nor a concert – when I slept through the whole night. Every other night I've been awake in the middle of the night, watching CNN at 4 a.m. – and I feel groggy each morning, as though my body thinks I should be asleep. Playing ten demanding concerts in these circumstances is not easy and, in my case, has used up as much energy as I had.

I'm proud of the quality of our playing on this tour, but I would say that the strain of touring exposes the fault lines in us as a social group. In a sense we are at our worst on these trips – missing our families, numbed by travel, trying to keep up with our private practice, constantly aware of having to economise (all our expenses here are paid for out of our concert fees, as they are on every tour) – and thus often not in a very cheerful or sociable state.

After the last concert, we go for a drink with the staff and some of the board members of Chamber Music New Zealand. One of them tells me that a distinguished elderly lady in the audience leaned over to him after our performance of the Fauré and said, 'The pearl *was* revealed' (a reference to my spoken introduction). And that pleases me greatly. Several people make an effort to tell us how much our playing – individually or collectively – has meant to them over the years, and how delighted they are to have us there in person – one woman asks if she can hug me, as she can't quite believe I am actually there. Someone thrusts a note into my hand which says what a thrill it has been to hear me playing 'live' after years of listening to my records. I find it amazing that complete strangers on the other side of the world should have been aware of our activities for such a long time without making themselves known to us. Often we feel isolated from the support of listeners, and these occasions are startling in their sudden revelation of longstanding affection. At such moments it feels worthwhile to have made this long journey.

Mostly, however, I fear that the response here has not made it feel worthwhile. Though the response has always been warm and friendly, I do wonder how much of what we were trying to do has been understood. The tone of most of our reviews in local papers has certainly borne this out: 'In Schubert's B flat trio there are some quite tricky passages for the piano, while the cello part is also demanding.' 'His colleagues' support came across as pertinent rather than mundane', etc. It feels as if the music – and our interpretation – has had only a shallow meaning for the audiences.

And after all, their European roots get more and more diluted as time goes on. Their parents and grandparents, who started these organisations in the hope of getting European artists to come and play to them, were emigrés themselves, but the next generations are Australians and New Zealanders. Recent changes in educational policy have meant that they are encouraged to feel their neighbourliness and links to the countries round about them, so that instead of learning French and German as foreign languages, they might now learn Japanese, Chinese, or Maori. Their links to European 'art music' are fading gradually away.

This is a different sort of problem from the problem of building and keeping audiences in Europe itself. It's a cultural reality which means that the kind of music we play will inevitably have more and more of a 'historical' air for Antipodean audiences now revelling in the fact that they are no longer exiled Europeans, but proud citizens of the Pacific Rim. For us, however, it means that travelling this long distance to play to them will have inevitable jolts of disappointment. I strongly felt that whether we played our pieces like this, or like that, was more or less irrelevant. They certainly appreciated the standard of our instrumental playing, and our 'togetherness', but I could not say whether they sought or found much beyond that.

We're always searching for listeners who understand our approach and our identity as musicians – and, frankly, I long for them to be able to distinguish between us and other players, otherwise it is not worth spending the amount of time we do on arriving at 'our' interpretations. Yet I have the feeling that, as long as the players are highly competent, many people can't distinguish between interpretations of different kinds, and I often feel that they might have been just as happy with any other competent group playing the same music.

For me this produces an unbalanced feeling between the effort that we put in, and the depth of the audience's response. I fear that the preparatory work for our performances is more for our own benefit than anyone else's – essential work to safeguard our own morale and integrity, of course, but if not matched by an audience response, making the whole thing feel unpleasantly self-indulgent and narcissistic. Furthermore, I often have the feeling that our specific identity – where we are on the

worldwide spectrum of performers – will remain a locked secret for audiences who
have grown away from their European roots, or who never had any.

During the very long journey home I muse on this. We've worked out that in ten
concerts we probably played to six or seven thousand people. Of those, we only
spoke to a handful in each place, so perhaps it is unwise to base any summing-up on
their reactions. The people we spoke to were either involved in the organisation, or
were those who were impressed enough to make the effort to come and talk to us.
Their views might therefore not be representative, but I suppose we could assume
they were on our side. They were kind, friendly, open and welcoming. Yet with a few
exceptions, what they said left an empty feeling. It left me asking myself whether as
players of European art music of other centuries, we have to accept that only in
Europe – and only in certain places in Europe – will we find listeners whose understanding nurtures ours. I wonder whether foreign touring is more and more
destined to bring a sense of cultural dislocation.

With a different mindset I imagine it would be possible to enjoy the feeling that
one was exporting a precious European resource to other parts of the world. Yet for
me the work of interpreting and performing is indissolubly linked to a wish for a
matching depth of response. To bring something complex and rare to an audience
who doesn't know much about what they're hearing is to be doomed to frustration.
In my group I'm the one who feels this most strongly. Indeed, I think my colleagues
would contradict me and say that they are proud to be illuminating the European
tradition in other places. But I am much more like the musician in the Chinese
anecdote which tells of a talented harpist whose greatest friend was a talented
listener. The harpist liked nothing better than to play to his friend, who understood
every nuance of his performance. Then one day the listener died. The harpist cut the
strings of his harp and never played again.

October 2001

PART TWO

Preparing and Performing

Sandor Végh and György Sebök –
a Tribute to their Teaching

Sandor Végh

If I had to say which teachers influenced me most in my musical approach, I would have to pick two, both Hungarian – the violinist Sandor Végh and the pianist György Sebök. Ironically, I didn't meet either until my studies were officially over. It was in my first year of professional life, after finishing university, that I met Sandor Végh at the International Musicians' Seminars at Prussia Cove in Cornwall. Végh had been famous for his leadership of the Végh Quartet, and in later years had built up a huge reputation as a teacher, based at the Salzburg Mozarteum. It was one of his proudest boasts that a recording of the Végh Quartet playing Beethoven had been sent into space orbit by NASA together with other items in a collection representing the best of twentieth-century life and achievement. I never heard anyone confirm this, but his telling of it impressed us all deeply.

Some years previously, Végh had visited Prussia Cove in the company of Hilary Behrens, a former student of his whose family owned the estate. Its dramatic location – a series of cottages and houses sprinkled around the lonely cliffs by an often wild sea – had impressed him immediately as a place for a music course, and he had begun a series of Easter masterclasses, which very quickly attracted international interest. To this far southwest corner of England, not easily accessible, talented string players were soon travelling from all over the world. In time Végh gathered around him colleagues who taught masterclasses in viola, cello, double bass and then chamber music, both piano-based and string-based. In the autumn, a second seminar was developed which drew together some of the finest players from the Easter seminars, along with more established international artists, who were invited to rehearse and perform chamber music in ad hoc groups. Both seminars have been hugely influential on a generation of string players and pianists, and continue today under the artistic direction of Steven Isserlis. All my colleagues in both Domus and the Florestan Trio were devoted to the Prussia Cove courses. For many years, at the start of my professional career, they were a highlight of my life.

When I first heard about Prussia Cove, there were only string classes available. As a pianist I was obviously not eligible for a place in Végh's classes, but Krysia Osostowicz suggested we apply as a violin and piano duo, and Végh agreed to teach us both. His classes took place each morning in the Great Room, a beautiful spartan drawing-room with long windows looking out on two sides to the sea just yards away. Each morning the class would gather to await the arrival of Végh, whom someone would fetch from his cottage nearby. His arrival was always an event, for he was so large and majestic. At that time he was in his late sixties, very overweight (which he constantly lamented, for it had brought on diabetes), bent forward from the waist, and waddling with his feet turned out 'at ten to two', one arm flung behind his back and the other dangling in front of him, or with both hands clasped behind his back in the manner of Beethoven in the famous contemporary sketches. Students would melt away into adjacent rooms to let Végh pass down the corridor. Because of his bulk and the way he leaned forward, he always gave the impression of being about to topple over unless someone was at hand to steady him. There was something anachronistic about his appearance; in an era of dieting and fashionable thinness, Sandor seemed like a statement of other values from other times. A German friend once described him as 'over-dimensional', which summed him up perfectly. His large, imposing head had a touch of the mediaeval Boar's Head in the carol of that name.

Végh was born in a part of Hungary that he always referred to as Transylvania. To us he was the epitome of central Europe, and of a country that was steeped in musical culture and respected musicians highly. He took it for granted that being a musician was an important and honourable calling, worthy of support and respect from everyone around. This made a big impact on us. Sadly, being a musician in Britain does not quite have the same flavour. We drank in his certainty that devoting your life to music was one of the finest things you could do.

Végh's favourite throne-like chair in the so-called Great Room was always placed in front of the rows of listeners' chairs, looking straight out to sea. This was very important both for him and us, and indeed it was the link he made between music and nature which was probably his most enduring legacy in the minds of many of his students. During the lessons, so many metaphors came from the water and the wind. It seemed very natural for him to point with his bow at the rolling waves outside. 'Look!' he would say to the student, drawing shapes in the air to mimic the motion of the sea, illustrating a rhythm, a series of waves in music, the way the trees moved their branches, the breathing sound of the tide as it sighed over the beach, the rise and fall of a long phrase in Beethoven. The closeness of the sea and of nature in general provided a whole inventory of images which seemed entirely natural for him to use. If we were lucky we might find that the motion of a particular piece of music was actually in time with the motion of the sea outside. Talk of 'natural shapes' and the 'rise and fall' of musical phrases was easy to understand. We somehow felt that as musicians we were engaged in a process no less important than making a flower bloom or a tree produce fruit. A piece of music would come to life in the room, and to the counterpoint of wind and waves close by. All this elevated the teaching of music to a grandeur I had not experienced before. My previous teachers had spoken of the importance of playing something beautifully, but their manner implied that music was a delightful enhancement of life, not an expression of life itself. Now, with elemental forces in evidence all around us in Prussia Cove, music seemed to be such a force too. We all felt its power, and that made us feel powerful.

This way of tying everything to natural, organic movement or speech applied to a single note as well as to a whole movement or piece. A single note had a rise and fall, a curve, an onset and a decay – which he liked to say was why the bow is made with a curved stick. He disapproved of the simple 'up bow, down bow' terminology of the

English, preferring the 'tirez, poussez' of French, which to him was more dynamic. On the other hand he disapproved of the German word 'Satz' (which literally means 'sentence'), preferring the English 'movement'. 'Slow *movement!*' he would say. 'How beautiful! Slow *movement!*'

Végh did not speak English well, and over the years he had evolved a unique blend of the various languages at his command. If he couldn't think of the word in English, he would just anglicise a word from German, French or Italian. His English had a highly distinctive stamp, partly because of his habit of translating idioms direct from other languages ('I feel me like a fish on the dry', for example) and partly because of his speech intonation. Two examples: his use of the word 'Quasi!', pronounced 'Kvasi!' and meaning 'That's on the right lines!', and his phrase 'That is!', meaning 'Now you've got it!' Both were delivered in a kind of falsetto, the syllables hugely drawn-out, the second syllable dropping almost an octave below the first, like two loud, slow emphatic minims in music.

I was a Scot used to a quieter style of teaching, and Végh's manner was a shock. For a start, there was no question of dialogue: he spoke, you listened. He was very personal and free with his comments both good and bad. Furthermore, he was very capricious, and would subject everyone to his bad moods without shame. If you had your lesson on a bad day, you could be fairly sure that some gratuitous insults would be thrown into the pot. He could be noble and generous with praise – 'You are like the young Ysaÿe!' (a reference to the distinguished Belgian violinist) – but also mean and unfair without cause. He was quite capable of reducing a nervous student to a state where they lost all their poise, and then he would pounce. For example, he once told a student in front of the whole class, 'Between you and music, my dear, there is a brick wall forever fixed.' This unkindness was something I never got used to, and it was my first close encounter with the paradox that sometimes runs through the behaviour of great artists. I admired his musicianship greatly, and I had always imagined that great artists would be great people. That this is often not so has been the subject matter of many heartrending books, but it remains a paradox.

Sandor was well aware of the brutal side of his nature, but he allowed it free rein nevertheless. Once in a lesson he reduced a student a state of nervous terror with his merciless comments. Watching her face, he leaned forward and said in a more detached tone, 'Don't show me you are afraid. When I see you are afraid, *I am like the biting dog what come always nearer.*' The remark was not addressed to me, but I took it to heart and tried to remember not to cringe in difficult moments.

Though I started out as a student, after that first Prussia Cove seminar Sandor asked me to work with him as the official pianist for his classes, both there in and other European countries where he held summer masterclasses. I did this for several years. The lessons were ostensibly for the violinists, but they might as well have been for me, as all the musical comments could be applied to playing the piano as well. Absorbing what he had to say, hour after hour and day after day on those courses, was as important a slice of musical education as I ever had.

But working with him was a strain as well as an opportunity. His sudden changes of mood and of plans – of which he often neglected to inform me – made life difficult, and I often had to take a deep breath and remind myself that I was fortunate to be working with someone of such magisterial musical experience and insight.

Shortly after I first met him, he asked if I would play for a mastercourse in

Switzerland. He told me that I would be paid a fee, and that he couldn't remember quite how much, but that the administrator would sort everything out when I arrived. At that stage I was not experienced enough to ask for an agreement in writing. When I arrived in Switzerland, the administrator broke the news that there wasn't a fee and never had been; they relied on us young professionals doing it 'for experience'. I had counted on a Swiss fee to tide me through the summer, so this was a serious blow.

But when I plucked up courage to approach Végh at his dinner table to ask him to intervene on my behalf, he kept on eating and grandly informed me that the experience would no doubt be useful for me in other ways, and that one shouldn't only focus on money. Although his remark may have been true in an absolute sense, I felt it was hypocritical. The next day I took a cable-car to the top of a mountain and wandered round on the top for hours, hoping that my anger would blow away in the wind.

On another occasion, in Italy, he asked me if I would like to perform a programme of Beethoven and Brahms sonatas with him at the Maestros' Concert, which closed the summer course. He told me that we'd have time to rehearse towards the end of the course. I was very excited and spent days practising the piano parts of the sonatas, one of which was new to me. One afternoon, just before our rehearsals were due to begin, I was passing the main square and saw a poster for the Maestros' Concert, but to my dismay it stated that Sandor would be playing unaccompanied Bach sonatas. There was no mention of me. That afternoon I asked him if there was some mistake, and he told me that he had concluded he didn't have time to practise the Beethoven and Brahms violin parts, and had decided to play solo Bach instead. I protested that I had spent many days practising the piano parts, but he only looked cross and said, 'Such work is never wasted.' These were bruising experiences for a novice, and I wasn't the only one who had them. But I don't mean to sound ungrateful; it was also an unparallelled opportunity to learn the repertoire quickly in the presence of an expert. And in fact it was not very different from the age-old apprentice system, though without the master being frank about the terms and conditions.

One had to learn to see things in perspective. I particular remember an occasion in Italy. There was a Japanese girl in the class who was greatly in awe of Végh, and she told me she was inwardly trembling in all her lessons. He seemed to smell her fear and subjected her to a merciless spate of criticism, mocking her demeanour, her femininity, the way she wilted under criticism, and telling her that she didn't understand music at all. Naturally, her playing got worse and worse. One night towards the end of the course the students gathered in a square in the village and sat round in a big circle. Someone had a violin with them and played a folk tune on it. Someone else suggested that the violin be passed around the circle, and that other people might contribute folk songs from their own country. And so the violin eventually came to this Japanese girl. To everyone's great surprise, she played some sad Japanese folk songs in an entrancing style, sweet, poignant and natural with no trace of the physical stiffness we had all seen in her lessons. This was a very important scene for us all to witness, and I think everyone understood then that a powerful teacher can inhibit as well as inspire.

Végh could be equally powerful in praise, of course. Years later I can recall some of the things he said to me when he was pleased. For example, he once said that he had been feeling tired and out of sorts when he arrived for his class that morning, but that my playing had restored him to a sense that everything was all right with the world. He would say, 'I don't know anyone who makes the piano sound more beautiful.' Going even further, he would compliment me on my playing of his beloved Bartók, and say that I 'must have Hungarian blood to understand it so well'. When he was particularly pleased he would swivel round in his chair to make sure the whole class was paying attention, and with a delighted expression he would indicate me (or whoever he was pleased with) and, beaming, would repeat, 'That is! That is!' in rapturous tones. To be thus described felt like a kind of blessing, and the effect would last for days.

I went back to Prussia Cove many times to be the official pianist for Végh's masterclasses, and I played the piano parts of all the sonatas and concertos that violinists brought to lessons. As I had no advance notice of what they would play, I was forced to sight-read whatever I didn't know. It required strong nerves to play in public, and in front of a roomful of talented musicians, a piece one had never seen before and make it sound plausible. Végh was quite aware of this, as he used the same system in his Salzburg masterclasses. Nevertheless it didn't stop him, when in a bad mood, from shouting at me in front of everyone, 'Why you play wrong notes! Why!' If I dared to answer, 'Sandor, I'm seeing this for the first time!' he would wave me away with an imperious gesture and a Dickensian 'Pah!' or 'Pshaw!' At other times, in a good mood, he would halt the poor violinist in mid-flow and treat the audience to a glowing disquisition on my many virtues, declaring that he had never come across such a fine chamber musician. The kudos of that would tide me over until the next time he pointed his bow at me and shouted, 'Why you play blah-blah-blah? You don't know Bartók's Second Sonata? You never studied this great piece? Eh?' I daresay even he couldn't have sight-read Bartók in public.

Each morning Végh taught for three hours, and during that time he was scheduled to teach three violinists. If he got carried away with the first student of the day, he was liable to go on for a couple of hours, during which the second and third students would start to make frantic gestures at me from the back of the room, pointing at their watches. I would try to interrupt Sandor in mid-flow, but once he became engrossed it was like trying to stop a juggernaut from rolling down the hill. Eventually I would have to stand up and announce that it was time to let someone else play. Even though he himself had asked to teach three students each morning, he never ceased to be cross with me for reminding him.

Végh had certain obsessions that he would indulge in one lesson after another. For example, anyone daring to bring Brahms' G major violin and piano sonata, opus 78 would be certain to be stopped after a few bars and ruthlessly subjected to Végh's classic speech on the subject, which I heard so often I could have sent him out of the room and delivered it myself. His concept involved a circular bowing action that caught up the dotted notes of the opening violin melody, and he took this as a microcosm of the approach needed throughout. Any hint of straight lines and non-breathing was immediately stamped on. His own playing of the opening bars was so extreme that it seemed a caricature (and indeed it was caricatured by many of the students in private) but often once it had been digested by an intelligent student, a diluted version would seem just right.

Végh had many Oriental students – mostly Japanese and Korean. He would often congratulate them on being Asian. They would smile politely, and then listen as he explained how much he valued the peaceful serenity of Buddha statues. He would contrast the smiling meditating Buddha with the traditional icons of Christianity, particularly Christ suffering on the cross. He asked us all what kind of religion would confront believers with this cruel image of suffering, and whether we wouldn't prefer instead a religion symbolised by the smiling, peaceful Buddha concentrating on inner beauty. At such moments I think we must all have recognised the resemblance between Végh on his throne in the Great Room, listening with his eyes closed, and an image of the Buddha – except that Végh would have been a grumpy Buddha.

Another tirade, perhaps his lengthiest, was prompted by any American player or anyone playing in 'the American style' he despised. Constant, unvarying vibrato, an attitude of big tonal projection that had nothing to do with the music – this would inspire a long speech about the importance of the Austro-Hungarian tradition. Situating himself in a line which went back through his teacher Hubay to the violinist Joseph Joachim and Brahms, he would explain that all these people liked music to have a 'speaking' quality about it, a way of phrasing and articulating that was in proportion to the music and what it expressed, an unbreakable link between content of music and manner of performance. He emphasised that we must all follow natural patterns of speaking or singing, the shapes of phrases that follow nature's shapes, the vibrato following the shape and rising or declining with it. He stressed the importance of phrases linked to one another like phrases in grammar, building into larger structures, delivering *meaning* above all. What meaning? The meaning of breathing, of musical life sustained by rise and fall, taking in and giving out; speaking to the audience through the music, and telling them something about life. He called it 'giving, not showing', and complained that Americans were seducing us all into showing off, being image- and beauty-conscious above all.

The beauty he was after had ugliness mixed in as well. To him, roughness where roughness was required was part of beauty. When he got started on this topic – 'You people never realised you are the heirs to the Austro-Hungarian tradition!' – the poor violinist would stand with violin still on shoulder and bow in hand, ready to continue as soon as Végh stopped talking. As the minutes ticked by, the student's violin would droop and eventually the player would tuck it discreetly under his arm – but still had to stand in front of the class while Végh orated, oblivious to the student's discomfort. I was sitting at the piano, and used to push my piano stool quietly against the wall so that I could lean against it while the speech unfolded. It never ceased to amaze me that he could deliver it each time with exactly the same gusto and sense of mission. In this sense he was a great teacher – in that he retained such a lively sense of the importance of what he had to tell each student. He never seemed to think, 'I said all this yesterday. I can't be bothered to say it again.' Every student was an irreplaceable opportunity for him to get certain messages across. Indeed, when I think back on it more than twenty years later, I think his speech on the disappearing European traditions – which we all mocked affectionately – was probably his most important legacy. He was right to stress the importance of linking oneself to a tradition of speaking and sharing rather than shining and dazzling. Already at that time big careers were being made in America by 'dazzlers', and such playing is now so commonplace and so widespread internationally that for many listeners, this is what violin playing is all about. Indeed, the American style of playing (big, strong, beautiful tone above all) has become dominant in the world. For some time I've been aware that Végh was right to warn us that a tradition of playing could actually be lost unless a new generation consciously carried it along. He felt that a new generation was sanitising and glamourising great music.

Today, when the media often try to present classical music as 'de-stressing' or 'relaxing' or 'soothing', there is a real danger of losing touch with music's ability to run the whole gamut from despair to joy, with all manner of light and dark in between. Végh was instinctively aware of this, and of music's power to represent our experience of life – not just the soothing moments, but the painful, crooked, searching ones as well. Great music encompasses all these, but one could easily forget it when listening to today's radio stations telling us to 'lie back and relax to the classics'. 'Had a rough day? Unwind with Brahms's Second Symphony!' Even Végh didn't imagine that development. He probably would have agreed with Brecht that if truth was not beauty, then beauty could not be truth. Sometimes when I listen to adverts for 'chill out with the classics' discs I imagine Sandor hearing them and saying, 'My mouth is o-pen!'

When I knew Sandor he was around 70, though we could never be sure because different works of reference gave different birthdates for him. His playing, never a textbook example of tonal beauty in any case, had become eccentric. His violin – disappearing into the folds of flesh around his chin, and dwarfed by his enormous hand – looked tiny, and his sound was thin and often rough or scratchy. His intonation was rough too, usually on the flat side. Yet he was quick to pounce on students with poor intonation, first complaining, then demonstrating the 'correct version' in a way that made them open their eyes wide with surprise while trying to keep a respectful expression on their faces.

People who had never heard any recordings of Végh in his youth were amazed, sometimes dismayed, when they heard him play in concerts, as he sometimes did during the masterclass course. One seemed to hear through a glass darkly what he must have been like as a younger man, though right to the end he retained that powerful sense of communicating meaning to the audience which for me was his finest and most vital quality. I still can count on the fingers of one hand those artists whose playing can make me feel that I am not only hearing music but also, mysteriously, *being given information*. Végh's playing was like this. It certainly demonstrated that uniform beauty of tone, projection, and perfect tuning are by no means essential for communicating the inner essence of a great work of music. How this can be so remains a paradox, one of many surrounding him.

György Sebök

If Sandor Végh was larger than life and overwhelmingly physical, the Hungarian pianist György Sebök was just the opposite. Even now when I think back to our first meeting, I have the feeling that perhaps he wasn't there at all. He was a small man who moved carefully and economically, spoke quietly, and harboured his powers. Sitting at the piano, with his short stature but his surprisingly long arms, and his bright eyes twinkling at us from his merry, wrinkled face, there was the tiniest hint of a super-intelligent simian creature. You might not have noticed him in the street, but in the realm of his piano classes he exerted quiet but total mastery.

His method contrasted strongly with that of Sandor Végh, for instead of dominating with his personality and insisting on being the centre of attention, he almost seemed to subtract himself from the room so that only the student was there. Indeed, one of the most remarkable things about György Sebök was how differently he approached different students, somehow sensing what it was they needed to hear. Perhaps all gifted teachers can do this, but what I particularly cherished about Sebök was his ability to put things into words. And what words! I still feel a sense of awe that anyone could phrase things so beautifully in what was, after all, his second language. Perhaps, indeed, it was the fact of English being his second language that expunged all sense of superfluous words or small talk from his lessons. He perhaps didn't know how to say things casually in English, and thus everything emerged in lapidary form, with no waste to cut away.

Having had regular lessons since early childhood, I thought I had experienced the full range of verbal expression that piano playing could draw from teachers. I had had teachers who spoke about technique, those who concentrated on musical matters, those who were analytical, those who were theatrical, and those who related things to the history of music. Nevertheless I still remember the amazement with which I heard György Sebök speak about aspects of playing and performing that I had no idea *could* be spoken about. He was the first, and so far the only teacher I ever met who was able to leap from matters of piano playing to metaphysics. His métier happened to be the piano, but I felt that he could have taught anything he had decided to focus on.

I met Sebök when Domus spent one winter semester at the Banff Centre in Canada in 1983. The Banff Centre hosted a roster of visiting arts staff; nobody was there all the time, but a succession of interesting people came to teach for a week or two. One could apply to have lessons with whoever seemed relevant to one's programme of study. Many of the names were well-known in North America, but not to us, so we randomly signed up for lessons with Sebök, of whom we had never heard. After those lessons I wrote the following pages about him, which I include here because they give an impression of the powerful impact he made on me.

'Sebök says he sees his job to be like a mirror. Sometimes he is exactly that, a pure description without judgement. Sometimes he is the cruel mirror of fairytale, the mirror which shows the splintered heart, the cracked smile. Other times he is the mirror hung in kindly light. His powers of reflection seem to get colder and more penetrating as the student is more gifted. When he smiles easily and compliments on little things, it usually means that he has made a judgement about the futility of going further or dealing on a higher level. When he uses his powers of observation like a surgical knife to cut away dead tissue and incise fine lines so that blood appears on the surface, it often means that he respects that student's achievement and considers that they can go even further.

'But he does not seem perfectly in control of that caged animal, his lion of instinct. He sits there with his mild urbane European manner, his cool rational smile, his discreet grey clothes proclaiming his self-control. He makes himself empty and then the lion wakes up in him and prowls out of his head while he listens to the student play. Sometimes it knocks the student senseless with a powerful sweep of the paw. Sometimes it is like the lion Aslan in C.S. Lewis's Narnia books, a loving protector. I had two lessons with him, one by myself and one with the group. By myself I had a wonderful feeling of repose in his presence, as one has with someone whose insight and observation one trusts completely. I felt that he sympathetically entered the world of my imagination, and from the inside, so to speak, opened me outwards.

'In the second lesson, though his observation was working just as keenly, I felt that he was incising lines from outside, digging into us with objective skill, not aligned with us in our search. I saw a mixture of these approaches, the objective and the subjective, with many of the students. I saw him with great dignity step away from a talented student, sum them up with the implied judgement that something fundamentally was wrong. Conversely I saw him labour lovingly over a half-talented student with an open mind, working marvels in the course of a single lesson. I saw him revert coldly to being a descriptive mirror with a girl whose manner implored guidance, and who was certainly intelligent enough to take it. I saw him judge and abandon a shy player who, he thought, did not really want to stop being shy. Yet he never did these things with contempt, or overt dislike. He just smiled at them in a certain way and the audience knew that his spirit had drawn away.

'Krysia and Robin asked him if he had ever written a book. He said that he never would, and hated the idea of repeating himself or condemning himself to a formula. He said he tried to make himself empty and let things come to him, and thought that his great gift as a teacher was the ability to respond exactly to a person and a situation. In general he spoke of his gift as though he was the medium and not the message, and he kept the instrument finely tuned so that the message could take any form, instinctual, intellectual, imaginative, emotional. All these faculties in him seemed razor sharp, and his manner suggested that he viewed himself like a valuable set of lenses always sparkling and perfectly organised.

'He had no strong personal manner but a quiet intense vigilance. He was not a modest man, and would never hesitate to pronounce an opinion on any topic; at meals, in answer to small talk or mild questioning, he would pronounce with merciless authority on any topic from psychology to the nuclear arms race. All his observations were delivered as though self-evident; he never made preamble or apologised for a strong opinion – everything he said had an unspoken "of course it is the case" in front of it.

'It usually was the case, too, but I had never heard anyone except Peter Brook so certain of the veracity of his opinions. He relayed them, as Brook did, like simple facts as though he was telling you the answer to two times two, whereas he was answering a question like What is the right way to overcome indecision? or How should I work on a new piece? No question seemed to surprise him, and it was inconceivable that anyone could have such faith in the powers of his own judgement unless he believed, as Brook perhaps does, that he is not the author of his own opinions, that he simply lets his mind hear the collective unconscious.

'He was talking one day about the eminent pianist Clara Haskil, how he heard her play a Mozart concerto on the radio and had the strange impression that he was listening to Mozart himself playing the piano. It was as though Clara Haskil had disappeared and that no human intermediary was coming between Sebök and Mozart. But, he said, there are ways and ways of disappearing. This window, he said, disappears when I look through it and yet I do not respect it for disappearing. It adds nothing to my appreciation of the nature which I see through it. But there is a way of disappearing so that the music becomes more perfectly itself and at the same time the performer is perfectly himself too.

'This reminded me of Peter Brook, and how he spoke of assimilating the role and giving it back to the audience. Sebök was always against playing which demonstrated how beautiful were the feelings of the performer, rather than how beautiful the music was. You can draw attention to yourself or you can draw attention to Mozart, he said, and was always alert for gestures and hand movement which illustrated both these types of playing.

'He told us one day that when he was young, and still living in Hungary, he had a feeling that nothing could go wrong for him. He had a feeling of special privilege, and was so sure of his inviolability that he used to sight-read things "live" on the radio, as a kind of proof. He told us that he had a regular spot on radio, and as a kind of "dare" he would wait until the red light went on before opening a volume of piano music he had chosen at random from the library, and sightreading it on air. "I don't know now how I had the nerve", he commented. After he left Hungary, he said he lost that feeling of special protection, and at the same time lost the certainty of his technique on the piano. He realised that anything could happen to him. "It was really like being chased from Paradise", he said with the cool wry émigré's smile behind elegant smoke.

'These were the moments about him that moved me most, when he spoke words that an angel might have spoken, but spoke them with the demeanour of a dry lawyer. Suddenly in lessons he would start to speak of God or the spirit or gravity or poetry with the same manner that he had been using to speak of pedalling a moment before. I used to feel slightly breathless, as though I had been magically transported to a very high altitude. He did not change gear or tone of voice or quality of smile when he passed from the mundane to the stratospheric.

'There was no theatrical climax to his lessons as there was to Végh's lessons, no audible build-up of excitement. But very often what he was saying would become more and more rarefied, would probe deeper into the mind, become more poetical in substance. His voice purred on in measured tones, so that the shape of the lesson was worked only in the imagination of the hearers. It was a little like playing a Mozart sonata pianissimo throughout, so that the lyrical moments, or the moments of culmination, simply had to be expressive because structurally they *were* expressive, not because of the expressive manner of their performance.

'He did not indicate to his listeners mundanity or ethereal poetry. Yet there was a theatrical quality about his lessons, and the shape of them often stayed in the mind like the shape of a piece of sculpture. Listening to his lessons was like reading the script of a Shakespeare play to yourself in a private room. Pure content divorced from manner. Deep, shallow, fast, slow, all mockingly equalised on the printed page and only you, the solitary reader, to realise what was really being said.

'Sebök says that he has no special technique of piano playing to advocate; he just tries to see where the reality of someone's playing falls short of the dream, and he tries to help them bridge that gap. This gives a clue as to why he sometimes abandons someone to the fate of their own playing: when he senses that there is no dream, or that the reality (inadequate as it usually is) is perfectly satisfying to the player. For example he lost interest in one student's playing of Mozart, saying that he had stepped back from the music in the wrong way, not into objectivity ("and in my opinion objective love is the greatest love") but into indifference. The student tried but couldn't break through to another level, and perhaps Sebök judged that he had no dream of better playing.

'With a Canadian girl he also thought there was a problem with the ideal vision. She played, he said, as though she had read about ideal Brahms interpretation in a book and was trying to reproduce someone else's idea of the music instead of her own. He said that he definitely felt it was not "her" Brahms he was listening to; he said he felt as if he was eating the cookbook instead of the meal. She listened carefully and he seemed intent on breaking through her barrier, but with a little experiment it emerged that perhaps "her" Brahms was not accessible even to her.

'With some students the dream of better playing was always there, ready to be tapped just as soon as he had convinced them that they were allowed to play beautifully. Sometimes the student merely seemed baffled by the notion that their ideal was, or might be, different from what they were actually doing: Why would I not be playing it if I had the idea in my head? they seemed to say. He always forgave someone boring playing if he thought that self-confidence was all that was needed to permit them entry to their own imagination. Indeed it often seemed, as in the case of a Japanese girl who mechanically clattered through a Mozart sonata, that a student only needed to be given permission to play well, and would then immediately start doing so. Sometimes he would strive to give someone the freedom of their imagination, and then they would appear perplexed, as though not sure why he would think that their worked-out interpretation and their "ideal" interpretation were different things.'

After meeting Sebök in Canada, we asked him where we might find him when we wanted to have further lessons, and he told us about his summer courses in Ernen. This was a village in the mountains of Canton Wallis in Switzerland where he had established his own masterclasses, teaching in the schoolroom, with students billeted in chalets and small hotels all around the village. There were people who travelled there each summer, some from America, just to listen to the classes though they were not pianists themselves. For several summers we went there and had lessons both as individuals and as a chamber group. It was a slightly strange experience because, although Sebök was the only teacher and the entire focus of the course, he did nothing to try and draw it together socially. One felt that he was happy if his students liked one another and became friends, but again, he had subtracted himself from that side of things. He would appear just in time to teach the classes, and disappear at the end, not to be seen again for the rest of the day. Once or twice Krysia Osostowicz and I, who were sharing a chalet, plucked up courage to ask him and Mrs Sebök to tea. This was regarded with amazement by the old-timers: 'you asked Sebök *to tea*!!?' The Seböks came, but I don't think they enjoyed the experience. Small talk was not Sebök's idea of a good time, and indeed it seemed important for him to maintain a distance between himself and his students. I don't think this was done to maintain status; I think he had to be like that to preserve his ability to look at them clearly. No doubt one can get close to someone and still see them clearly, but this was not his temperament; he needed to be detached. Some of his students were with him for many years, at the University of Indiana at Bloomington in the USA, where he had a professorship. Yet even for these long-term students he remained, I believe, an enigmatic figure. More than one of his Bloomington students told me how strange it was to be so close to and yet so remote from such a brilliant professor.

He would pronounce in public on the most intimate facets of one's musical personality, but conversation with him did not become easy or natural as a result. I always felt that he 'switched on' to people during lessons, and 'off' when he was not teaching. I never felt, for example, that I could go to ask his advice on a personal matter, despite the fact that he had seen deeply into my musical character, and by extension, into my life. I did keep up a sporadic correspondence with him during the years after I stopped going to his summer masterclasses, but our exchanges consisted of me telling him things, and him responding that he hoped I would continue to do so – not, of course, reciprocating with any news of his own, except for a brief outline of his itinerary that year. It was always daunting to see how many countries he planned to visit and how many students he planned to teach.

Sebök's teaching had a curious double effect on me, an effect that he would no doubt have enjoyed analysing and describing. On the one hand, he suddenly gave me a glimpse, followed by a long look, into a world of teaching that I had not imagined could exist. This was inspiring, to say the least. And I can honestly say that I have never stopped thinking about the principles he enunciated in his lessons. On the other hand, his example inhibited me terribly. I felt he had set a standard that I could never live up to.

When I started teaching, several years after I stopped seeing him, I tried to prepare myself by reading through the notes I had made during his lessons. This, as he would have said himself, was a bit like eating the cookbook instead of making the meal. I felt him hovering over me, but in a spirit of amusement rather than encouragement. I tried to listen to my students and ask myself, 'What would Sebök say if he were here?' It didn't work, of course. I found eventually that my own way was different from Sebök's in any case. I don't have his capacity for ruthless forensic investigation in public. This may be a blessing as well as a drawback.

One aspect of Sebök's teaching that puzzled us all, and I daresay puzzled him too, was that his career as a performer was not more successful. During lessons, he was the best demonstrator I ever heard. His playing was perfectly matched to the wonderfully precise and colourful descriptions he had just given the student. Indeed, his demonstrations of how to make certain sounds, how to present certain composers, how to function at the keyboard were so right that they very often provoked gasps of admiration or gales of laughter, whichever was appropriate.

Mostly these demonstrations were fragments of pieces, or just single bars or groups of bars. When you heard him give these illustrations, you couldn't help thinking, 'My God! He must be the best pianist in the whole world.'

And yet when you heard him play a whole work in a recital (an opportunity I only had a few times) there was something strangely disappointing about it. The magic of his illustrations seemed to desert him when he himself was the performer, not just the agent of someone else's performing. Everyone noticed it, and I think we were all slightly at a loss to know what to say to him after concerts, when he seemed quietly avid for reassurance. His concert playing was indeed absolutely authoritative and competent, but it lacked the *ne plus ultra* quality of his playing when he was 'demonstrating' to us. Perhaps his was the sort of power that functioned best through the medium of another person, an object rather than a subject. I don't doubt that this aspect of György Sebök has deep significance for any future biographer.

Sebök's death in November 1999 gave me a peculiar feeling of sadness. I was stunned to think that his insight would be no longer available to us, his students, but at the same time I realised that he would in no sense have welcomed or even recognised that we felt personally bereft. He did not acknowledge that one had become close to him, but I can certainly say that I had formed a bond with the way his mind worked, whether he liked it or not. I think that because he saw himself as 'the medium' through whom the message came, it did not seem appropriate to him that one should form a bond with the medium instead of the message. Or there may have been less high-minded reasons for his indifference. I always had the feeling of being kept at arm's length, and in fact it may be that he did not know how to accept friendship.

After he died it occurred to me that many people would never have the chance of hearing him teach, and that my notes on his lessons might be interesting to people who are curious about his approach. I then stopped feeling so guilty about all the times when I sat in the classroom in Ernen, Switzerland, writing down his comments in my notebook. As far as I remember I was the only person to do so, and it seemed to annoy everyone around me, who could not understand why I was not content to bask in the reverential atmosphere of the class. But I think that my notes, which after all represent just a tiny fraction of his teaching, demonstrate the extraordinary range of his knowledge and understanding. More than that, some of his comments still give me the *frisson* of being in touch with transcendental thought. Here is just a tiny selection of them, to give a flavour:

'If you want a student to think in longer units, you have to give them more material for thinking. If you don't, they will simply stretch the music like chewing-gum, which when stretched is not more chewing-gum, but just thinner. With long-unit thinking, you also need amplitude.'

'Before a difficult passage, it helps to unfocus slightly. This doesn't mean that you should go on automatic pilot, but that you should loosen the vision, the concentration slightly so that it becomes peripheral. Many people concentrate fiercely in order to get through the passage, and allow themselves to relax afterwards. But they should relax *before* it. Then knowing – rather than concentration – can take over.'

'Total participation in one's playing doesn't mean heaving around. Imagine meeting someone and shaking hands with them. If they pump your hand up and down manically, will you think them more sincere? If they squeeze your hand and grip it for a long time, will you believe them more? A warm handshake is far more likely to convince you. In other words, the *character* of the participation is important. The warm handshake *has* total participation. The hyperactive handshake doesn't have more participation, just a different kind. It may have even less participation!'

'Some things one can't practise slowly. Water-skiing is an obvious example!'

'Two balancing forces rule every natural movement; thus, all good ritenutos have an accelerando somewhere inside them. A good crescendo has a piano somewhere; an upbeat hints at a downbeat, and vice versa. So music becomes like life, or *lifelike*.'

'Pianists are often too influenced by the fact that they play the piano sitting down. Their wave of movement goes from their head to the piano stool and stops. But there should be a longer wave which goes right down to the ground.'

[This is a treasured memory of mine – Sebök trying to persuade a Spanish cellist to be less nervous about performing:] 'You know those statues of the hero on the horse? *You should look like the horse.*'

'Some people don't play long notes – they play short notes and hold them. A long note should have an internal life.'

'Any fixed idea becomes a blurred spot in your vision or thinking. It may even start by being a good idea: you can be a pianist who marches under the flag of phrasing, or one who cares deeply about dynamics. But even a good idea can prevent you from seeing things as they really are. When you [a Japanese pianist] play, I don't hear anything *but* phrasing; I don't hear music.'

'A sound is something you mean. Your hands should not be independent of you.'

'Many pianists don't think of their hands as having weight. Thus the work of sound can be done by the weight of the finger dropping onto the key. Some people's hands behave as if they are skimming the surface, unaware of their weight. Others put the weight in with effort. Horowitz always found time in between notes to relax his hand and to use the whip motion, the focused drop that made you feel the notes were falling through the keyboard. [The class laughs as he demonstrates Horowitz's characteristic hand action and then looks under the keyboard for the notes which have dropped onto the floor.] Use the weight and the right effort, let the forte happen, have the courage of the "*now*" forte!'

'There is a basic fear of attacking the key, descending in the key. We fight this unconscious fear with a conscious courage. But I can't really use conscious courage to persuade my fingers to *trust*. If I am not afraid, I don't need courage. What you must develop is trust, not courage.'

'[On string playing:] A player is identified with the instrument at three points – the left hand, the right hand, and where the bow is in contact with the string. The third of these is very interesting because it does not involve the hand *holding* or *moving*. This third point is like standing in a river with water pushing against your legs.

You're not aware of water flowing away and past you, though it is. You're aware of the constant pushing of *new* water. In the same way, a string player has to focus on this *staying-point* of the bow on the string, always going away and yet staying. Don't go with it, stay with it! Don't travel with the sound or the bow; *be in the point of contact*, focused there, although your hands move on the bow and the string.'

'You must transfer your thought from one note to the next, participate in the *information* conveyed by the note F going to the note C. The letters 'T,O, B,E,O,R,N,O,T,T,O,B,E', etc. are *information*. 'To be or not to be' is the *message*. You must first convey the information in order to convey the message as well.'

'Remember the aim is to know more, not to concentrate more. When you know more, you concentrate less.'

Reading of his death in 1999, I picked up a volume of Beethoven violin and piano sonatas and opened it at the slow movement of opus 96, where after the lesson I had scribbled down a series of consecutive comments he made, *sotto voce*, in my ear while listening to me playing the piano part:

1. 'Technique must disappear.'
2. 'The instrument must disappear.'
3. 'Don't have a tempo.'
4. (a moment later) 'But don't be neutral!'
5. 'Don't give it a shape – it *has* a shape.'
6. 'Don't be a soloist' – (and, wickedly, a moment later) – 'or accompanist.'

The weightless, limitless sensation that these observations produced in me was a profound and unforgettable experience.

December 2002

A Performer's Experience of
the Recording Process

In May 1998 I was invited to Jerusalem to give a talk at a conference about recording. Most of the contributors were academics and historians, and the organisers decided that they needed a view from the other side of the microphone, as it were – to show what recording is like for players. My speech focused on my first experience of recording, which came as something of a shock. Since then I have made many records and have grown used to the process, and I have enormous respect for the producers and engineers with whom we collaborate. In particular I pay tribute to the meticulous producer Andrew Keener, who has become so attuned to the working methods of the Florestan Trio that he really seems like a fourth member of the group when we are making a record.

After I had given my talk in Jerusalem, I found that many of the listeners, expert though they were in various fields of study connected with recordings, were unaware of what actually goes on in a recording session. If this is so, then many record-buyers must be in the dark as well. For this reason I decided to include my conference paper in this book.

My experience of recording began by being taped at concerts and rehearsals throughout my student years. These were always negative experiences; I never thought that the result sounded 'like me'. This was partly due to the poor quality of the recording equipment and the lack of knowledge of where to put the microphone in the room, but I always found that beyond being a simple proof that the concert took place, there was no pleasure to be had from listening to a recording.

Although I now have the best of recording equipment, fine venues, and superb producers and engineers at my disposal, I still have a very distrustful relationship with records, and almost never listen to my own once I have given my suggestions to the producer after hearing the 'edited version'. Why is this?

It is partly that a record conveys *only* the sound, and therefore your eyes are not there to help you while you listen. When you go to a concert you hear *and* see the player; body language can be expressive, and you add the information you get from seeing to the information you get from listening. A player's relationship to his instrument is something that can be hinted at, but not completely conveyed, by a sound recording. And personally, as someone who is often told that it is interesting to watch me play, I feel diminished by the knowledge that a record is 'only' the sound.

When I am at a concert, I see how the player makes the sound, and I can also observe the rapport between the players, which certainly expresses itself in the sound, but also in lots of other ways, not transferable to a disc. Therefore I don't feel entirely happy about people listening to my chamber music records in a faraway place. Will they glean anything about the way we relate to one another?

I asked several of my colleagues if they are happy to be represented on disc *only* by the sound of their playing, and they said yes, so perhaps I am in the minority on this question. Essentially they felt that the part stands for the whole, that there's nothing about their musicianship that would be absent from a record. Nevertheless my own special musical memories, of other people's playing, all derive from occasions when I have been present in the room, or at least able to see them. I understand things from their faces that may not be immediately apparent in what they are playing. I intercept and understand the looks that pass between them. I forgive them wrong notes and technical slips if I can see what happened, or perhaps they have charmed me with a wry smile or a self-deprecating look at that moment. Of course this is not possible with a record, where nothing will ever mitigate an error; an error, moreover, destined to be repeated whenever the disc is played.

I must, however, declare an inconsistency in my attitude: I would not like to have a video/sound recording of my group instead! I find that recording engenders a tremendous self-consciousness because of the process of repeating and polishing and selecting, not to mention the drive to eradicate imperfections. And I feel that if the same process were applied to our appearance – indeed, if 'ugly' or 'flawed' expressions were deemed to be unacceptable, and the performance repeated until the player were able to achieve facial beauty as well as musical accuracy, the whole process would be unbearable. It would increase our self-consciousness to a maddening extent.

As things are, I expect that a lot of our good playing has been done with rumpled hair, sweaty faces, grimaces of all sorts and a floor strewn with biscuits and old coffee cups, none of which matter as it is 'only' the sound which is being recorded.

So – I feel uncomfortable with my records because they are only a partial document about us. Another reason for discomfort is that I know the finished product presents a performance which never in fact took place. This is for me a much more serious objection to records, one which I have had to accept – and sometimes appreciate – but still feel peculiar about.

Unless one is exceptionally lucky, and can play accurately, musically, and without mishaps and background noises in one single 'take', any record is going to be made out of 'bits' strung together. If these 'bits' were all the best bits of our playing, amounting to an ideal portrait, this might be a good feeling. All too often, however, I know that the bit which is finally selected is a bit which is accurate, blemish-free and free of extraneous noise, but not necessarily the bit on which I played my best, or indeed the bit on which we achieved musical unanimity.

Over the years we have discussed this with our producers, and have agreed that a compelling musical sweep, or an inspired risk, should be preserved on disc even if it has technical problems. The producer's tendency, however, is to identify those compelling sweeps and, if they have technical flaws, to make us do them again until 'the same' musical result is achieved but with less inaccuracy. And I know very well that some of my best phrasing, some of my most finely judged tone colour, has not been included on a record – for non-musical reasons.

Therefore, when listening to a record, I often have to sigh, because it presents a blemish-free but antiseptic picture of our playing, and it gives the impression that we have mastery over nerves and fatigue, which is of course absolutely untrue. I also have to smile, because I realise that never in a concert have we negotiated every difficulty with the sovereign ease that we seem to have on our records. But what will the listener think? Will it raise expectations of our concerts which we can never fulfil? Will people find our concerts less authoritative than our recordings? Or will they welcome all the human and technical muddle of live performance, which makes them an experience in real time *and* in a real atmosphere?

This aspect of recording has always made me uneasy, and we used to argue with the producer about whether it was 'moral' to iron out mistakes and problems in the way that they do. Isn't a bit like the old portrait painters, who painted flattering pictures of ladies in faraway lands and carried them to prospective husbands, who would make a decision on the basis of what they saw, and then be horribly disappointed by the appearance of the real lady?

As far as I understand it, producers' attitude is that the medium of recording allows one to remove *transient* defects. They feel that if the artist is indeed capable of playing the music with insight and accuracy, then their mistakes in a recording session are just transient mistakes, not ones which happen on every occasion. If they did happen on every occasion, it really would be a lie to produce a perfect version on disc! Most mistakes, however, are transient and not repeated in the same place at the next attempt. And therefore, if the artist *has* a musical message, the recording process allows him to give his message without things getting in the way.

Assuming that someone who buys the disc will want to hear it more than once, he won't want to hear poor intonation every time, or a wrong note every time, so (the producers claim) it just makes sense to eliminate these kind of accidents. It allows the artist to capture his thoughts at a certain point in time, but without physical distractions. I have tried to argue that as long as a performance has integrity and is compelling, I wouldn't care about 'accidents' on the disc, but I am assured that if I listened to more records, I wouldn't feel that way. Record collectors have agreed that it is intensely irritating to be compelled to listen over and over again to a slip which the artist and/or the producer could have corrected. To iron out mistakes is therefore acceptable because the listener's perception of the player's fatigue or nervousness would outweigh perception of his musical intention. In that sense the medium is not a lie, but an opportunity to create an enduring picture without ephemeral defects.

So – records 'have to be as perfect as possible', or the resources of recording will not have been used properly. So why is it, I wonder, that everyone seems to love the 'old' recordings best? The early, the historic recordings, the ones where players can be heard grunting and wheezing, the ones with wrong notes, background noises, memory slips? Would they be acceptable today? Or does our liking of them depend on our historical knowledge that recording was in its infancy, that they didn't 'correct' things then? Do we like them precisely *because* of their imperfections?

I think there is another factor in old recordings, namely that those players had no other recordings to listen to, perhaps not even other performances. So when they came to make their recording, they had no other versions 'in their mind's ear'. They may not have conceived of any approaches other than their own. Our position today is very different. My trio might wish to play the Schubert B flat Trio just as the famous trio of Cortot, Thibaud and Casals played it in the early decades of the twentieth century, with just their rubato and phrasing, but even if this is our preferred interpretation, there is no way that we can actually play it like that *today*. Indeed, there is no way we can be unaware of several different well-known recordings and versions of different kinds, on period instruments, version that have become modern classics, versions that were rejected by the critics. Our position as interpreters is therefore not a 'carte blanche', for we may feel that certain claims to interpretative territory have been marked out by others.

We may feel that even if our ideal tempi are identical to those of the Beaux Arts Trio, for many years considered the world's leading piano trio, we cannot use exactly those tempi without being accused of plagiarism or weak-minded copying! Equally we may know that period recordings have claims to be 'different' because they play fast and light, with a certain balance between the instruments, so that too is an approach we cannot take. It is in fact increasingly difficult to be original, and all too often the disc ends up by being compared to other versions and described as 'faster than X's recording' or 'more mellow and warmer than Y's, yet without being as leisurely as Z's'. My own group makes a conscious effort not to listen to other recordings when we are preparing a work, but even if *we* don't, others do. Critics always attempt to present one's new recording along an interpretative spectrum where certain other musicians are already situated at the extremes, and at various places in between. In fact this is something we rather dread when the disc appears – to be judged not on how successful our approach is in itself, but on how successful it is relative to others' success.

I don't think this happens so much with concerts, where one is much more likely to be assessed on the merits of the occasion, and not explicitly compared to other concert performances. But with a record, everyone knows that it has been worked on, perfected as much as possible, and is designed to last, so it seems to move out of the realm of the evanescent and into the objective, where it can be compared and judged as if it were a piece of furniture.

My recording career began in 1984 when my group Domus was asked to record the two piano quartets by Fauré – a record which, incidentally, later won the Gramophone Award. We were pleased but scared by the offer. At that time we did not see our disc as being a snapshot of our thoughts on the music at that time. We saw it as a kind of monument, something solid and irrevocable, which would fix 'our Fauré' in the ears of the musical world. An interpretation that must, in fact, transcend the temporary.

None of us had made a record before, and we were confronted with many factors that had not entered our lives as concert performers. When I describe these to friends, I find that many are unaware of how a record session 'goes', so I thought I would dwell on that side of things in the next part of my talk. Even though a group has prepared scrupulously for the record, there are new things to take into consideration.

Firstly, what the microphone hears. This is something we have had to learn and use. When you are sitting at an instrument and playing it, you don't hear what the microphone hears. In fact, the 'mike' is usually located in a position where no listener ever sits (typically, about a metre away from the group and a metre above our heads) and so its view of the situation is a new one for all of us. It hears resonances, overtones and also mechanical noises that the player may never have heard before. A pianist may be surprised by how much bass there is, or how much cloud there is around the sound. A string player may be disconcerted by how much is audible of bow on string, fingers shifting on the fingerboard, squeaking of the bow – things that would not be audible to anyone in a normal audience seat. Everyone may feel that the balance they hear in their seats in not the same as the balance they hear when it is recorded a few feet above their heads.

These are mechanical things. We were also surprised by how the microphone hears finesse of touch. Notes that seem solid and clear at the piano may seem crude and insensitive over the mike. Notes that seem pure and quiet may seem plain and timid. A volume that feels just right for accompanying the other players may suddenly seem too much or too little. A colleague whose playing seems just fine in the hall may seem too reticent on the tape. A violinist may sound aggressive and raw as the mike picks up more high frequencies in the sound than we are aware of at floor level.

Over the years my own technique has changed because of recording. My touch has become more accurate, my ear has become more alert to unevenness. I know I can play more quietly in a recording than I can in a concert, and be heard perfectly. I know I have to be careful about stamping on the pedal with enthusiasm, or bringing the pedal up too slowly so that a soft hissing sound can be heard. I know I can't turn a page with abandon if the sound of the paper will rustle in a silent beat. I know I don't have to 'project' the sound to the back of the hall. Of course, a mike does collect ambient sound as well, but basically it hears what a person on stilts would hear if they were standing where a conductor stands in front of an orchestra.

Another difference in a recording studio is that there is no audience. This can affect the players greatly. In a concert, your consciousness embraces all the listeners as well as your colleagues. You see them, they see you, you catch their eyes. You become aware of your own place in the room relative to them. You extend (or should extend) your mental field to include them. So what happens when they are not there? The focus shifts to oneself, to one's instrument. Of course this is normal in private practice and rehearsal, but not when being heard by others. The subtraction of 'others' from the performance context can give a sterility to the occasion. In the absence of people in the room, you have to imagine people at home listening to the eventual record. At the recording, however, it can give a strange 'bell-jar' effect, isolating each player in over-concentration upon himself. Once you have heard some of your playing on tape, you realise that no matter how important a colleague's musical line, and no matter how beautifully they play it, the microphone will at that moment also be ruthlessly attentive to how you yourself are playing. This tends to distract the attention that you would normally give to a colleague in performance, dropping your own 'laser beam' to a lower intensity in order to listen to someone else. In a recording, I find, one almost has to drop the colleague into a lower layer of one's consciousness in order to ensure that the accompaniment is free of blemishes. Of course, this may alter the degree of sympathy with which one plays the accompaniment!

The microphone also hears something I hardly ever notice in a concert – background noise. It impartially records tube trains, dogs barking, piano stools creaking, planes overhead. It records the dustbin lorry manoeuvring round the corner while you are playing a quiet transition. It hears the central heating clicking as it cools down while you are ending the movement with a poignant silence. It hears the pianist's foot tapping gently on the floor along with the music.

None of these things would be unacceptable in a concert. Nevertheless record producers feel very strongly about them. For them it is a matter of professional integrity that no silence shall have a lawnmower trundling away in the street beyond. And they are super-sensitive to noises on the platform: page-turning, cello spike slipping, inadvertent touching of the strings when not playing, moving of mutes.

On our first recording, I was shocked when a particularly fine 'take' was deemed unusable because a bus had passed by outside while we were playing it. As the session wore on, we became all too familiar with the producer's voice over the intercom: 'Sorry, dears, but there's a plane overhead – we'll have to do it again.' In anguish we asked, 'But does it matter?' and were assured that it is profoundly irritating for a listener to have a background noise, especially an ugly noise, glued permanently to a moment in the music. I took his word for it, while still privately feeling that I might not even notice that noise myself.

Many times in London we have sat in the recording venue (usually a church) trying to record 'a bit of silence' to go at the beginning or end of the disc, or to fit between movements, and have been amazed at how difficult it is. A bird suddenly sings on the roof, a police siren wails by, a door bangs somewhere downstairs and you have to start again.

So when we start to record, do we feel that the interpretation is 'finished' and ultimately polished?

Certainly this was how we approached our first disc. And yet, the instant we go backstage to listen to the first 'takes', the finality of our approach starts to crumble. We hear it through the observer's ear and with his perspective – and things seem different. The tempo that you felt was moving and stately suddenly seems lethargic; the attention to detail seems pedantic and overdone. The ideal balance that you heard in the church seems to have vanished too: why is the cello line submerged? Why is the violin louder? Why does the piano seem to be in another room?

Painful discussions with the sound engineer ensue. His dignity is wounded by the suggestion that his judgement is at fault. He may parry your suggestion of a change to the microphone with a counter-suggestion that his recorded sound is an accurate picture of the way we play. Inner security begins to crumble within the group. The producer and engineer begin to indulge in techno-speak, hinting that perhaps they should artificially enhance one of the players by electronic manipulation at the recording unit. The pianist wants to be 'brought forward' in the sound. A microphone is placed at the end of the piano to pick up more direct resonance. Now the pianist is happy, but the string players feel that *their* sound is now indirect in comparison. Now the cellist is put on a small podium to raise him up towards the mike. Another take is done, and this time the violinist feels that he is hearing more cello sound than he's used to, and the sound picture is distorted. The engineer retorts that he can do anything *artificially*, but didn't we 'want to sound natural' on the disc? Finally an acceptable balance is achieved, but usually with at least one person unconvinced that the best result *for them* has been found.

So, on to recording 'our interpretation' of the music. After listening to some of the takes, we decide that the tempo really is too slow. However, we may never have rehearsed it at a faster tempo, so some lightning adjustment is needed. When we next come down to listen, it seems to us that the opening theme is too glibly presented, not 'special' enough; the whole opening section sounds like a 'received idea', not fresh and inspired. Back to the platform we go, to re-think our way of playing it. Next, a transition that seemed delicate and subtle in our rehearsals now seems shallow when we listen back to it. How could we not have heard this? Or does it seem different because we just changed the opening?

Because the tempo is now faster, and the transition now more emphatic, we have to play the movement several times to get used to the new feeling, and during these several times, someone starts to get tired. We realise this when they start making mistakes. We have not yet got a single bar that we could release on a disc. Should we go back to the original conception, as time is short? Should we record alternative versions, and then go downstairs and compare them? Do we need to lie on the floor and rest for twenty minutes?

We play the exposition again until it settles. All of these attempts are recorded, but the producer informs us that they are all slightly different in speed, or attack, or tonal projection, and therefore cannot be used to 'cut between' different takes, as they will not match. (Of course we have long ago rejected the possibility of digital wizardry to 'make things match'.) So now we have to decide which of the new versions is our chosen one, so that we can start recording in earnest.

We choose one, and then play through the whole movement again, to get the sweep of the big structure. By this stage it is lunchtime; we have been working hard for three hours and nothing is yet on tape that could be used in a finished product. We have only two, perhaps three days for the whole record. Where is the 'polished interpretation', which seemed inadequate at its first exposure to our critical ears in the listening room? We adjourn for lunch telling ourselves that the new version is better, more advanced, and that recording helps things to evolve.

In the afternoon we plough on. After playing through the movement perhaps six times, the producer 'takes stock' and then informs us that as far as he is concerned, we now have bars 1–8 'covered', unless anyone knows any different. So we can proceed with attention to detail, starting with bar 9. This is always a shocking moment, a moment to dread. Has the attention to detail not been enough yet? Surely there is enough material from which to stitch together a perfect version? Sadly, it seems not. Every phrase that someone played beautifully seems to have a squeaky chair, a cough or a wrong note from someone else.

Individual players start to tell the producer, 'I thought I played the second subject pretty well just now,' and he replies, 'You did, you did . . . but I'm afraid there's a split note in the piano part during that phrase: I can't use it.' Or the pianist will say, 'I think there's only one time that I played that difficult run in bar 58 correctly', and the producer says, 'That's right, but unfortunately the strings were out of tune while you did it.' Dark looks now begin to pass amongst the players. People begin to resent the fact that their shining moments have been nullified by someone else's lapse of concentration.

'So, let's go from the second subject, and what I need is: bar 32 without without a split note from the piano, bars 34–36 with good octaves between the strings, bar 38 without a page-turn noise, and a really good attack from all of you at the same moment in bar 42. And Sue, be careful with the pedal when the music gets loud.

Let's just try to cover these bars.' We give great attention to these bars, but self-consciousness intervenes, and as one flaw is fixed, so another surfaces. Eventually, after half a dozen attempts, the producer assures us he has enough material to work with, and we go on to the next bit. Basically the idea is to repair all the little flaws and then 'drop in' flawless elements into a complete take of the movement.

At this stage the players are very vulnerable, beginning to feel tired and despondent, and this is where their relationship with the producer is crucial. Producers are interventionist to varying degrees. Some wait for us to say what we think needs to be done again, but often our judgement has been become shaky after hours of playing things over and over again. I certainly am not one of those who has good recall of what went well, or which version had more character, and I certainly don't recall which takes are compatible in style and tempo with which other takes! So we really rely on the producer to tell us what he thinks has not yet been heard in an acceptably accurate way. Some producers have remarkable recall in this respect.

Apparently the first record producers did not see it as their role to influence the artist in any way. They thought of themselves as 'holding up a microphone to history', and if the artist rushed, or played wrong notes, then so be it. The first 'interventionist producer', I am told, was Walter Legge, in the 1950s and 1960s, who would tell the artist if he felt they were singing their best, or should move their position in the room, or have a break and try again.

Since then, some producers have come to see themselves as essential artistic contributors. Some players feel that they need a producer who understands their personality and aspirations, because otherwise he will not be able to guide them through a forest of alternatives at the end of the sessions. Producers themselves have become very conscious of their compatibility with the artist, and sometimes say that they 'can't work with so-and-so' or that such-and-such an artist 'always insists that I am there for his recordings'. Clearly, then, the producer does a lot more than just hold up a microphone. On a simple level he has to help the artist to feel at home in the recording environment. During the sessions he has to develop a fine sense of when to ask for more, or when to keep his mouth shut. And after the sessions are over, he can actually determine which portrait of the artist will reach the public. His own preferences and principles come into play; he has to walk a fine line between going for pristine, scratch-free sound, and going for musical sweep and energy.

Technology now offers the means to engage in all kinds of games in post-production. Just to take one example, a fast movement can be speeded up at pitch to make it sound more brilliant. This wasn't possible before, when speeding up a recording meant that the pitch would rise. We made a decision early on that we wouldn't indulge in any of this. Correcting mistakes is one thing, but making people sound better than they actually are is quite another. It is widespread in the pop world, but we are stubbornly old-fashioned. We always feel that it is important to be able to turn up in person and play at least as well as we did on our records. How depressing for listeners to say, as they do about pop musicians, 'They sounded far better on their CD'!

During recording sessions I have come to feel that the producer is like another member of the group. In my heightened mood of concentration, I find that once a take is over, it's over, and I have already forgotten it when we pass on to the next one, so I rely very much on the producer's ability to recall other takes in detail. Trying to capture a virtuosic passage, for example, he may say, 'But wasn't it really good on the take we did this morning before the break?' or, 'I know we've got it up to bar 112 on the first take we did this afternoon – so just concentrate on the second half of the passage.' This is invaluable when one is preoccupied.

Similarly, I know I lose my perspective completely when we come to record the tiny excerpts the producer calls 'patches', which often occur at the end of sessions. He may come out with a list of bars where one tiny thing is wrong, and has never been right on any take. We find ourselves doing minute corrections without, in fact, knowing where they will be grafted on to - which version, which character. Will the little corrections be compatible? I never know how the final version is achieved, but I know that sometimes a single note has been 'dropped in' to correct a tricky bar. At this stage, where someone has to create a mosaic of best bits, clean bits, quiet bits, inspired risk-taking and so on, I'm glad that it is not my responsibility any more. As a concert performer I am used to delivering one version on one occasion for one audience, and the multiple variations of recording just shatter my simple wishes!

A serious point arising from all this is that I don't think recording is compatible with being musically profound. The whole drive of recording sessions – these days – is towards more and more alertness, more accuracy, more irreproachability. Recording definitely makes everyone more self-conscious – more selfish, too, determined to succeed with their own parts regardless of what is happening in other parts. These are not the conditions in which profundity is likely to be achieved.

In my experience, to be profound you have to let go of surface thoughts and allow something deeper to guide you, for but for me this is not possible in recording because you have to control the surface more than at any other time. I suppose it should be possible to be accurate in minute details *and* profound in mood, but I don't know any artist who feels they can do this under recording conditions.

And speaking of conditions, I must mention the inadequacy of the time allotted to making a record. Every time I make one, I have the feeling that I am struggling against time limitations that have been imposed simply for reasons of economy. Typically, two to three days are allocated to record over an hour's worth of music (these days it can be 79 minutes of music) – and it must *be* over an hour, or the public will feel that it is not 'value for money'. That means recording a four-movement work in a day, usually. When my group recorded the complete Brahms piano trios in 1997, we had six days for five works, one of which was forty minutes long. In other words, we had to record twenty movements in six days – more than three a day. Compare this with the world of film or TV, where they think it's good progress if they get a few minutes' worth out of a day of filming!

Listeners who have been present at orchestral recording sessions may not be aware of the intensity with which smaller groups, and soloists, hurl themselves into the recording process. In a large-scale undertaking like a symphonic recording, there are all kinds of rules governing how long the players can be asked to work without a break, how long the breaks must be, how long the whole day can be. An orchestra will work typically from 10 a.m. to 1 p.m. and from 2.30 to 5.30 p.m. – and that is the end of the day. And I think I am right in saying that on some orchestral records (in London, at least) the recording sessions may be the first time that the orchestra has played the work. This contrasts painfully with the months of preparation, the personal practice and the soul-searching that goes into making a record of solo or chamber music.

With a chamber group there are no union rules, and as long as the producer and engineer are willing, we can start as early as we like and continue as long as we like, working late into the night if we choose, and starting again early the following morning. Very often we have worked 12 hours on a recording day. Not all of this is playing; a considerable time is spent trying out different microphone placings and alternative seatings, and listening to the balance between the instruments, and a considerable time is also spent in traipsing up and down stairs to listen to what we have already done, and deciding whether it matches our 'Platonic ideal'. Even with these long days, and with everyone's willingness to play until their muscles rebel, I have always had the feeling that there wasn't enough time. In fact the very end of a record session is often determined by a non-musical factor: the piano transporter comes to take the piano away, the janitor comes to lock the building. And often we are then in a most peculiar, unsatisfactory state of mind, because it may have been hours since we played anything 'properly' – we may have spent hours at the end trying to correct the notorious 'transient mistakes.'

When I was preparing this talk, the producer Andrew Keener asked me to think about the following questions:

1. When you go into the studio, do you feel you have a 'finished' interpretation to commit to disc?
2. If not, is the process of exploration still going on?
3. Is recording, therefore, different from a concert?
4. Is it more interesting than a concert?
5. Does it create advances in your understanding of the music and of yourselves?
6. Does it make the next concert different because of what happening in the recording sessions?
7. If the answer to most of these questions is 'Yes', does it make recording an important facet of twentieth-century musical life?
8. Could recording be considered 'an art-form' rather than 'a lie'?

If it is an art-form, then it is a collaboration between artist, producer and engineer, none of whom really have control over what the others do, so I can't feel entirely happy about it, as my own contribution is essentially a series of building-blocks. I know that the producer would contend that he builds the structure according to the plans laid down by the musicians, but I know there is more to it than that. I can accept it as a process of exploration, but it's a process achieved against tremendous constraints, not a process undertaken in a relaxed spirit of enquiry. Perhaps, therefore, it is a process that should properly be undertaken *before* the interpretation has been 'polished' – if its principal benefit is to advance the musicians along the road of knowing the music, and themselves as its performers. This would not result in a product that anyone wished to buy, of course, and so it could not be commercially funded.

Finally, I suppose I do feel that I and my colleagues manage to persevere with the interpretation that we wanted to record. The adjustments we make in the recording sessions probably seem more extreme to us than they do to anyone listening. Therefore I am glad, on the whole, to have a way of publishing 'our version' to faraway listeners, and I am glad when people want to make contact with us because of a record they have heard and liked.

But I do suspect that a record is, to quote William Wordsworth's *Elegaic Stanzas*, like 'the light that never was, on sea or land'. And therefore I do still have the feeling, as I did when I was a child, that the record is 'not like me'!

May 1998

Rehearsing Beethoven's Trio, opus 1 no. 1

It's the Florestan Trio's first rehearsal of Beethoven's E flat trio, opus 1 no. 1. We've been concentrating on his late trios, but are now repairing the gaps in our Beethoven repertoire, preparing for concerts this summer, and eventually for a complete recording on Hyperion. Although we've never actually played the first trio with one another, we all know it backwards. Or so we thought, until it becomes clear that we don't know it forwards.

'But surely the first chord should be "Woompf!", not "Waaah" or "Boom!" And surely the arpeggio should not be *melodic*, but short and abstract. And surely it shouldn't have an accent on the top note? The whole thing should be "Woompf! Pa-pa-pa-pa-pa-pa!" so that we feel we're in the key of E flat major, but without wallowing in it. Not "Waah! Bom-bom-bom-bom-bom-bom!" That's too soggy. And then the arpeggio shouldn't sound thematic, because the theme is actually embedded in the chords that we all play together during the first four bars.'

Clearly it wasn't going to be a straightforward task to learn the first of Beethoven's opus 1 piano trios. We had little time to learn it, but from the first rehearsal it felt as if we were climbing a mountain. Motivated largely by our cellist, Richard Lester, who also plays in period instrument ensembles, we tried to look afresh at this famous work and go right back to whatever it was that seemed so bold and daring when Beethoven produced it.

'That sudden loud chord in bar 25. String players can't attack it as suddenly as you can on the piano. We need time to recover and prepare our bows. So there needs to be a fraction of time before the loud chord.' 'But if there's time, it destroys the element of surprise.' 'The loudness after a little gap will be surprising enough, if we're really together.' 'Well, couldn't you recover from your quiet notes more quickly?'

Anthony then remarks that the second subject is the first *pianissimo* in the piece, but claims that it doesn't sound any different from the *piano* passages we've had already. I point out that the word *rinforzando* is written over the third chord. Doesn't that mean 'make it stronger tonally'? He thinks it should perhaps be brought out melodically, or emphasised in the timing, but not played louder, otherwise it ruins the pianissimo. 'Well, why did he write a complicated word like *rinforzando* over just one note?' 'Maybe it's supposed to apply to the whole phrase?' 'No, it can't mean that. Maybe it's to ensure that the emphasis doesn't fall on the first bar of the second subject – he wants it to be on the second bar.' 'He could just have written an accent or a *tenuto* mark if that's all he wanted.' 'Let's lean on the rinforzando chord, then, but without coming out of the basic pianissimo.'

Anthony points out that eight bars later, when the same thing is repeated an octave higher, Beethoven writes *piano* instead of *pianissimo*, so the sound should develop. 'You don't think he just means "keep it quiet – don't let the sound level creep up?" ' 'No, I think he means "take a tiny step *up* in tone".' 'But it will sound "up" anyway, because the theme goes an octave higher. Could the *piano* be a mistake?' 'No – this is supposed to be the Ur-text Edition, with all Beethoven's original markings, and nothing added by editors.' Richard says that there's a new edition out now, published by Baerenreiter. 'They have markings that don't appear in the so-called Ur-text [original text] edition, so it doesn't mean that every marking in the Ur-text is right.' 'How can we work, then, if we can't rely on the Ur-text?'

'Good Lord – we have to play all three of these opus 1 trios in about two weeks' time. If we go on working at this rate, we won't even get through the first one in time.' 'Well, we have to do this work. There's certainly no point in just churning them out automatically just because we all know them by ear.' 'But aren't we in danger of looking for things to look for?' 'Well, so far everything has sounded completely routine. There's no point in going to the Bergen Festival and playing like this.'

We ponder the row of *sforzando* chords which begins at bar 74. 'Shouldn't they be additive, each one being a little more?' 'No, I think they should all be little explosions within a quiet volume.' Someone refers to the theory that a sequence of *sforzando* markings in Beethoven implies a *crescendo*. 'It's only a theory, surely, not a fact. We have to decide what makes musical sense.'

'But if we don't do a crescendo through those *sforzando* chords, the forte at bar 78 will be a sudden one, and yet it only lasts for half a bar.' 'Yes, half a bar, and then there's half a bar of diminuendo, and then in the next bar he writes *fortepiano*. Does that mean at the level that the half-bar of diminuendo has reached, or is it a jump up again in volume?' 'I think a jump up, but then instantly followed by quiet, as if all the energy of the passage before has just been swallowed.' 'How many notes should be forte, then, before the piano?' 'I think just one.' 'I thought maybe the forte should die away during half a bar.' 'If he'd wanted that, he could have written a diminuendo.'

We're getting cross now because we're all hungry, but we don't want to break for lunch until we've finished at least one movement. 'This piece is bloody impossible. It's as difficult as the opus 18 string quartets. Everybody thinks they're straightforward, that it's obvious how to play them, but they're so concentrated, so minimalist, it's impossible to bring out all the details that he wants.' 'Well, let's not sound as if we're bringing out details.' 'We have to go into this kind of detail before we can find the right shapes.' 'But doesn't this sound incredibly self-conscious?' 'It's much better to sound self-conscious, or at least conscious, than just to plough through this piece like everybody else does, just playing eight-bar phrases from start to finish and ignoring all the variety within them.'

And here's a very difficult thing. Until the archive of recordings was built up, nobody had any idea how other people usually played anything. They might never have heard anyone else playing a particular piece of music. Certainly they wouldn't have known how people in other countries approached it, let alone how people in previous generations did. And they couldn't have been aware of changes in style, of performance practice which goes in and out of fashion, linking its performers irreversibly to the year they did it, and all that that implied.

In the case of Beethoven, we are in the unfortunate position of having a vast array of recordings available to us. We also know how the Beaux Arts Trio play on the recordings now generally dubbed the best available. Clearly there's no point in aping them, but on the other hand there's no point in distancing ourselves consciously from an approach regarded as a benchmark. Our instinctive approach might be just like theirs, in fact, but that avenue seems to be closed to us, since we couldn't prove that we had arrived at our interpretation independently.

We know, too, that even today in London there are probably groups playing them on the correct 'period' instruments, groups trying a mixture of old and new ingredients, like violins and cellos with modern set-ups, but with gut strings, or modern pianos specially picked out because they sound more delicate than the full-blown Steinway grands, yet not as fragile as the pianos Beethoven would have known. We know, too, that there are probably temporary liaisons of three soloists coming together to play these trios without spending much time on them. Their preoccupations will be very different from ours, and though we may deplore their lack of immersion, we also know that their glamour and big sound will fascinate London audiences, and is not to be sneezed at. So it becomes increasingly difficult to step up to this core repertoire with an innocent mind.

While digging away at the glittering mine of motifs, allusions, sub-phrases, cross-rhythms and the like, it crosses my mind in a naughty way that, without all this accretion of other people's performances in the background, we might actually go for the simple, eight-bar-phrase approach, and let the tiny cross-references sink down into the subconscious, where quite possibly they *should* reside. I might, anyway. But my enquiring colleagues are highly motivated to uncover through this work just why Beethoven is famed for his compositional rigour, his grasp of structure, his wild dynamics. This piece is, as one of them says, 'Beethoven's calling card'. Let's pretend, then, that we are his ideal interpreters, and try to grab these notes hot off the press as he writes them, and as he wants them to be heard.

This process is a little like the essay about the fictional Pierre Menard in Jorge Luis Borges' book *Labyrinths*. Pierre Menard, a writer obsessed with Cervantes' *Don Quixote*, casts aside the original and tries to 'write' fragments of the book, using only his own experience of life as his prompter. His ultimate success comes when he writes a sentence or two in the exact words of Cervantes, not by copying Cervantes, you understand, or 'remembering' the original, but by identifying himself so much with Cervantes and his world that in the end the same formulation of words occurs to him.

This is what we aspire to do with Beethoven – or, indeed, any other composer we're serious about. We try to get so far under Beethoven's skin that his musical ideas become our ideas. Not just our ideas about his ideas, but all of us thinking the same ideas. He thought them two hundred years ago, of course. And perhaps it is a dangerous *folie de grandeur* to think that one can think his ideas at a distance of centuries, not to mention all the other kinds of distance between us and Beethoven.

Yet there is occasionally, just occasionally, a true *frisson* that occurs when you've really worked at trying to understand something, and you suddenly feel that *your performance has actually coalesced with the composer's original idea*. This fleeting sensation is not only hard to describe, but is very much the exception, of course. It happens maybe once in a performance for one or two phrases, and then not again for ages, maybe not for years. It's also a different sensation from simply giving a convincing performance, or trying to play it as the composer would have liked to hear it. It's some kind of deep bonding with the musical material, so that your brain starts to produce the same brainwaves that the composer was having when originating this music.

This is, I suppose, the goal of all rehearsal, and yet it occurs so rarely, because we all lack time for reflection, and for letting our reflections mature. Yesterday one of us was playing a concerto, one of us was flying back from America, and the third was playing in a period ensemble. Now we're together again, and we have to settle down and remember where we had got to with this piece. In the interpretation of music, 'ripeness is all', but in the professional player's life these days, one hardly ever stays still long enough to ripen.

August 2001

Recording Schubert's E flat Trio

The Florestan Trio has just spent three cold winter days recording Schubert's great trio in E flat, the most monumental work in our repertoire. It's also the work I have most dreaded recording. Now that it has been safely committed to disc I feel that a milestone has been passed – or should I say a mountain climbed?

The Schubert E flat Trio has always been associated in my mind with a winter journey. Years ago when I first got to know it, and rehearsed it with Domus, there was a lot of discussion in rehearsals about the right tempo for the slow movement, one of Schubert's finest inspirations. Some were in favour of a very slow tempo to bring out its tragic character. Others wanted a flowing tempo to honour his marking 'andante con moto', but an easily moving tempo seemed too flippant for the great sadness in the music.

That Christmas we visited a friend in rural Scotland and continued to rehearse the trio there. There was deep snow, and I went out for a walk in it one sparkling winter afternoon. Suddenly it occurred to me that the tempo of my footsteps trudging in the snow was exactly the right speed for the opening chords of the slow movement. At the same moment it seemed clear to me that the trudging steps of the slow movement were analogous to a winter journey. It was one of those moments where a musical gesture seems to have its roots in a physical one. Since then the piece has retained its 'winter narrative' character for me. And the recording process this week seemed like a destination of some kind, completing a stage of the journey begun in the snowy Scottish landscape of twenty years before. Not an ending, of course, since pieces go on developing in everyone's minds, but certainly a significant milestone.

Interestingly, although I hadn't told anyone in the Florestan Trio about my winter associations with the Schubert E flat, when we started to record the slow movement, a friend listening in the producer's studio said to me, 'Those opening bars! As soon as you started to play them I saw the whole thing – the snow, the light, the loneliness of the landscape.' This was thought transference of a kind – from me to him, perhaps, or from Schubert to us!

The E flat Trio takes fifty minutes to perform, making it probably the longest piano trio we know. It also contains some of the most technically difficult passages of individual and ensemble playing, especially in the finale. Yet these things don't constitute its main challenge, which is that of understanding the huge structures and making them clear to the listeners. The work is so episodic, and appears to be so rambling and discursive, that it's easy to get lost in the beauty of each subsidiary idea and to lose track of where you are in the whole structure. As Anthony, our violinist, said, he often doesn't know exactly where he is in the piece except when he's performing it. Then it comes alive in an extraordinary way, creating folds of events and chains of emotional links, which lead back eventually to the original point of departure, only seen from a heightened perspective.

When we first started performing this work, it seemed endless, fully the fifty minutes of clock time that it occupies. As we have got to know it better, and to digest it more, it seems to get shorter in performance. Instead of understanding it as a long sequence of episodes, we now understand it more as a complex sculptural shape. When we play it we are creating layers – some high, some low, some dark, some light, some inner, some outer. We sense how the layers fit into the whole shape. The piece still takes time to perform, but the time has become detached from clock time, and has transformed itself into artistic time. Curiously, when this happens the clock time seems to get shorter as well, and members of the audience have even reported having this same sensation.

An intriguing fact about this music is that getting to know it better has not stilled debate about how to play it. Like all great works in any medium, it seems to go on developing as the participants develop, and to keep pace with one's ability to understand it. One can take things at face value and find them beautiful. Equally, one can see them in a complex way and find that beautiful too. The opening page of the score used to seem quite simple and straightforward to me. Later, it came to seem austere and monolithic, and at other times, reserved and noble. It has seemed abstract, but sometimes also very direct and confiding. I've also gone through various phases of thinking that it should have one pulse per bar, three pulses per bar, one pulse per two bars, one pulse per four bars, and so on. I've liked it to have 'swing', and at other times I've wanted it to be dignified and stately. All these changes must reflect changes in me, but the piece is so multi-faceted that it responds easily to new perspectives.

My own understanding of the work has to be blended with that of the others in the trio. This creates endless discussion in rehearsals of it, which only ever seem to reach a temporary stopping-point, holding still just long enough for us to perform it. We may hold the same views about it for a run of performances, but then someone will suddenly say, 'I don't like the way we do such and such any longer', and someone else will say, 'Yes. I've been feeling uncomfortable too . . .' and we're off again on our interpretative debate.

How soft is 'soft'? Is there an absolute, or is it only soft in relation to loud? How soft should it be if 'very soft' is still to come? What does *con moto*, 'with movement', really mean? How much accent should there be in a 'forzando', and how is it different from a 'fortepiano'? How do we distinguish between the various kinds of accents – triangular 'hat' shapes, 'wedge' accents? Which edition is better, Henle or Bärenreiter, both allegedly based on the original manuscripts? How much lilt should there be? If there is a hint of the dance, does that make it more touching or less? Which is sadder, the minor or the major? Perhaps only great composers can create such ambiguity in their harmonic colourings, and perhaps among great composers Schubert is the most sensitive to major/minor inflections.

When you record a piece you have to make decisions, for even if you feel you are engaged in a journey of understanding, you have to put your cards on the table during the recording process and say that *this is where you think you are*. Committing ourselves to this decision is rather painful, but at the same time there *is* a consensus about how we like to perform the trio at the moment, even if we are all likely to suggest something else next year. So there is certainly a version we're all prepared to put our names to on disc. Secretly, though, I think we'd all like to have a qualifying remark like '2001 vintage' included on the cover. The recording will be no more or less than a taste of our thinking at this particular time.

The process of recording does not stop discussion going on. Right through the three days of recording, all three of us still argue about how much edge there should be on particular accents, whether a certain 'forte' is positive or aggressive, and whether harmonic colourings indicate a turning inwards or a turning outwards. The sense of possibilities is still so active that we even record different versions of some passages and go backstage to listen to them with the producer, waiting to see what sort of effect they will have on us. Luckily we always seem to agree on this. One version clearly fits into the overall shape of our performance, the other to be misleading, and it gets discarded.

It's very hard to record a piece with such a broad wingspan as the Schubert, because of the nature of recording. We have argued many times about whether mistakes are acceptable on a record. Nobody is perfectly accurate all the time in a performance, and when there are three people involved this is three times as true. Therefore, when we have played a whole movement two or three times, to 'get down the basic shape', we are then faced with a very long process – several hours per move-ment, of playing shorter sections again and again.

When each section has been satisfactorily 'covered' we find ourselves doing yet smaller sections, often ending with so-called 'patching', when tiny mistakes are corrected. With luck the producer will be able to use our recording of the whole movement as a template, and will be able to slot in more accurate versions of indi-vidual bits and pieces without altering the shape of the whole. But of course in the process of focusing on smaller and smaller sections, a certain change in energy may be imparted to them, so we have always to try to remember 'where we are in the piece', and to play with the appropriate degree of 'electric charge'. And although while focusing on small sections the accuracy rate may rise, we may lose expressive power.

We used to say that we'd much rather be musically 'right' than technically right on a disc. But Andrew Keener, our producer, points out that while we always say that in the recording sessions, when he sends us the 'first edit' six months later for our comments, we always pounce on any wrong notes or mistakes and implore him to correct them. We too have become consumers of the artifice, and think that performances on record should *at least* be technically perfect. Now that we are all pretty experienced recording artists, we know that we have to build as much accu-racy into our recording sessions as possible, so that with luck, musical and technical purity will go hand in hand. I'm a far more accurate pianist than I used to be, though I sometimes wonder if this is a good thing.

One thing is certain: it's very bad to spoil someone else's most beautiful perfor-mance of an important passage with errors in an accompanying part. I hate it when I do it to them, and I hate it when they do it to me. In that respect altruism, or 'chamber music pride', has motivated all of us to be as much in control of our indi-vidual parts as we can be. There's nothing more shaming than forcing your colleagues to play a passage over and over again because you haven't got the fingering mapped out in your mind.

Recording often focuses on small details and short sections. But surprisingly, the process can also reveal things about the large shape that we hadn't realised. An example of this occurs towards the end of the last movement. We find ourselves recording the last pages at the end of a very strenuous day. Each time we play them, our accuracy rate seems to decline, and finally Andrew suggests that we should all go home, have a rest and return the next morning to 'have another go at it'. So we adjourn for the night. The following morning we listen to what we've done. It's clear that, because the last movement is so long and so physically tiring, its climax is underdone in our performance. Just before the theme of the slow movement returns wearily for the last time, there is a series of 'sighs' (bars 665–693 in the Henle edition), which signal a last outburst of defiance before the inevitable sadness returns. In the context of the whole movement, we feel that these sighs should increase in intensity, the last carrying a huge emotional charge, the roar of a caged lion.

But in practice I find this very difficult to do. My hands are so tired after almost fifty minutes of playing. I've just negotiated two or three extremely difficult fast passages, and my left hand hardly has the strength for another section of fast repeated quaver chords, perhaps easier to control on Schubert's light-action piano, but something of a feat on today's heavier Steinway grands. In addition to this, we have to gather energy for the final 'roar'. In performance this musical gesture is often dictated by our level of physical fatigue, and one might think that this is all as it should be. However, listening back to what we've recorded – and particularly from the night before – it's clear that tiredness has actually robbed that climactic final 'sigh' of its power. It sounds feeble, not defiant. Our performance, with its 'real-time tiredness', underplays this important moment.

Approaching it freshly the next morning, with new energy, allows us to tackle the last pages on their own and to record a powerful version unaffected by performance fatigue. Here is one instance of the recording process actually helping our artistic vision. Recording can create an opportunity one would never have in the concert hall. Some might think that it's a false opportunity, an illusion. Yet one might also think that the composer didn't intend physical fatigue to ruin one of his greatest emotional expressions in the piece. He composed independently of the physical process of playing, and away from real musicians; he probably imagined everything played at full intensity – or with the *right* intensity – *all the time*. As the beam of his concentration passed across the notes as he wrote them down, he would of course 'hear' them in ideal form, not coloured by the muscle fatigue of mortal interpreters. Thus sometimes the process of recording can actually allow us to brighten the beam of our own concentration, doing more justice to the composer's idea than perhaps we do in performance.

This is not to say that physical fatigue is a bad thing in a concert performance. The sense of being at the extreme of physical possibilities can be very powerful, both for players and listeners. Even if accuracy and power are lost, the sense of effortful involvement can be emotionally right. However, I think most players now feel that listeners will only accept a sense of struggle if it happens in front of their eyes in a live performance. It might also work on disc as a recording of a live performance, but even then the 'wobbliness' might pall after a couple of hearings. Our record of the E flat Trio will have an accuracy and freshness it doesn't have in concerts, and the recorded performance will be more enduring as a result – though it won't therefore be more human.

The recording process also helps us to play the very last pages, where in the piano part the syncopated pairs of descending chords return. This passage is technically very hard, and in performance – and at the end of a fifteen-minute fast movement – it's always shot through with wrong notes from me. However, I can't bring myself to end our recording with the usual shower of errors. So this passage also benefits from being isolated and tackled after a cup of coffee and quarter of an hour listening to the playbacks.

During this final passage, there's a very important moment, which often eludes us slightly. After being in the minor key for a very long time, Schubert suddenly turns to the major (bar 721) for the last page of piano score. It's a gesture which, coming so close to the end and after so much emotion, can seem almost trivial, like a reader closing the storybook with a glib, 'and so they all lived happily ever after'. What does it mean? We've tried all sorts of ways of playing it. Is it a moment of relaxing and warming, or a moment of triumph? Should it be a gentle 'forte' or a surprising one? Does it need extra time in that bar? Should the string players sing out or *blare* out? Whatever we've tried, there is always a suspicion of 'acting' about it.

So it is educational to listen to what we've recorded. As observers we can hear that this moment of turning back to the major key is also underdone in our performance. It sounds unconvinced and unconvincing. What we hoped was noble reserve sounds like timidity. And because it is such a long movement, it is clear that this last-minute turn to the major must have immediate affirmative force, with nothing sentimental about it. Timing and tone are crucial here. Listening to our own performance we realise that we need a moment of expanded time at the arrival of the major chord, a very positive assertion of it from everyone, no cracking or wobbling in anyone's tone. There must be a sense of having turned the corner towards safety, but without any hint of gloating. We must 'come home' and realise it too.

At least, that is how we feel it on 20 December 2001. Other players will find other solutions. But for the moment we end our recording with the feeling that we have achieved the shape we wanted, the shape we understand. And so our recording becomes a portrait of us painting a portrait of Schubert.

December 2001

A Puzzling Schubert Quintet

Last night I attended a private concert, at which I heard a puzzling performance of the Schubert String Quintet, one of my favourite pieces of music. It was played by five professional musicians, members of reputable London orchestras, who described themselves on the programme as getting together as often as possible to play chamber music. Their performance was confidently presented; they brought along a lecturer to introduce it, and microphones were set up to record it. Yet from the very first chord – mis-coordinated, and haphazard in tone – it was clear that no-one would be able to lose themselves in it.

Immediately, my head began to buzz with devil's advocacy. 'Oh, come on, this is just a social occasion. Stop being critical. This is just *fun* for them – they probably haven't had much time to rehearse. Maybe they were just "hired" by the leader, and don't play together regularly at all. Just relax and listen to the music, and don't be so judgmental!' But the prevailing feeling was one of resentment on Schubert's behalf, and on behalf of the listeners too. 'How dare they take up an evening of our time with this dabbling?' It felt a bit like being invited to a meal, and finding the ingredients all laid out on the table for our admiration, but no attempt to cook them – as though the hosts hadn't realised the difference between acquiring the ingredients and cooking the meal.

In legal cases, you have to 'prove intent' to achieve a particular result. The same should be true of concerts. Of course all players would say that they do intend to give a good performance, but their playing has to be the *proof* of that. In other words, one should be able to sense their motivation and commitment to the task, but also their effort to get under the skin of the piece and make it come alive. One should be able to sense that 'analysis' has occurred during their preparation. Alfred Brendel puts this so well in his essays *On Music*: analysis is something that you can only do when you have become deeply familiar with a piece of music and how to play it. It is not a way of breaking down the music into its little components. It's an understanding of the nature and inner meaning and emotional contours of the whole work; in other words, an understanding of the way it *adds up*.

Philip Radcliffe, one of my university tutors, used to say that the test of a great piece of music is that a bad performance cannot ruin it. And so I focused my mind on that. But I found myself thinking that had I not known the work already, and had I been hearing it for the first time, I would have wondered why it is so celebrated.

I found myself studying the five faces of the players in the hope of gleaning some information about their involvement in this intensely spiritual work. And this increased my sense of puzzlement. The five faces were like a series of studies in how to undermine the audience's trust. All looked detached in a most peculiar way, as if they were sitting round the outside of a huge goldfish bowl containing Schubert, but could only look through the glass, not swim in the water with him. Often when you hear a good performance, you realise the performers feel that the music resides *in them*. Whatever happens, they *possess* their interpretation. Yet in this case the five players all had expressions that showed that they already felt defeated by their task, or locked out from it. Some looked complacent, some blank, some humble, but as a group they gave a strange collective impression that Schubert's Quintet did not reside in their hands, but elsewhere – on an ideal plane, perhaps, to which they didn't have access.

At least this was how I felt. And because their playing was so plain, and from an ensemble point of view so haphazard, I wondered what they could possibly have said to one another during their rehearsals. Did they stop and express wishes or feelings? Did anyone express dissatisfaction with the results? It was as if they all thought that by playing the notes, something composite would emerge, the greatness would be there without their seeking it. And this is what began to puzzle me. The greatness *is* there in the notes, of course, but the notes are also a kind of cipher, or a set of signs which stand for something greater. To continue the earlier analogy with food, a musical score is like a recipe. The composer gives the instructions, but the player has to supply the ingredients that make it come alive, *now*, in the world of sound.

Musical notation is very limited, and Schubert doesn't use words to describe the changes of mood and atmosphere that he envisaged, perhaps because there are so many layers of feeling and so many interpretative possibilities, for which words would be too concrete. Yet when you hear a performance by people who have immersed themselves in this music, it seems so clear that the piece abounds in contours, in light and shade, in earthly and heavenly, in sudden outbursts and sudden consolations, in narrative and in abstraction; it's hard to listen to a performance where none of this appears to have occurred to the players.

And yet these were all professional musicians, dealing every day of their lives with good music, playing to audiences, explaining things to students! Probably they had even coached students on this very piece. So were they satisfied with their own performance? Watching them afterwards, laughing and chatting over a glass of wine, I saw no sign of misgivings. This was somehow depressing. Yet at the same time I had to think that just playing the notes in that workmanlike way, with so little sense of enquiry – far less of discovery – had been satisfying for them, as though Schubert's inspiration had leaked through somehow, because they looked happy and relaxed. And I felt guilty about being disappointed. After all, they may not have made a great impression on the music, but the music may have made a great impression on them.

I felt as though the players had felt their task to be one of playing the notes, keeping together, sorting out bowings – practical tasks, essentially, which stopped well short of what I would describe as 'interpretation'. In fact the effort seemed to stop at the level of physical coordination with the others. Perhaps for some people the enjoyment of playing is predominantly a physical pleasure, and the chief pleasure of playing chamber music is to be part of a coordinated physical effort, like in a team game. It was chamber music as a participant sport: well, certainly that's an element of a successful performance, but it should not be what the performance is primarily *about*.

When we listen to a performance, perhaps we subconsciously ask ourselves: what's this performance *about*? If you feel that it's *about the music*, then you can forgive or forget all sorts of distractions. You can overlook physical mannerisms, you can ignore technical shortcomings, if you feel that the player is the composer's interpreter. But if this feeling is absent, you might feel that the performance is *about* something else entirely. It might be about egocentric display. It might be about physical effort and reward. It might be just about conquering the notes. It might be a demonstration of the performer's obsessions and needs. All of these are perceived by the listener as the primary material of the performance, and prevent the listener from losing himself in the music.

That opening chord to which I referred at the beginning, for example: I said it was random in tone colour. What actually happened was that the first violinist lunged forward and gave a huge physical gesture, an upbeat, designed to grab the audience's attention and galvanise his team into action. But the gesture was so huge that it destroyed his ability to control the sound. His bow dropped onto the string with a momentum that made it land before the others had touched bow to string, and with a ragged sound caused by his bow almost bouncing on the string. The sound that came out was far too loud in itself, and too loud in relation to the other players.

Moreover, his gesture was far too large for a group of four friends sitting no more than a few feet away from him. It was the kind of gesture learned from leading an orchestra in a very big hall – and an orchestra whose eyes had to be caught in order to make anything happen. But this was not such an occasion. The gesture, which to me said, 'I'm going to impose my will on you now', was entirely wrong for the start of a long and intimate piece of chamber music. It would have been far more convincing if he had matched his body language and bow use to the quiet and magical C major chord, which intensifies into a painfully ambiguous diminished chord before settling back into the major again – and so on.

How much more satisfying if the players had tried to imagine the right sound for the opening of the piece, and then worked out the physical movements needed to make it. But this was just what didn't happen throughout the performance. Watching this group, I felt rather as if each player had a repertoire of physical movements that they made regardless of the content of each phrase. They didn't let the inner meaning of the music direct their effort; instead, they let their physical habits limit their expression. And they didn't interpret the 'conversation' of musical phrases as an exchange of information, such as one would have in a spoken language. Yet this kind of exchange is analogous to the way we talk to one another, and as in a spoken conversation, musical dialogue should have a sense of natural timing and meaning.

It may be that if you play in an orchestra you have to learn how to make yourself a blank canvas so that the conductor may paint his own interpretation on the orchestra. Clearly the individual players will have their own views on the music, but they can't determine the collective approach of the orchestra, so they must in a sense learn to subtract their own wishes from the rehearsal situation. If this goes on over many years it must be hard to cling on to a sense that the performance is in your hands.

So perhaps these five players were 'in search of a conductor', so to speak. Indeed, what they gave us was a bit like the blank canvas of the piece, from which their own wishes had been subtracted. Or maybe even a blank canvas onto which their own wishes had not been added. In a way, one could imagine that this might be the result of excessive respect towards the music. 'Who are we to impose a shape on this great music?' It could even be that they assumed Schubert's wishes were innate in the writing, and would automatically emerge if they played the notes – that it was irrelevant what they thought.

And certainly there is a kind of great playing that appears to have some of these characteristics. All concert-goers must have had the sensation of hearing someone really good who has the knack of making themselves 'disappear' so that one seems to be hearing just Schubert, not so-and-so playing Schubert. This could even be described as the performer subtracting himself from the situation. Yet it can only be done successfully when the performer has *already done the work* of interpreting and mastering the piece. Somehow the listener has to sense that the performer has previously brought all his hopes, dreams and willpower to bear on the understanding of this music, even if he eventually reaches a stage where he can stop concentrating and just relax into the music.

I had a cellist friend who went through a phase of 'letting the music speak for itself'. His method was to learn the notes, work out the bowings and work on intonation and so on, but not to impose any 'shape' or 'tone colour' on the music, let alone allow us to know how he felt about it. I was in the audience for one such performance, and I was taken aback by how unsuccessful this approach was. His idea was noble: not to interfere with Bach's original ideas. But somehow his 'non-interventionist' performance was little more than making the printed page audible, and was about as touching as a mute glimpse of the printed page.

It's a strange reality of music that in order to write it down, the composer has to switch from the aural to the visual mode. A composition, conceived in the inner ear, cannot be written down in aural shorthand as there is no such thing. Therefore to pass from the composer's inner ear to the performer's, it has to be encoded in the visual medium of the score. From the visual medium the player has to decode it again into sound, but this is only part of his task. He also has to decode it so that he and the listener can grasp its inner meaning. This is the main work of 'interpretation'.

Yet time and again one hears players who stop short of interpreting. They transfer the printed score back into sound, but without appearing to ask themselves what more they have to do to re-vitalise the music, in many dimensions, so that it becomes as the composer originally imagined it. I find it helpful to say to students, 'What do you think the composer heard in his mind when he wrote down this passage? If you played it like that to him, would he be likely to say, "Yes, that's exactly how I imagined it would sound"?' Usually they smile pleasantly, and say 'no'. But although they seem aware that there's a gap between their version and the composer's ideal, they don't reproach themselves for not having tried to bridge it. And quite often embarrassment is a controlling emotion. Really bridging that gap – making yourself expressive – would require some sort of cultural permission, easier for some cultures than for others. Well, that's a big subject on its own, of course.

Musicians have an enormous task when they undertake to bring the printed page to life. So many decisions have to be made, using the printed page as a map. But there's a huge difference between reading a map and travelling through the countryside that it depicts. A good performance should make us feel that the player has seen through the map to the countryside, and can share the vision with us. But he has to bond with the piece, or this alchemy cannot happen.

There are paradoxes involved in performance. I once discussed some of them with a class of pianists at the Guildhall. One student told me that he aimed to 'stand back and let the composer speak for himself'. But curiously, after he had demonstrated his idea in class, none of his friends thought it worked. We concluded that even if you are scrupulously respectful of the composer's wishes, insofar as you can work those out from the printed score, your performance will never seem authentic *if you are not there*. We talked about various ways of letting your listeners know that you are 'there'. Some performers can do it by movement and energy, others by stillness and concentration. The right way may even vary from piece to piece, and era to era. But the main thing is that your involvement must be felt. Your listeners must hear that you have taken the trouble to study and plan, though it may be a good thing if you cover your traces afterwards. As the Chinese saying goes, 'he who excels in travelling leaves no wheelmarks'.

I can only think of one category of performers who can sometimes let the composer shine through without doing anything themselves, and that is talented children. I do remember sitting on an exam panel once and hearing a most beautiful performance of Haydn by a boy of about twelve. He presented it so simply, and didn't appear to be 'doing anything' to make it work, and yet one had the impression that Haydn was suddenly alive in the room. Perhaps certain kinds of gifted young people are able to be a conduit for music they instinctively like. Yet even here there are paradoxes: on the same exam panel, I heard plenty of performances by youngsters of the same age which, similarly, didn't appear to be 'doing anything', and the result was that nothing was done.

Helen Fielding, in *The Edge of Reason*, the second of her Bridget Jones diaries, jokingly quotes a Zen self-help book as saying that 'you must not do the washing-up in order to get the washing-up done, but *simply in order to do the washing-up*'. In the same way, perhaps, you must not play Haydn beautifully in order to give a good performance of Haydn, but simply in order to play Haydn beautifully. This would imply that there is no manipulation of the audience by the performer, and no interest on his or her part in the power relationship between him and them.

For so many performers the performing situation is about this relationship. Either they relish the power they have over the audience, or they fear it and wish to withdraw from it. And many students have expressed the feeling that the audience has power over *them* – the power to make them make mistakes, for example, or the power to make them play less than their best. With some young players, however, it seems that their self-consciousness has not yet increased to the point where it's painful to have listeners, and therefore their relationship in the concert situation is *with the music*. Of course this can have wonderful results.

In the Schubert Quintet I've been talking about, I am not sure how I would describe the principal relationship that was going on, but I didn't feel it was between the players and the music. Nor did I feel that it was between the five players, or even – with a few momentary exceptions – between one player and another. On the other hand, I didn't feel that they were out to dazzle us, nor did I feel that they were afraid of us. Indeed, it was this lack of any perceived relationship that was disappointing. I felt as if we were all taking part in some social event that was designed to stay superficial in order to be acceptable.

As Alice Munro says in a memorable short story[1] about a children's concert, 'we are accustomed to notice performances [at Miss Marsalles' parties], but it cannot be said that anyone has ever expected *music*'. It was like a pact in which the players guaranteed not to be embarrassingly involved, and we were excused from being involved too. It was a musical version of avoiding eye contact, as we so often do when we are conscious that the subject matter is emotional. Hovering over it was the source of this emotion, Schubert, who couldn't quite make contact with us mortals. Those players would have had to be willing to enter Schubert's world in order to share it with us. Indeed, *they would have had to enter it*.

Summer 2001

---

[1] *Dance of the Happy Shades*, in *Selected Stories of Alice Munro*, Chatto & Windus, London, 1996.

Making Small Music in a Big Kiln

Friends in the BBC Symphony Orchestra tell me that during certain contemporary works, the noise level in the rehearsal studio is so great that it breaks health and safety guidelines. In theory, workers exposed to these levels must wear ear plugs, but this would be self-defeating for musicians. Some of the players most affected – those who sit right in front of the loudest instruments, such as brass and percussion – have taken to putting their instruments down and sitting with their fingers in their ears until the noise level drops. A sympathetic management is nevertheless unable to prevent composers from demanding these massive effects.

The taste for high noise levels is not confined to contemporary music, as anyone who goes to nightclubs or pop concerts will confirm. What is it, I wonder, that fuels this desire for music on a scale far beyond the human? Music at this kind of volume delivers not so much an emotional as a physiological punch. Call me a miniaturist, but I'm still far more attracted to music at the other end of the noise spectrum. Solo or chamber music, played on just a few 'acoustic' instruments, has all the drama of the interior monologue or dialogue in musical form. It's powerful on a human scale, and thus far more emotionally meaningful than loud music that deprives us of the power to think.

Now that style gurus have told us we all need corner shops again, to restore a sense of human scale after years of wandering hollow-eyed round hypermarkets as big and anonymous as airports, perhaps other small-scale endeavours will become fashionable. Chamber music, in my view, is ripe for reassessment. It's the medium in which many composers give us their most intimate portraits of themselves, let us eavesdrop on the working out of their inner thoughts about life. It also provides a unique opportunity for players to share their thoughts among themselves. This is relished by 'vocational' chamber musicians, though not always by people who spend a lot of time playing solo music.

A friend has just returned from an unusual tour of chamber music concerts with an eminent solo pianist. Greatly to his surprise he noticed that the pianist, renowned for his focus and mastery when alone, was seriously discomfited by the presence of other 'equal voices' on the stage. Other people's ideas about tempo and character were received as implied criticisms, and their seizing of the musical initiative provoked outbursts of technical insecurity from the great man.

Many soloists seem to get anxious when they leave the Olympian plateaux of solo recitals and plunge into the lively currents of chamber music. Even a good-natured discussion about how to play things can be perceived as a challenge to their usually sovereign authority. They're a bit like the Zen monk who was noted for his serenity in the temple. So famous was his calm that the emperor invited him to conduct a ceremony in front of the court. But finding himself in unfamiliar surroundings, he panicked, began sweating profusely, and forgot his words. He realised that his composure was accessible to him only in the temple, and was not as profound as it seemed.

Last weekend I took part in the Gaudier Ensemble's annual festival at Cerne Abbas in Dorset. This delightful event – given by instrumentalists who are all principals of major European orchestras – seems unknown outside Dorset, not a practical disadvantage since all the concerts are sold out weeks in advance anyway. But it is galling to be present at music-making of such outstanding quality, ignored summer after summer by the same press that doggedly prints a review of every single Prom concert whether it was good or not. Surely things shouldn't command attention just because they're in a large venue? In the literary world, books are reviewed because they're interesting or original, not just because large numbers of people are going to read them.

Most of the works we played were chamber music, but I also played the solo part in a Mozart piano concerto. This is a work which Mozart said could be played just with a string quartet instead of the usual orchestra. Having performed both, I revel in the chamber version. When you've practised the piece alone in your room for many weeks, the addition of an orchestra can be disappointingly heavy. A large body of players has an inertia that precludes spontaneous changes of speed or character from the soloist. Not so with the quartet version, however: there was a swiftness of sound and response that made me feel as if we were flying.

Yet I also noticed that these same players, who an hour before had been in the throes of debate with me while rehearsing the Schumann piano quintet (exactly the same grouping) were respectfully silent during the concerto, as though tradition informed them that a soloist doesn't want or need their input. At the end, they even tapped with their bows on the stand, orchestral players' way of saying that they appreciate the soloist's playing. I realised that, because it was 'a concerto', we had flicked a mental switch and were no longer 'colleagues', but master and servants for those twenty minutes.

If you are a soloist, never subjected to the cut and thrust of democratic ideas in rehearsal, it produces an isolated state of being. On the one hand, nobody questions your interpretation. On the other, the responsibility for it is yours alone. No light will be thrown on it by an imaginative colleague or someone with experience outside yours.

Chamber musicians, who work without any kind of director, thrive on the exchange of ideas. Indeed, there's no other way to arrive at a result where everyone feels important. Players must feel 'listened to' in every sense. Therefore in the professional world everyone has to learn how to give and receive criticism – the former a lot easier than the latter!

A string quartet colleague told me that he woke up one morning recently and thought what a peculiar way he spent his life – going to rehearsals every day to criticise other people and be criticised himself. As he mused on other professions, he couldn't think of another where this kind of openness and vulnerability is the norm. Actors are criticised by directors, of course, and many employees are criticised by the boss, but it's rarely a two-way process, even on occasions when it should be. Rehearsing chamber music can be painful, but there's something special about an interpretation that emerges gradually from the ebb and flow of the participants' egos, and the complex interaction of their energies and ideas.

At its best this process is like the kiln described by the Japanese potter Shoji Hamada. When asked why he fired his pots in such a big kiln, he replied, 'Because in a small kiln I can control everything exactly. In a big kiln, the power beyond me is necessary. It's only with the grace of this power beyond me that I can make my best pots.'

August 2001

Looking Involved

At our chamber concerts, listeners often say that it's fascinating to see how we communicate with one another, and, in particular, how we 'look involved' and 'look as if we're enjoying ourselves'. This seems to give them the permission to enjoy themselves too.

Yet paradoxically, 'looking involved' is not always attractive, as I realised recently when watching other musicians. The most striking was a group of Irish folk musicians playing in a Bantry pub. The music was lively and cheerful, but I was struck by the miserable expressions on their faces. Their shoulders danced and their fingers flew, yet had the music suddenly become inaudible one might have guessed that some arcane rite was in progress – like the Norns weaving the rope of fate. Though they sat facing across the circle, they grimly avoided one another's eyes. Clearly there was no sense that they were there to please listeners.

I mentioned this to a man who turned out to be the father of one of the lads playing. He told me that when Irish folk musicians play, they believe that they communicate not with humans, but with the fairy realm, in an enchanted sphere far from everyday life. Apparently a leading Irish folk fiddler, Martin Hayes, had recently compared the belief in a fairy realm with what nuclear physicists now tell us about the behaviour of particles: sometimes observable, sometimes not, and following the mysterious laws of 'strangeness' and 'charm'. Watching the players, whose behaviour was the reverse of showing off, I couldn't help thinking what a disaster it would be for my own group to appear so sullen and remote on stage. And yet the listeners' enjoyment was not marred by the players' indifference to them. Indeed, I would guess that the sense of eavesdropping on a private ritual positively enhanced our sense of authenticity.

Soon after this I saw other examples of musicians detached from their listeners. One was a hurdy-gurdy player of traditional Breton folk music in France. Looking like a mediaeval woodcut, he sat perched on a windowsill in the street, gazing impassively with a slight frown into the distance as his fingers tapped out merry tunes. Here was no pretence of enjoying himself for our benefit, and yet his strictly detached expression seemed, if puzzling, somehow soothing and familiar.

I also watched some excellent jazz musicians who made no conscious bridge to the audience. Absorbed in their task, curtains of hair falling across their faces and hiding their expressions, they seemed to be saying, 'the relationship here is between us and the music. You may watch if you like.' In jazz there is, perhaps more than in any other kind of contemporary music, a strong desire to avoid melodrama. Players of this charismatic music pay homage to its painful origins in eras of slavery and sorrow by taking it very seriously no matter what its surroundings. Today this seriousness has been translated into 'being cool'. For reasons of style, they might actually restrain natural impulses to behave exuberantly when playing exuberant music. But again, the votive rituals of jazz don't alienate fans.

As a listener on these various occasions, I wasn't troubled by the players' apparent remoteness. I took it as a sign of their meditative state, or even their idealistic desire to subtract their personalities from the artistic event. I wasn't offended that they didn't smile at me, or map out their feelings about the music to guide me through it. And yet I also knew that if my chamber groups behaved like that, it would be perceived as snobbish, unkind, as yet more evidence that classical music is 'difficult' and requires special initiation.

As a performer I know I have to strike a balance between drawing people in and reaching out to them. Concentration and absorption are necessary, and work their own spell on people. But to rely entirely on the listener's ability to interpret my absorption would seem arrogant. At least, I've come to feel this after years of being told that audiences relish our signs of enjoyment. But how to guarantee that these signs arise genuinely from spontaneous feeling, are not 'painted on' or engineered for the audience's benefit? I know I sometimes consciously reach out to include the audience in key moments of a favourite piece. At the same time, I know some listeners will be more touched by private moments, which they witness, but know were not contrived for them.

In classical performance, there's a range of 'looking involved', from the skilfully charming variety to the grotesquely off-putting. It depends so much, also, on the innate character of the player. Audiences may not always know the music, but we've all been trained by ordinary life to interpret body language, and we can sense the degree of artifice used by a performer.

Some musicians both feel and show – even perform – an intense love of their instrument that may seem unhealthy, certainly not always feeding into their understanding of the piece. Others betray their obsession with the music; they sing tonelessly along with themselves, grunting and moaning in an alarming way; their jaw muscles clench and work in time to some inner commentary; they hunch over the keys, portraying their sense of abasement to the instrument. All these are physical trappings, distracting to observe and not actually helping to convey the music. True absorption is usually satisfying to watch, but obsession expressed in physical behaviour is not.

Some listeners will latch on to the player's theatrical identification with music or instrument, finding it as satisfying as watching a film romance. Others, those who like me are by temperament somewhat Lutheran, will find it ugly.

When I think of pop and commercial performers, I realise that 'looking involved' is the absolute minimum required by the fans. The emotional simulacrum here is everything. To imagine a pop singer 'letting the music speak for itself' is ludicrous. So perhaps the key is the type of music – how consciously was it composed for a performer and an audience? In this sense one might put folk music, the ancient traditional kind, at one end of the spectrum, and pop music at the other. Some people may be surprised that I separate folk and pop in this way. After all, both are supposed to be 'music of the people'. Yet in the way they arise, and they way they're performed, there's an unbridgeable gulf between them, for pop music is cynically designed to be short-lived and entirely commercial, two things that folk will never be.

If folk and pop music are at the two ends of the spectrum, classical music lies somewhere in between. It is meant to played and heard, but isn't composed *for public performance* above all. It could be enjoyed by someone quietly reading the score in his private room, or indeed by people quietly playing it in their living-room. On the other hand, it could be brilliantly performed to great acclaim on the concert stage. Perhaps this straddling of the private and public worlds is what makes classical chamber music ambiguous for the performer. Should I, as a performer, relate to the composer or to the audience? To the other players? Which aspect of the music is more important, the public or the intimate? Should we look or not look involved?

It seems to me that the older, the purer and more timeless the music, the less relevant is 'looking involved' and calculating the audience's need. An ancient lullaby or lament will be at its most potent with a minimum of participation from the musician. Imagine the lone Scots piper playing a lament on the castle battlements at dusk – for him to mime his sense of drama would be offensive. His remoteness is essential.

August 2001

Practice makes Imperfect

A recent report on athletes' preparation came to the conclusion that whether they warm up or not doesn't actually make much difference to the result. This must have come as a surprise not only to athletes but to their fans, who regularly watch them warming up until the moment before competition begins. Perhaps warming up is not physically essential, but for athletes it seems to be psychologically important, a sort of inventory of their powers. For musicians the process clearly works on a number of levels, but as with athletes it's not at all clear how much the ritual of preparation has a direct effect on the performance itself. After all, the performance is as much mental as physical. Does the ritual help to keep thoughts in, or does it help to keep them out?

When I was a violinist in the National Youth Orchestra, every rehearsal and every concert was famously preceded by a two-minute silence. Having tuned the instruments, we all sat quietly until the arrival of the conductor, whose entry was always timed to perfection. I rather liked this enforced silence before an intense burst of music. For me, whatever sound came next was more meaningful if it emerged from a still background. However, for many of my string-playing friends the silence was torture. They resented the interruption to that physical bonding process with their instruments, feeling that they would have to start all over again when the rehearsal began.

How musicians psyche themselves up for performance has fascinated me ever since. Some like to prepare months ahead of the concert, whereas others deliberately leave preparation almost too late, to generate more adrenalin. Some like to be left in peace to assemble their thoughts before a concert, while others practise right up to the last minute. Indeed, many are still practising while standing outside the door to the platform. Only seconds of silence separate their off-stage practice from their on-stage performance. They seek to create a continuum of sound in which the concert is only the last and most vivid segment. This applies particularly to string players, who seem to bond with their instruments more than other musicians do. Perhaps because of the strong tactile elements of playing a string instrument, they develop a sensual hunger for their instrument that is only satisfied by continuous physical contact with it.

Silence before concerts is often imposed on pianists because there isn't a piano backstage. As a pianist, therefore, I'm often forced to sit quietly and watch other people preparing for the concert. Mostly what they do is to practise the difficult bits. They play them over and over again, trying to nail the tricky fingering into their subconscious so that under the strain of platform nerves, the patterns will remain.

However, the effect of repeating difficult passages is by no means calculable. In terms of statistics, repeating something many times backstage will have no effect on the likelihood of the stage version being successful. A player may feel he's increasing his chance of success by multiple repetitions in the minutes before the concert, but statistically it makes no difference to the chances of success onstage. Obviously more than just chance is involved, but perhaps we would do better to prepare mentally rather than physically. A classical ballet dancer told me that performing a complicated manoeuvre, such as a pirouette, in the wings may actually lead to a false sense of physical security. On stage, the dancer may rely on physical memory rather than instant calculation of the degree of control needed at that moment, with the result that over-confidence may lead them to overshoot the turn fractionally. Most classical dancers, it seems, accept that they need all their finely tuned senses to perfect a difficult movement at the right moment (i.e. onstage), and they may even feel superstitious about throwing that fine edge off balance by trying it out beforehand. That most musicians are not like this may show that playing music is felt as an emotional rather than a physical task.

Many players feel that they have to concentrate intensely to get difficult things right in performance. If you could get inside their consciousness you would feel the outside world fading away every time there was something challenging to play. Such an approach seemed normal to me too until I watched the Hungarian pianist György Sebök demonstrating to students that concentration isn't always the answer. He believed that if you have done the necessary practice, it would actually help to de-focus your concentration at the relevant moment. It was funny and instructive to see him deliberately distract a student while they were playing something terribly hard. If he intervened at the right moment, they would look up in surprise while their hands, unhampered by the mind, whizzed effortlessly through the difficult bits. He had similar results when he asked someone to concentrate on one hand while the other was playing something hard. Assuming that the student had actually worked out the necessary fingering, it worked like magic to let the hand find its own way without conscious supervision. The student's expression of delight and amazement at such moments made us all laugh, but there was a serious underlying point. Concentration was clearly a mixed blessing, and could even create problems. There were other parts of the mind and body that knew what they were doing. 'Think nine times and play once', was Sebök's wise advice.

This extends beyond the concert platform. Music conservatories are full of people who think that the more they practise, the better they will be. All day long the honeycomb of practice rooms buzzes with their industry. To impress their teachers, students set themselves arduous practice goals. I know students who start practising at 7 a.m., grab a coffee at 10 a.m. before classes begin, and practise again in the evenings. Not many discover how to practise productively, and most people spend long periods 'practising' what they can already play. A college health adviser recently told me that his days were full of students seeking advice about their aching backs, shoulders and hands. Yet if they did more practice away from the instrument, focusing on the mental instead of the physical, they would benefit greatly.

How even well-prepared musicians approach a concert day varies enormously. Some of my colleagues get themselves keyed up by telling themselves they haven't yet done enough practice, even at 7.25 p.m. There are still minutes to go, in which something could be achieved! Their sense of responsibility towards the audience expresses itself in trying this and that right up to the moment of walking on stage. To stop tinkering around with things would seem like dangerous complacency. For others, however, it's essential to interpose some peaceful time between rehearsal and concert. Some like to think about the whole shape of pieces, or, if they are about to play from memory, to run through things in their head quietly. Some like to distract themselves by reading a book or chatting. I myself like to go and wait at the side of the stage where I can hear the murmur of the audience and get a sense of their mood. For me the relationship with the piano is secondary to what I hope to do as a musician. My focus is on the music and on communication of it to the audience. I need to play the piano to achieve this, but playing the piano isn't the *sine qua non* of my musical life. Perhaps performers of my temperament hope to create in themselves an appetite for the music by holding it at arm's length for a while. We're aware of the audience sitting in silence waiting for the music to begin. If the artist sits on the other side of the curtain in silence too, the music may come as a gift to audience and artist alike.

Clearly some players have to make themselves uncomfortable in order to perform. By questioning themselves as much as possible before the concert, they instinctively build up a performance tension that is released in the presence of the audience. Telling themselves that they are not ready heightens their sense of occasion, sometimes with excellent results. But other musicians, like me, need to feel comfortable in order to perform. It's important for us to tell ourselves (if it's true) that we have done and thought enough, that we should stop now, and look forward to giving our best onstage. For this type of player, self-doubt has a harmful effect on their playing. They need to feel and draw on a sense of trust.

I loved the anecdote I once heard about the distinguished German pianist Wilhelm Backhaus. A fan of his gushingly asked him, 'Mr Backhaus, you never seem to play wrong notes in your recitals. How come you never play any wrong notes?' He quietly replied, 'I only practise the right notes.' When I first heard this story I immediately had a sense of all the time that we spend in effect practising the wrong notes; thinking the wrong thoughts, doubting our ability to get it right, watching ourselves for failures of nerve. Backhaus's approach seemed to indicate a mind at peace with itself. To practise 'only the right notes', and only in the right way, would eliminate whole areas of unproductive work of the kind that occupies practice rooms in colleges and concert halls throughout the world.

November 2002

Pay and Display

I sat and gazed out of the window for a while after hearing the newsreader say that unskilled workers on Heathrow's Terminal Five are to be paid more than I am. Well, I admit he didn't put it like that; he merely stated their salary. The same week, Polly Toynbee wrote with feeling in *The Guardian* about the miserably low pay of compassionate care workers who look after the sick and elderly. We live in a peculiar world where nurses struggle by on basic rates of pay, but corporation chairmen can earn bonuses of millions even though their company makes a loss, and even if it has been implicated in public disasters like rail crashes or the wholesale loss of ordinary people's savings and pensions. Footballers, film and TV actors can be millionaires in their twenties.

Clearly there is no straightforward correlation between how important a job is, and what society will pay. There's no panel of wise men sitting down with a list to work out which jobs are the most meaningful, worthwhile and skilful, and how they should be remunerated. We are all working in a fog of traditions and assumptions (sometimes unjustifiable) about how much we have to pay to get someone's attention. And somewhere in all this muddle are artists – musicians, poets, painters – often financially constrained, and constantly wondering why it is so difficult to get a good price for their work. But some people would say they don't have a right to be paid at all for something they would do for love anyway. It isn't a proper job, is it? They could keep it as a hobby if they liked, couldn't they?

All the evidence is that for hundreds of years musicians have played out of love for their art, and no doubt they will go on doing it. They are pleased if they get paid, but philosophical if they don't. It doesn't stop them from planning the next rehearsal. So as a society we don't have to try and buy musicians' loyalty with salary scales, health benefits and company cars. We don't have to give them golden handshakes when they leave, not even if they've been superb. What's more, musicians and artists could never bring society to a stop by going on strike. They're a luxury, something to spend money on when times are good. In any case, now that we're all obsessed with gourmet food, we're more likely to spend our disposable cash on a meal than on a concert.

Britain has a thriving culture of amateur music-making. Many people, for whom music has been important since childhood, are devoted to their local orchestras and choirs, to their summer music courses. Amateur chamber musicians meet regularly to read through piles of quartets and the like. The spontaneity of these events is important to the participants, many of whom positively don't want to know in advance what they are going to play, so that it can't turn into work. 'Having a go' is the primary goal, and it enables people to gain a nodding acquaintance with lots of music.

It does, however, also militate against people who want to go considerably further. Music probably has a larger amateur following than any of the other arts. It includes people who could have been professional players, but were too sensible to launch themselves into that financial void. These are often the very people who are unsympathetic to the financial difficulties of full-time musicians. Having made their own pragmatic decision to keep music as a hobby, they find it perverse of professional players to keep banging their heads on that brick wall and complaining about how hard it is to make a living. Indeed, the very fact that we have a flourishing amateur scene makes it harder for professionals to claim their dues. This is particularly so in Britain where there is a tradition of muddling through, of having fun, glad to be spared the anguish of doing something supremely well.

Music is unusual because one *can* do it on an amateur basis. Who has heard of an amateur lawyer, dentist or architect? Such dabblers would be up in court in a trice. Many professions jealously guard the fact that only a highly paid adept may engage in them. But in music there is room for everyone from the child with a few notes on the recorder to a soloist delighting a connoisseur audience. And so it should be.

But doing something for fun, now and then, is not the same as committing yourself to it seriously on a full-time basis. The results are very different, and most concert-goers would agree that the deepest satisfaction comes from listening to a performance that has been nurtured, studied and lived with by serious artists. This is not to belittle amateur music-making, but to point out that there are realms of musical revelation only accessible to those who commit themselves to intensive rehearsal, and to a level of skill and self-mastery achieved often at great personal cost over many years. In a sense many full-time musicians do not 'have a choice'. There are truly gifted musicians who, though they might rationally accept it would have been 'more sensible' to pick a desk job, believe their lives would have been wasted had they done so. They can't put a knife between their musical selves and their selves. They can't choose to become dentists or architects instead, no matter how advantageous a decision that might be; it would seem *irrelevant* to what was really going on in their heads. Non-vocational musicians don't understand this.

In the last few years I've had various reasons to consult lawyers. In doing so I encountered a world in which people charge £200 an hour for routine administration. Even if I am calling to tell the lawyer something, I have to pay for the time they spend listening to me on the phone. If they call me to confirm that they've got my letter, I have to pay for that too. The contrast with my own world couldn't be more marked. If I started charging £200 an hour, the phone would stop ringing right away. We 'need' lawyers in a way that we don't 'need' musicians. When people brush up against the law, only a lawyer will do, and we realise it costs money to get a good one.

On the other hand, how people brush up against music and what they get from it is incalculable. As E.M. Forster pointed out in his essay about the National Gallery concerts during the Second World War, 'experience proves that strange filaments cling to us after we have been with music, that the feet of the birds have, as it were, become entangled in snares of heaven, that while we swooped hither and thither so aimlessly we were gathering something, and carrying it away for future use'.[1] A

---

1   *National Gallery Concerts*, National Gallery, London, 1944.

quick burst of Classic FM might yield something as delightful as would a trek to the Royal Festival Hall. A remark your music teacher made years before may come to inform all your practice. Therefore there is no way that we can assess the value of a musician's hourly labour and put a price on it.

Many musicians discover their talent as youngsters. They are often fêted for it within their social circle. People take it for granted that a very talented player will become famous and that material success will follow. The player him- or herself, once they discover how long it will take to perfect the skill, may spend years believing that all this effort will one day be highly rewarded. After all, to play supremely well is something that scientists tell us is remarkable, and remarkably difficult to analyse. The fastest of typists is a beginner on the keyboard compared with a good pianist. The musician's fingers move faster and in more complex patterns, the capacity to learn is quicker, the memory works better, than in the average person.

Furthermore, the musician makes music, the art that many people turn to when they need emotional feedback. Some musicians, particularly in popular music, become heroes to their audience. In classical music the audience is much smaller, but still relies on its favourite players to be their emotional mouthpieces. I can't say why the audience is small; for me, this has always been the most interesting kind of music, even though there were no outreach programmes to coax me in as a young-ster. After devoting myself to it for years, I grew up and discovered that its fanbase is small compared with that of pop. Yet its fans are truly devoted: people write to me from different parts of the world to tell me what an impact my playing made on them. Sometimes they write about a concert they attended ten years before. Those are the times when I wonder why an art that evidently has the power to change people's feelings about the world is paid so modestly.

Within the world of classical music there are, of course, extraordinary differences in what musicians are paid. In former times, talented musicians were looked after by wealthy patrons. Beethoven was only one of those who wouldn't have got far without them. More recently, top artists in some countries, notably the old commu-nist ones, were supported by the state. Today there are some European and Scandi-navian countries who support their artists with grants and lengthy sponsorship amounting to a living wage. Britain, I need hardly add, isn't one of them.

A friend of mine in a symphony orchestra told me that an international conductor is often paid as much as all the members of the orchestra put together, though he doesn't make a sound. Promoters justify this by saying that the conduc-tor's name has the power to put bums on seats; just the orchestra's name won't do that, except in rare cases. Similarly, opera stars have the commercial power to make people splash out £100 for a ticket. Going to the opera is expensive partly because the singers are so highly paid. A chamber concert isn't expensive because the players aren't. There is, of course, no guarantee that an expensive event will yield more musical rewards than a cheap one; musical revelation is quite independent of celeb-rity and of cost.

What about that imaginary panel of sages who might sit down to allocate the right wages to the whole spectrum of human activities? Obviously they'd sever the link between 'celebrity' and high fees. They might, I suppose, decide to pay everyone the same, be they barrister or childminder. But they might look at how certain professions enhance the quality of people's lives, and they might re-define what society needs to spend its money on. They might consider how much people 'need' the things for which they pay. A manicure or a couple of hours of Schubert? A prescription for sleeping-pills or a weekend of string quartets? An hour with the lawyer or a term of violin lessons? 'O reason not the need', says Shakespeare. So need is irrational; unfortunately income is irrational too.

January 2003

Am I too soft?

When pianist Mitsuko Uchida toured with violinist Mark Steinberg performing Mozart's duo sonatas a few years ago, they decided to be billed in that order: pianist first, violinist second, just as Mozart lists them in the score – 'sonatas for piano with violin'. But this was perceived as subversive in an artistic scene where the pianist is generally named after the violinist, and many people felt it was, well, stridently feminist of Uchida to want to be first. But I thought that it was just putting right a relationship that has been inexplicably wrong for a long while.

Last week I received the French review of a recital disc I made with the distinguished viola player Thomas Riebl. All the works we played were duos, conceived by their composers as intimate musical conversations. Our interpretation took months to prepare. Yet our first review spoke as though only Thomas had played: 'his choice of programme . . . his tone . . . his interpretation . . . his rhythmic sense . . .', and in the last sentence it said something like, 'in all this, he was ably supported by the delightful Susan Tomes'. Supported! I could have sworn that we were playing duos.

This review was one more brick in the wall against which I have been banging my head for years. Almost every day one can read the review of a duo recital in which the poor pianist is caged into the final sentence. Nothing seems to have changed in this respect since Artur Schnabel complained about it in 1945: 'How often have I seen reports, in America as well as in Europe, telling at great length and with enthusiasm about a famous violinist's or cellist's performance of a sonata and adding at the end: "The accompanist played with good taste", or something similar. Actually, the piano part is always more substantial and the pianist should, from a musical point of view, be the leader – in chamber music as well as in songs.'[1] It may well be that the pianist has taken months to learn the difficult piano parts, and is the one who knows the whole work inside-out, but the press insists on turning this reality upside-down and focusing on the person who isn't playing the piano. Why, for heaven's sake? Don't these people have any ears? Just as feminists had to scream that women were doing most of the work and getting none of the credit, pianists should fight until everyone recognises their contribution for what it is. Instead of labelling ourselves feminists we could call ourselves . . . well, pianists.

I often wonder how we arrived at the point where pianists in duo partnerships with string players, wind players or singers have become semi-invisible. If they play on their own, pianists are lionised. If they play in a trio, quartet or quintet they are

---

1 *My Life and Music*, Artur Schnabel, published by Colin Smythe, Gerrards Cross, 1970.

again acknowledged as having the lion's share of the music, and often as being the driving force. But, uniquely, if they play in a duo they suddenly become 'an accompanist'. This point is illustrated by the current edition of *Grove's Dictionary of Music and Musicians*, which in talking about Rubinstein's chamber music activities describes him as 'Ysaÿe's accompanist, and the partner of Heifetz and Feuermann'. The acccompanist in a duo, but the partner in a trio! Why is he not described as Ysaÿe's partner? You may well ask.

The downgrading of pianists to accompanists would shock the composers, mostly pianists themselves, who conceived these pieces as works for piano with an important parallel role for a single-line instrument. Look through the scores of any duo sonatas from Mozart or Haydn onwards through Schubert and Beethoven and Schumann and Brahms . . . all called them pieces 'for piano and violin/cello', not the other way round. This was no more than a recognition that the piano carries the main burden of the musical thought and has the more demanding part.

The rot probably began with Paganini, the first and one of the most important in a line of celebrity soloists that continues to this day. Their glamour derived from their dazzling performances of virtuoso pieces, but it also threw their pianists into shadow, and that was the way many soloists liked it. They continued to think of themselves as soloists even when playing pieces clearly designed as a dialogue between two players. They adopted a style of stage presentation where they stood out front, boldly facing the audience, often moving theatrically about while the pianist was, naturally, obliged to sit in profile to the audience and nailed to a perch like the Monty Python parrot. This reached absurd heights when Richard Strauss, playing the piano part of one of his own songs for his wife to sing, was banned by her from playing the postlude for piano alone, because he would draw the audience's attention away from her. Strauss was obliged to abridge his own song, drawing quietly to a close as the singer did. I don't wish to undermine the skill and subtlety of good singers and string players, who have to create every note, and whose mastery of colours and nuances are among the glories of music. But I deplore their elevation into heroes instead of partners.

Here's Schnabel again, protesting in 1945 about 'the duo calamity': the wrong-headed separation of duos into soloist and accompanist. 'A "star" singer or instrumentalist receives hundreds of pounds for a part, his or her pianist perhaps only ten to twenty or so. He may be more musical than the "star", but probably feels too depressed and degraded to try his best. Where he should lead, he has to obey. Almost all violin and cello virtuosos compel pianists to subordinate the requirements of the music to their vainglory – or limitations. Nearly every fiddler tells his pianist that under all circumstances he is too loud – he does not mean that he is too loud for the music, but too loud for his fiddle.' At around the same time, pianist Artur Rubinstein reported that the cellist Pablo Casals would sometimes divide the pieces in his cello recitals into 'serious' and 'lighter' items. For serious pieces such as Beethoven sonatas, an eminent pianist such as Rubinstein himself might be invited. For virtuoso cello pieces with an 'oompah oompah' accompaniment, a mere artisan pianist was enough. This would result in the curious spectacle of two different pianists appearing in the same recital, one to play the difficult parts and one to play the 'easy' ones. Rubinstein reported that he was grateful to Casals for treating him as an equal. How the other pianist felt is not recorded.

Fifty years later, when you might have thought that equal opportunities had taken hold, I was invited to play a duo recital with a famous violinist and found to my horror that his fee was *ten times* as high as mine. Our programme contained things like Beethoven's *Kreutzer* Sonata, legendarily difficult for both instruments. I assumed that he had invited me because he thought I was his musical equal, but this didn't extend to the finances. For me that was reason enough not to play with him again, but others took my place and he continued to get away with it.

Sometimes a very famous soloist can claim that the public is there for him alone, and that he can claim a larger share of the takings, but infuriatingly this same attitude crops up among some young instrumentalists who are no more experienced than their pianist partners and have no greater claim on the public's affection. Some of them seem to think it is 'their' recital, for which they happen to need a pianist. My policy is never to play a duo recital for anything less than half the fee, but such arrangements are not always transparent.

Some of my pianist colleagues, notably those who specialise in playing for singers, do not feel so evangelical about the pianist's role. They follow rather in the footsteps of Gerald Moore, whose famous books, such as *Am I too loud?*, gave listeners an affectionate glimpse into the life of the unashamed accompanist, as he styled himself. Gerald Moore accepted with wry humour the subsidiary role of a pianist who had to be careful not to step on the train of the soprano's evening robe as she swished ahead of him onto the platform. He took pride in his professionalism and craftsmanship, yet remained deferential to the great personalities he served, relating stories of their foibles rather like the guardian of some exotic aviary. Indeed, I think he felt that his down-to-earth good English sense was a necessary foil for their artistic flights of fancy. He was famous too, but famous for being the power behind the throne.

The cult of the solo singer has continued unabated and, in Moore's wake, many of their pianists have selflessly stepped out of the spotlight, not always with justification. Privately they may say, and some of them do, that in rehearsals they often have to teach the singer their notes, explain the text, suggest interpretations, correct intonation and follow them to voice production lessons (singers continue going to teachers long after instrumentalists have stopped). Though this would indicate to me that the pianist is the *éminence grise* of the partnership, singers seem to feel that when it comes to the concert they may expect their pianists to efface themselves while the singer bonds with the audience. Only today, for example, did I read in *The Guardian* that soprano Jessye Norman last night sent her pianist offstage to collect the music for her encores while taking the applause all by herself at the end of a duo recital.

Curiously, some pianists consent to be taken for granted, as I once found to my surprise when discussing this topic with some very distinguished *Lieder* pianists in the Wigmore Hall café. They felt that ultimately there was no point in pretending that a pianist could rival someone who uses the human voice, and, also crucially, has the words. A singer will always strike the public more forcefully just because of this. Any instrumentalist playing with a singer is therefore, they felt, fated to live outside the spotlight. Their own love of the song repertoire has reconciled them to the situation. But one might sometimes think that there is a tiny hint of masochism in the relationship between singer and pianist, all the more surprising when one thinks of the difficulty of many of the piano parts.

Non-musicians may wonder why I refer to the pianist knowing the music better than their partner does. The reason lies partly in the way that music is published. In the piano part, the other parts are also printed, so that a pianist may see at a glance not only his own notes but everyone else's as well. The violinist, on the other hand, generally learns his notes from a part that contains only the violin line, printed on a single stave with no clue as to what the piano is playing. The expense of buying music generally means that the two players will buy one copy of the sonata; the violinist will take the violin part, and the pianist the piano score with the violin line added. Right from the start, the pianist will know the score in the literal sense. The violinist may never discover what the piano plays until he or she hears the piano part at the first rehearsal. Naturally, a conscientious violinist or similar will acquire a copy of the piano score and study it before rehearsals begin, but I can tell you that in twenty years of professional life I don't even need the fingers of one hand to count the number of instrumentalists who actually do this. Thus it is that when rehearsals begin, pianists are way ahead of their partners, and I would contend that they generally stay that way.

In recent years I decided to wage war on the word 'accompanist' whenever it is wrongly used. And by that I mean wherever the composer meant the piano to be the equal of the other player, which in duo pieces is *all the time*. There may be a genre of virtuoso pieces where a single-line instrument is designed to thrill us, and the piano part is deliberately kept simple. But such pieces today form only a minor part of most recitals. So whenever I turn up to play a programme of Mozart, Beethoven or Brahms sonatas and somebody refers to me as the accompanist I immediately say, 'I'm the pianist, not an accompanist.' They make a face and I can see they're thinking: 'Oh, blimey – one of those feminist types'. But, as I tell my students, I've realised that if pianists don't fight for their own rights, nobody else is going to do it for them.

May 2003

Dark Matter

Recently I tried to teach someone how to read music. I heard myself saying, 'Notation is a pretty basic way of indicating music. It's really just a way of showing you how high or low a note is, and how long it lasts. Composers have a few other things they can show: long, short, fast, slow, loud, soft, happy, sad. Apart from that, we're on our own. There are lots of other things notation doesn't show.'

Later it occurred to me that these 'other things' are what we musicians spend most of our time grappling with. The notes are only a map of the music's landscape, but the journey through the landscape is hardly delineated by the composer. The dynamics of the performance have to be created by the players, using the composer's shorthand as a set of clues. We take the written notes as our starting-point, but once we've learned the basics, we diverge enormously from one another in our way of deciding where to go from there.

Composers who use conventional notation, for people to play, have never indicated the contours of the whole performance. These days there are composers who are so determined to control every aspect of the performance that they have done away with musicians altogether, and write on computers for electronic reproduction. But composers who like acoustic performance by real people are quite limited in what they can, or do, specify. Using their notes as a map, musicians have to use their imaginations to try and reach the land they describe.

How the music builds up, with what waves of energy, what it builds up to, and how or whether it ebbs away. Should it feel like climbing a mountain, or just going for a walk along a shore? Should it sound easy or difficult, and when? Are the voices equal, or who leads and where do they stop leading? How big should the changes of dynamic be? How quiet is 'quiet'? How loud is 'loud'? How big is a crescendo or a diminuendo? How much should we speed up or slow down where instructed? When an eighteenth-century composer wrote 'very fast', did he imagine something different from someone who writes 'very fast' in the age of the supersonic plane?

What is the élan of the music, its sense of flow, its eagerness to change? Is it introvert or extrovert and how do we decide? How to cope with the transitions between one idea and the next? Should links be hidden or made obvious? When should we just go with the flow, and when is it important to resist an oncoming change of pace? How big should a musical climax be? Should we allow ourselves to be overwhelmed by the drama, or should we remain in control? Should we play as if we know what's coming, or as if we're hearing it for the first time?

When composers have a musical idea, it probably doesn't occur to them in terms of notation, but multi-dimensionally. The act of writing it down is a serious reduction of the original inspiration. It has to be expressed in some kind of outward and visible sign, and composers express their ideas in notes because notes are what musicians know how to read. All the same, what composers want us to express is not the notes, but their idea. Usually they are flexible about how their ideas may be expressed, and in my experience they are even happy to be surprised, as long as the musicians make a good job of guessing at the original inspiration. Some composers are even kind enough to say that what the performer makes of the piece is what the piece *is*. But there is also a danger that, using only the notes, musicians will fail to realise the idea.

Would composers like to be able to indicate more in the score, or do they deliberately leave things unsaid? Is it just that nobody ever succeeding in devising graphic signs and hieroglyphs to express events along the feeling/timing continuum? Or is it that it may be counter-productive to tell the player too much? Edward Elgar, chatting to the pianist Ivor Newton on the day that Yehudi Menuhin had played him his Violin Concerto, referred to the punctiliousness with which he had written directions into his scores. 'Beethoven and Brahms', he said, 'wrote practically nothing but *allegro* and *andante*, and there seems to be no difficulty. I've done all I can to help players, but my efforts appear only to confuse them.' This was an important observation. The active collaboration of the player, linking his or her mind with the composer's, is a necessary part of the process. But there's no way of notating that either.

Using the written notes to divine what layers of spirit and expression lie beyond them is the most time-consuming, and usually the most interesting part of rehearsal. But it staggers me to think how little of this is indicated in the score. If we played literally what composers wrote and nothing more, music would only realise a fraction of its potential. Music probably has more power to move us than any of the arts, but only if the notes are linked to the spirit. That may seem like the self-justification of a professional interpreter, but I believe it is true.

Physicists now tell us that the universe, as well as being full of the matter we can see, is full of dark matter that we can't see, but which is vital in some mysterious way. The dark matter is observable because of its gravitational effect. In music, notation is the matter we can see. The spirit which lies beyond it is the dark matter. It can't be defined, but without it there is no music.

January 2003

Discography of Susan Tomes

Solo and Duo records

1. Susan Tomes plays the piano music of Billy Mayerl
   Virgin Classics CUV5613232, 1989
2. Recital with Thomas Riebl, viola
   Pan 120722 (Vienna), 1983
3. Fauré violin and piano sonatas, with Krysia Osostowicz, violin
   Hyperion CDA66277, 1987
4. Bartók violin and piano music, with Krysia Osostowicz, violin
   Hyperion CDA66415, 1990
5. Brahms complete violin sonatas, with Krysia Osostowicz, violin
   Hyperion CDA66465, 1990
6. Martinu, Milhaud, Prokofiev: music for two violins and piano, with Krysia
   Osostowicz and Ernst Kovacic
   Hyperion CDA66473, 1991
7. Mendelssohn complete music for cello and piano, with Richard Lester, cello
   Hyperion CDA66478, 1989
8. Saint-Saëns Carnival of the Animals, with Ian Brown and the Nash Ensemble
   Virgin Classics 59514–2, 1988
9. Franz Schubert part-songs with piano, with the BBC Singers/Jane Glover
   Collins Classics 14492, 1997
10. Dvořák Sonata, Sonatina, Romantic Pieces etc. with Anthony Marwood, violin
    Hyperion CDA66934, 1997
11. Brahms Clarinet and Piano sonatas, and Intermezzi op. 119, with Ulrich Zimmerman,
    clarinet
    Fine Classics 4429–2 Trenton, New Jersey, USA, recorded 1994 (released 2000)
12. Fauré 'Dolly Suite', with Ian Brown/Nash Ensemble
    CRD 3505, 1995
13. Schumann Violin and Piano Sonatas 1 and 2, with Anthony Marwood, violin
    Hyperion CDA67180, 2000
14. Schumann and Schubert works for viola and piano, with Thomas Riebl, viola
    Pan Classics 510149, 2001

Records made as the pianist of Domus

15. Fauré Piano Quartets nos. 1 and 2
    Hyperion CDA66166, 1985
16. Dvořák Piano Quartets in E flat and D major
    Hyperion CDA66287, 1987
17. Brahms Piano Quartets nos. 1 and 3
    Virgin Classics 90709–4, 1987

18. Brahms Piano Quartet no. 2 and Mahler Piano Quartet (together with preceding item, now available as VC 5616152)
     Virgin Classics 59144–2
19. Schubert 'Trout' Quintet and Rondo Concertante
     Virgin Classics VC790801–2, 1989
20. Mendelssohn Piano Quartets nos. 1–3
     Virgin Classics VC791183–2, 1991
21. Mozart Piano Quartets
     Virgin Classics VC791485–2, 1991
22. Suk and Martinu Piano Quartets
     Virgin Classics VC7 59245–7, 1992
23. Lekeu Piano Quartet
     Ricercar RIS 104091, 1992
24. Judith Weir Chamber Music
     Collins Classics 14532, 1995
25. Fauré Piano Quintets
     Hyperion CDA 66766, 1994

Records made as the pianist of the Gaudier Ensemble

26. Dvořák Piano Quintet (and String Quintet)
     Hyperion CDA66796, 1995
27. Franz Berwald Chamber Music volume 1
     Hyperion CDA66834, 1995
28. Franz Berwald Chamber Music volume 2
     Hyperion CDA66835, 1996
29. Jean Francaix L'Heure du Berger, etc.
     Hyperion CDA67036, 1997
30. Mozart Chamber Music (inc. Piano and Wind Quintet)
     Hyperion CDA67277, 2001

Records made as the pianist of the Florestan Trio

31. Dvořák Piano Trios in F minor and E minor
     Hyperion CDA66895, 1996
32. Brahms: complete piano trios
     Hyperion CDA67251/2, 1997
33. Schumann Piano Trios nos. 1 and 2
     Hyperion CDA67063, 1998
34. Ravel, Fauré and Debussy Trios
     Hyperion CDA67114, 1999
35. Schumann Piano Trio in G minor, Piano Quartet, Fantasiestuecke for piano trio
     Hyperion CDA67175, 1999
36. Schubert Piano Trio in B flat, Nocturne, Triosatz
     Hyperion CDA67273, 2000
37. Schubert Piano Trio in E flat
     Hyperion CDA67347, 2001
38. Beethoven Piano Trios opus 70 nos. 1 and 2
     Hyperion CDA67327, 2001
39. Beethoven Archduke Trio, Kakadu Variations
     Hyperion CDA67369, 2002

To be released in 2003/4

40. Beethoven Trios opus 1 nos. 1 and 2, WoO 38
      Hyperion
41. Mozart Piano Concertos K. 413–5, Susan Tomes (soloist), with Gaudier Ensemble
      Hyperion CDA67358
42. Mendelssohn Piano Trios/Florestan Trio
      Hyperion
43. Beethoven Trios opus 1 no. 3, opus 11
      Hyperion
44. Weber Piano Trio, Piano Quartet, with Gaudier Ensemble
      Hyperion

Awards

Gramophone Award 1985 – for Fauré piano quartets/Domus
Deutsche Schallplattenpreis – for Fauré piano quartets/Domus
Deutsche Schallplattenpreis – for Brahms piano quartets/Domus
Diapason d'Or – for Fauré piano quintets/Domus
Palmares des Palmares, France – for Fauré piano quintets/Domus
Gramophone Award 1995 – for Fauré piano quintets/Domus
Gramophone Award 1999 – for Schumann piano trios/Florestan Trio
Classic CD Award 1999 – for Dvořák violin and piano recital/ Anthony Marwood
Classic CD vote – for Schumann piano trios nos. 1 and 2/Florestan Trio as 'best chamber
    disc of the past decade'
Royal Philharmonic Society Award 2000 – to the Florestan Trio

Index